After the Cold War

Europe's New Political Architecture

Alpo M. Rusi

St. Martin's Press   New York

First published in the United States of America in 1991

Printed in Great Britain

ISBN 0–312–06114–5

Library of Congress Cataloging-in-Publication Data
Rusi, Alpo.
After the cold war: Europe's new political architecture/Alpo M.
Rusi.
p. cm.
Includes bibliographical references and index.
ISBN 0–312–06114–5
1. Europe—Politics and government—1989– I. Title.
D2009.R87 1991
320.94—dc20   90–26347
                                                      CIP

AFTER THE COLD WAR

Also by Alpo M. Rusi (in Finnish)

**PRESS CENSORSHIP DURING THE CONTINUATION WAR
FINNISH FOREIGN POLICY IN TRANSITION** *(editor)*

To Leena, Tanja and Inka

No one who examines the modern world can doubt that the great currents of history are carrying the world away from the monolithic idea toward the pluralist idea—away from Communism and toward democracy and freedom.

John F. Kennedy (on March 23, 1962)

International politics is something organic, not something mechanical.

George F. Kennan

Contents

Foreword

In 1989, the floodgates of revolution were opened in Eastern Europe. Today, Germany is reunited after 45 years of bitter separation. Glasnost and perestroika in the Soviet Union, the prospect of increasing West European integration leading to the further marginalization of Eastern Europe, and long-suppressed alienation of the public from the political leadership throughout Eastern Europe were among the immediate factors leading to the upheavals of 1989 and the massive changes that continue today. In this thoughtful, thought-provoking Research Volume, Alpo Rusi, Director of Planning and Research in the Political Department of the Finnish Ministry of Foreign Affairs, examines the history of the postwar East–West relationship in Europe, the underlying processes of change and the implications of the present period of transition to a new European order.

Dr. Rusi makes it clear that the drive for change in Eastern Europe goes very deep and is based on a fundamental desire to return to an "organic" Europe, undivided and interdependent. This book makes it clear that these tendencies exist in both East and West. In Dr. Rusi's view the events of 1989 are but a harbinger of a new security order in Europe. Dr. Rusi analyzes the rise of bipolarism, both during the conflict of the Cold War and during the growth of detente. But he also lays stress on the parallel process of an evolution towards multilateralism and the "Europeanization of the East–West system."

Dr. Rusi's view is that in exploring the prospects for Europe's future, analysts and policy-makers must take into consideration the implications of the revolutions of 1989, the reunification of Germany, social, economic and political turmoil in the Soviet Union, the growing economic and political power of the European Community and the decline of superpower influence. In *After the Cold War*, Dr. Rusi emphasizes that the aims of both East and West must include the development of a framework for common European security. The Conference on Security and Cooperation in Europe may be able to adapt to meet these requirements, according to Dr. Rusi. While he sees change as both inevitable and desirable in Europe, Dr. Rusi believes that without responsible decision-making and guidance, the evolution of European security structures could result in increased instability during the period of transition.

Dr. Rusi began this book while serving as a Resident Fellow at the Institute for East–West Security Studies in New York during 1988–1989. He would like to express his particular appreciation to Peter Volten, IEWSS Director of Research, Ian M. Cuthbertson, Senior Research Associate, former Institute staff members F. Stephen Larrabee and Allen Lynch, as well as the 1988–1989 Fellows team, for their helpful criticism. In addition, Dr. Rusi would like to thank Richard Levitt and Peter B. Kaufman, respectively present and former IEWSS Director of Publications, and Rosalie Kearns and Mary Albon, IEWSS Publications Editors, for working closely with him in the various stages of writing and revising the manuscript. Finally, Amy Lew and Jennifer Lee of the wordprocessing office deserve special commendation for typing the seemingly endless revisions of the manuscript during the past few months.

The Institute would like to extend its appreciation to the Ford Foundation, the John D. and Catherine T. MacArthur Foundation, the Rockefeller Brothers Fund, and the Carnegie Corporation of New York for their generous support of the publication and distribution of this Research Volume, as well as of the Institute's Fellows program. The Institute is pleased to sponsor *After the Cold War*, the first single-author study in its Research Volume series. Dr. Rusi's work is certain to make a significant contribution to shaping the parameters of the emerging debate on the future political architecture of Europe.

New York   JOHN EDWIN MROZ
October 3, 1990   *President*
                              Institute for East–West Security Studies

Introduction

This book is about the systemic and political processes involved in undoing the division of Europe. Europe was divided as the result of a failure to settle the outstanding political problems of World War II. For decades the division provided a relatively stable, although not necessarily just, security order for Europe. Although most Europeans—in particular the Germans—have been uncomfortable with the division, the superpowers have by and large been satisfied with the status quo.[1]

On November 9, 1989, the Berlin Wall—so long the concrete symbol of the Cold War—fell. Psychologically and politically, Eastern Europe was no longer conquered territory; Eastern and Central Europe began to "return to Europe." The military-political pillars of the postwar division grew shaky. Although the events of 1989 in Europe were dramatic, the earthquake in Eastern Europe constituted one of the final stages in a long and complex process. This book attempts to shed light on this development and to make some predictions about the future of Europe after the Cold War.

Europe's division and the subsequent status quo can be considered the first postwar peace arrangement, since no peace treaty regarding the status of postwar Europe was ever signed by the four powers—the Soviet Union, the United States, France and the United Kingdom. More recently, the Conference on Security and Cooperation in Europe (CSCE) has been viewed as a possible substitute for the missing peace treaty. The CSCE did not challenge the bipolar security order, however; rather it strengthened it. Nevertheless, the CSCE has also become a force for change, with the East European states particularly benefiting. However, although it de facto constituted a second postwar peace arrangement, the CSCE process never really touched upon the root causes of Europe's division. The military buildup in Europe could not be halted even after the signing of the CSCE Final Act in Helsinki in 1975.

In 1990, the European security order is still based on a bipolar structure, albeit a rapidly eroding one. The central source of power in this system is military might; consequently, Europe is very heavily armed. However, this military buildup is not the cause but rather the consequence of political conflict among states with an interest in

Europe, in particular the Soviet Union and the United States. Thus
the dismantling of the division of Europe is primarily a political issue
although the process toward a unified Europe accounts for
"nonpolitical" systemic and organic factors as well.

The bipolar European order emerged between 1947–1948 and the
mid-1950s, and has subsequently tended toward gradual depolariza-
tion.[2] Although the original frenzy of the Cold War waned with the
peaceful resolution of the Berlin and Cuban missile crises in 1961–
1962, the level of confrontation between the two military alliances,
the North Atlantic Treaty Organization (NATO) and the Warsaw
Treaty Organization (WTO), and the division of Europe did not
diminish at that time. The reason for this was simple: the political
causes of the conflict still existed almost completely unchanged. In
addition, since the mid-1950s, nuclear weapons have decisively
influenced superpower relations and the structure of the international system; the two leading nations have been reluctant to sacrifice
the benefits of nuclear deterrence by opening political wounds
inflicted by World War II. Although some authors argue that the
stabilizing effects currently associated with nuclear deterrence could
be achieved, with increasing feasibility, by non-nuclear military or
especially political means,[3] the crucial role of nuclear deterrence in
maintaining the division of Europe and military stability cannot be
disputed. Nevertheless, radical reductions in the level of Soviet forces
and conventional arms arsenals in Eastern Europe—to take but one
example—would, if realized, automatically diminish the need for a
nuclear option in Europe and would also have geopolitical implications with the potential to affect postwar political arrangements in
general.[4]

Consequently, the emergence of political premises for a post-
bipolar European security are directly related to the resolution of
the outstanding political problems of World War II. The postwar
bipolar security order was based on the so-called Yalta legacy,[5]
which entailed, above all, statecraft aimed at ensuring that no
European nation would ever again be able to dominate the
continent. In addition to restoring Europe economically and politically, it was also crucial to hinder the reemergence of Germany as a
major actor in European politics: a divided Germany was to
constitute an integral part of the more or less permanent peace
settlement. The result was a divided Europe, which "legitimized,"
among other things, the Soviet military presence in Eastern Europe.
Thus, developments in Eastern Europe and a solution to the

"German problem" have always been closely related. In the words of Josef Joffe, "To reassociate the two Germanies requires reassociation of the two halves of Europe by breaking down the barriers of bipolarity."[6] In early 1990 it became clear that the superpowers also agreed to the reunification of Germany basically on German terms.

For decades the maintenance of the status quo, as already mentioned, was a major goal of the leading powers of European politics. Yet in the long run a just and stable peace must be based on a more organic political structure, which may, if realized, disrupt the status quo. Indeed, as Zbigniew Brzezinski points out, postwar European stability actually has been more of a "metastability," a physically rigid condition which, if shaken, could suddenly shatter. "Its collapse would have drastic consequences for the East–West relationship,"[7] Brzezinski concludes. This study argues that the bipolar structure of the postwar European status quo is rapidly losing credibility and will be dismantled as a result of deeply rooted economic, social (or systemic) and especially political processes of change. Although the factors stimulating change in the European security order can be identified on systemic and global as well as national and subregional levels, this book narrows its scope to specifically "Eurocentric" processes of change that take into account the following factors:

1. A shift in global power relations started in the early 1970s and became more dramatic in the early 1980s, compelling the Soviet Union to introduce reforms as an attempt to catch up with the West and ensure its status as a world power in the 21st century. Instead, the gradual shift in the European balance, an effect of the growth and modernization in the capitalist West and the continuing stagnation and deepening crisis in socialist East, created the precondition for the revolution in Eastern Europe.

2. Both superpowers are increasingly aware that their postwar fixation on bipolarity not only prevents their policies from adapting to the real world, but also poisons their bilateral relations. Their motives may differ remarkably, but they nevertheless share a growing number of common interests vis-a-vis the rest of the world, despite remaining rivals in the international arena.

3. Political unrest will characterize life in Eastern Europe for years to come. The East European states, along with the

Soviet Union, are seeking a new pluralism. If this process
continues without major setbacks, it will address most directly
the root causes of East–West political confrontation.

4. The reunification of Germany is eliminating what is perhaps
the most difficult political problem related to the end of World
War II. Over the long term, this process could constitute a
solution to at least the postwar version of the German
problem, if not the problem as such.

5. Europe has not escaped the global phenomenon of increasing
interdependence among states, particularly in economic terms.
European domestic political structures seem to be in transition
as well. As a result, Europeans share an increasing number of
common values and unifying threat perceptions, which have
less and less to do with postwar political-ideological confrontation but instead reflect new security needs. Indeed, in the
mind of the European public, the continent is now less
divided—if it is at all—than at any other time since the
establishment of the split. Yet because of the stubbornness of
the military division, European interdependence has developed
primarily within an adversarial context. (The concept of
"adversarial interdependence" provides a theoretical framework for the major part of this study's account of systemic
processes.)[8]

6. Nuclear weapons in the final analysis have been the guarantors of bipolarity. Thus the elimination of the nuclear option
in Europe has begun to stimulate political change.

In the examination of political change in Europe, this book gives
special attention to intra-alliance developments. It is obvious that the
reassociation of the two halves of Europe cannot take place without
major political changes within both military alliances. One of the
purposes of this book, then, is to envisage, in light of the overall
process of change, the evolving geostrategic landscape of Europe and
the political premises of the emerging post-bipolar security order.

Prospects for dismantling the partition of Europe depend in large
part on a broad interpretation of security. Whereas the neutral states
in particular have traditionally shared such an approach to their
security strategies, a similar view is now gaining ground in both
military alliances. If the offensive capacity of the alliances were to be
eliminated, most of the political ramifications of the weapons
involved would be eliminated as well. The military instrument

could—and would—be used only for defensive purposes. However, since World War II security has been defined in excessively narrow and overly military terms, mainly because of nuclear weapons, which prompted an extremely static definition of security as merely the balance of power and nuclear deterrence. But security is no longer a static process.

In this age of growing interdependence and globalization, the source of security for any country lies increasingly in its ability to take part effectively in varied forms of international cooperation, rather than, for example, in its endowment of natural resources. Although military preparedness will remain one of the key factors— if not *the* key factor—in national security strategies, a broadening of security thinking is likely to become crucial for Europeans and, in turn, for the states involved in European security affairs. This study attempts to examine the development of the common security concerns of all Europeans. A central conclusion is that the overall process of change could constitute a third postwar peace arrangement, since it most directly addresses the unresolved political problems left over from World War II.

After the war, Europe's organic structures lay largely in ruins: national borders were erased, nationalities were divided and dispersed, and ancient political and cultural traditions were destroyed. Over the 45 years since then, the process of restoring Europe has been complex and characterized by a great degree of immobility. Many efforts to restore Europe have not respected the organic realities, such as national rights and traditions. As Winston Churchill stated in 1950 at the dawn of Western integration: "Europe is treated like a machine, not like an organic plant."[9] In the long run, the restoration of Europe as an organic whole should have been the guiding principle for all peace arrangements. George F. Kennan had already put forward this view during the war, when he insisted that American interests lay in "the broadest and most stable possible foundations for a reconstruction of Europe: in arrangements which would give maximum play to the natural and permanent creative forces of the continent and provide the least possible sources of national frustration and friction."[10] This study argues that both the political and systemic processes of change under way today are belatedly addressing the process of Europe's restoration in organic terms.

This Research Volume is divided into seven chapters. Chapter 1 describes the structure of the Cold War conflict and deals with the geopolitical issues that constitute the core of the East–West system. The second chapter analyzes the policy of detente, which added a cooperative dimension to East–West relations while having a divisive impact on West-West relations. The third chapter takes a general look at systemic processes that were dynamic influences in Europe in the 1970s. The fourth chapter focuses on the "Eurocentric" political processes that eroded the bipolar security order, while the fifth chapter attempts to describe the evolving geostrategic landscape of Europe. The sixth chapter attempts to knit together the conclusions of the previous chapters to envisage a new European security arrangement for the 1990s beyond the bipolar framework. Finally, the concluding chapter makes an attempt to predict the future, particularly in light of the revolutions of 1989 in Eastern Europe and the continuing disintegration of the Soviet Union.

Part I
The Status Quo Plus

PART I
THE STATUS QUO PLUS

For two decades, from the end of the 1940s to the end of the 1960s, the United States and the Soviet Union dominated the European scene. During this period the structure of East–West confrontation was established: military alliances were formed, economic organizations were created to promote integration among states in the opposing halves of the continent, and an ideological battle was fought to reinforce recognizable enemy images for decades to come. During those years—the classical era of the Cold War—the political struggle over the future of Europe was waged primarily between the two superpowers. The Europeans themselves were too weak to play any significant role, even in their own affairs.

During the Cold War the superpowers were generally satisfied with maintaining the status quo. Yet they also wanted to challenge each other geopolitically. This antagonism brought the world to the verge of nuclear annihilation in 1962. Thereafter, a cooperative dimension was self-consciously added to the East–West system—an innovation which, in the short term, only strengthened the East–West status quo. Nevertheless, the ideological competition did not cease. Later, however, it was precisely this element of cooperation and the eventual emergence of detente that triggered a process of reshaping the political landscape of postwar Europe. In short, the establishment of a postwar "status quo plus" order in Europe constituted the necessary precondition for change, which was played out in the following years at the national, all-European and systemic levels.

1 The Conflict in Retrospect

The French statesman Alexis de Tocqueville shrewdly predicted more than 100 years ago that Russia and the United States would eventually become antagonists in world politics because of their vast power resources and immense size. Although de Tocqueville was to a large extent right, the postwar East–West confrontation took place in a specific historical context that heightened existing Russo-American differences. Accordingly, mistrust superseded confidence in the relationship that developed between the "East" and the "West" in the late 1940s, and subsequently it has disappeared only temporarily.[1]

After World War II Europe needed to be restored both economically and politically. Although a consensus was never reached among the four powers on how to proceed, they regarded general stability as the main priority in European politics, whether the issue was economic growth, the arms race or a balance of political forces in national policies. Order superseded justice in most approaches of the decision-makers to the situation. In practical terms, the paramount problem was a dual one: restoring Germany to health and prosperity without creating a Germany that could constitute a serious threat to European security. The result was that a new intra-European balance of power and a stabilizing economic structure were eventually established.[2]

The liberation of the Eastern European peoples by the Red Army, and subsequent Communist take-over in Poland, Czechoslovakia, Hungary, Romania, Bulgaria and East Germany, gathered these countries into Moscow's "socialist camp." By this, "the power-relation between the two systems, the socialist and the capitalist, was radically changed in favor of socialism."[3] It was emphasized in the "socialist camp" that the world arena became divided into the imperialist and antidemocratic camp on the one side, led by the U.S.A, and on the other the "anti-imperialist and democratic camp" under the leadership of the Soviet Union and with the new "people's democracies" as their main members. In fact this interpretation of the origin of "world socialism" and of the changes in the global

power-balance remained valid for over 40 years, and it was even
confirmed by Mikhail Gorbachev at the 27th CPSU (Communist
Party of the Soviet Union) Congress in February 1986.[4]

The "camp"—later renamed "socialist community"—was perceived and presented to the outside as a monolith united by
"identical types of political and social–economic system, Marxist–
Leninist ideology, class solidarity, friendship and cooperation." In
the late 1980s the whole process of the unification and integration of
the Bloc was evaluated even by the Soviet leadership as a mistake
and failure. One could agree with Ernst Kux, who states that "it
remains no less a fact that the Communist take-over by Moscow's
puppets in its 'satellites', the imposition of the model on historically
and socially different societies, their separation by the Iron Curtain
from the other part of Europe and the subsequent military confrontation and the series of crises between East and West had shaped
the history of Europe over forty years."[5] And the "Eastern Bloc"
never was a stable political community. The first cracks in its
foundation had appeared as early as the late 1940s after the
defection of Tito's Yugoslavia, and they were enlarged during the
Sino-Soviet conflict during the 1960s. On the other hand, although
short periods of "destalinization" took place occasionally, the true
apogee of Soviet hegemony in Eastern Europe took place in August
1968, when Soviet tanks crushed the Prague Spring. That action
established finally the so-called "Brezhnev Doctrine", which claimed
the right of interference into the internal affairs of the fraternal
countries, limited their sovereignty and confirmed Moscow as the
supreme overlord in the bloc.[6]

The Soviet Union wanted to speed up the military and economic
integration by keeping quiet and order in its empire. From the
geopolitical point of view, while Stalin had wanted to gain his goals
by pushing America out of Europe and by keeping Germany down,
Brezhnev tried to achieve the same goals—to maintain the Soviet
hegemony in Eastern Europe—by detente with the United States
and, later on, with the Federal Republic of Germany.

It is clear that, despite far-reaching changes in military doctrine
and weaponry on both sides since 1945, the balance of power
between East and West has remained remarkably unchanged when
measured by its political effectiveness. This high degree of qualitative
strategic stability despite considerable quantifiable strategic change
goes a long way in accounting for East–West political stability in
Europe. Indeed, it is a situation of virtual immobility in the East–

West system; maintenance of the status quo, which was at first considered merely a temporary solution, turned into the goal as such. This state of affairs was most striking during the 1950s and 1960s. Since then the superpowers' eagerness to maintain the status quo has repeatedly been a source of conflict between them and their respective allies. Particularly since the early 1970s the fragmentation of attitudes towards the status quo has constituted a central political problem within the two alliances.

THE STRUCTURE OF CONFRONTATION

The historian Gordon A. Craig has observed that when the Iron Curtain descended between Eastern and Western Europe soon after World War II, the event was tragic for "not merely the political and economic significance. It presented a barrier to the free exchange of ideas, to mutual stimulation, and to scholarly and scientific collaboration that was virtually insurmountable."[7] Quite naturally, neither East nor West Europeans have accepted the division as a desirable or permanent condition. Nevertheless, for more than four decades the East–West structure of European relations has proven highly resistant to change. Now, however, the situation is evolving rapidly, with dramatic results.

The structures of a divided Europe that emerged in the late 1940s and early 1950s reflected ideological, power-related and economic conflicts within the relationship between the two superpowers. The most important consequence of Europe's division was the formation of lasting and opposing political–military alliances. Although Europe also has been to a large extent divided in terms of its economic, social and cultural life, the political-military split has until now been the most decisive aspect of the division.

It is obvious that there is no single, objectively verifiable answer to the question of why Europe has been divided. For years the debate has ranged far and wide; what does seem clear, however, is that, as already mentioned, the military buildup of Europe is not the cause but the consequence of political conflict among states involved in Europe.[8] The victors of World War II never managed to solve all the political problems resulting from the war. In the end, no clear-cut solution was reached regarding the status of the occupied territories. Joseph Stalin commented in a conversation with Yugoslav leaders in April 1945 that "this war is not as in the past. Whoever occupies a territory also imposes on it his own political system . . . as far as his army can reach. It cannot be otherwise."[9] Such a legacy, however, was disputed by the United States. As Ralph B. Levering points out: "With Stalin's Russia reluctant to abandon its dominant position in several neighboring nations, and with Truman's America reluctant to concede Soviet hegemony anywhere, the stage was set for the Cold War."[10] Yalta became the symbol of the unfinished struggle for the future of Europe.[11]

In sum, the original Cold War structure had three main characteristics: 1) a fairly fixed and pervasive East–West bipolarity, which derived from a fundamental ideological and socioeconomic confrontation; 2) the balance of military, and in particular nuclear, terror; and 3) an atmosphere of international tension arising from preparations for war by both parties, their ideological animosities, their tests of strength in crisis situations, and their mutual suspicions and misperceptions fed by the scarcity of interbloc communication.[12]

In spite of its many shortcomings, however, the bipolar security system also has certain indisputable merits. For one thing, Europe has in fact experienced the longest period of peace in its modern history. As a result of World War II, Europe was more or less doomed to division; however, the division created stability which, in turn, provided a starting point for peaceful change at a later stage.[13]

THE COLD WAR AS GEOPOLITICS

The driving force behind the Cold War is geopolitics: conflict over territory and its control. In the historical perspective, it is evident that the superpowers have to a certain degree competed to implant or impose their own political systems beyond their borders. Within the European framework, however, the core issue of the Cold War has been Soviet domination of Eastern Europe, a situation that threatens West European as well as U.S. security. Thus all plans aimed at improving the European security situation—not to mention dismantling the partition itself—make reference to the establishment of a new relationship between Eastern Europe and the Soviet Union. In short, the principal requirement for the end of the Cold War has been self-determination for Eastern Europe.[14]

But Soviet domination of Eastern Europe must also be seen in historical terms. Hitler's policy had already destroyed the European balance of power in the early 1930s. By its end, World War II had created a power vacuum in Europe, which was filled jointly by the Soviet Union and the United States, the only powers capable of both reconstituting a stable equilibrium on the continent and decisively upsetting this balance each to the disadvantage of the other. Historical experience as well as political theory should have indicated that tension and discord were inherent in such a situation, however.[15]

In the aftermath of World War II strong pacifistic sentiments gained ground in most of the West European countries. As had been the case in the years following World War I, power politics were once again rejected, blamed as a root cause of the war. Many hopes were raised by the founding of a new world organization, but it was soon realized that the United Nations would not be able to establish a better balance of power in Europe. The Soviet military machinery was deployed offensively throughout Eastern Europe, and the Soviet Union was not about to change its posture on international relations since it was modeled on the Leninist concept of class struggle and systemic antagonism. Indeed, many scholars date the origins of the Cold War from 1917.[16]

The postwar Cold War, however, was triggered by a U.S. counter-offensive to stave off another hegemonic enterprise in Europe. The main thrust of this U.S. effort was the economic program known as the Marshall Plan, which was designed to restore the war-ravaged economies of Europe and was implemented in 1947–1949. Because the Soviets prevented the participation of Eastern Europe in the Marshall Plan, this American campaign created the overall political, ideological and military division in Europe, which was consolidated into the structural basis of the bloc division. Institutionalized confrontation, brought about by the militarization of the Marshall Plan, was not, however, one of the original goals of the planners. George F. Kennan, the plan's main strategist, regretted in his memoirs that he had failed "to make clear that what he was talking about . . . was not the containment by military means of a military threat, but the political containment of a political threat."[17] Kennan defined his doctrine of containment in an article published in *Foreign Affairs* under the pseudonym "Mr. X" in 1947. He stated that, "In these circumstances it is clear that the main element of any United States policy toward the Soviet Union must be that of a long-term patient, but vigilant containment of Russian expansive tendencies."[18] The ultimate outcome of the Marshall Plan—the Cold

War structure— was not in anyone's interest. In retrospect, it is clear that the de facto economic, political and cultural isolation of Eastern Europe and the Soviet Union from the rest of Europe that resulted from the implementation of the plan may in fact constitute a major cause of the current economic and systemic problems in those countries. However, the militarization of the Marshall Plan was not a cause of the Soviet threat, but its consequence.

To understand recent efforts to undo the division of Europe and, by extension, of Germany, a closer look at the geopolitical context of the collapse of postwar negotiations among the allied powers is necessary. The major outcome of that collapse, the partition of Germany, is not a normal state of affairs, although many prominent politicians in both the East and the West long defended the partition as the best possible arrangement for maintaining stability in Europe.

Paradoxically, World War II deepened the Germans' sense of unity. Some observers recognized that all attempts "to keep the country partitioned in a Europe where most other linguistic and ethnic bodies would be unified would only be to recreate the aspirations and compulsions of the mid-nineteenth century, and to place a premium on the emergence of a new Bismarck and a new 1870," as Kennan remarked in 1967. Rather than seeking a model for the unification of Germany by looking to the past, Kennan hoped to discover a new solution. In his view, a united Germany could be possible only as part of "something larger than herself" and would only be tolerable as "an integral part of a united Europe."[19] In a nutshell, an organically restored Germany should only be established within the framework of an undivided Europe.

The overall Western strategy, then, was meant to cope with the process of European integration, which in turn would constitute a major means of promoting unification. But the German question was always handled separately, without a deeper sense of the larger processes of history taking place in the aftermath of World War II. It was generally understood that Germany's prosperity was vital to the prosperity of Western Europe, but there was no clear understanding of how best to achieve European integration in a politically satisfactory way. Furthermore, the link between the need for European unification and a solution to the "German question" was never acknowledged. Nevertheless, from the outset, in all deliberations about the future of Germany the problem of its geopolitical location was never far below the surface. Would a new Germany tilt toward the East instead of playing a role in the strategy of containment? Would a united and independent Germany in fact pose a threat to the West? As U.S. Secretary of State Marshall noted in the winter of 1948: "This Government is determined not to permit reestablishment of Germany's economic and political unity under conditions which are likely to bring about effective domination of all Germany by Soviets."[20]

Accordingly, the Western allied states—the United States, France and the United Kingdom—put the question of German reunification on the back burner during their meeting in London in the spring of 1948. Since they were frustrated by the USSR's refusal to implement unification on terms acceptable to the West, the three powers agreed at the London meeting to permit the formation of a German government in their zones of occupation without relinquishing occupation control. This decision was a decisive step toward the establishment of two German states and the eventual division of the continent. In contrast to the opinion of most Western elites, Kennan presciently described in August 1948 the ultimate outcome of this breakdown of negotiations over the "German question":

> If we carry on along present lines, Germany must divide into eastern and western governments and Western Europe must move toward a tight military alliance with this country, which can only complicate the eventual integration of the satellites into a European community. From such a trend of developments, it would be hard—harder than it is now—to find "the road back" to a united and free Europe.[21]

Although the division of Germany did not hinder the positive development of the Federal Republic of Germany, in the longer term, as Kennan was to diagnose years later, two problems arose. First, the instruments of containment were allowed to overshadow the policy's ultimate objective, which was to change the Soviet conception of international relations and thus make possible a negotiated settlement of outstanding differences. A strategy of encircling the Soviet Union with military alliances could hardly move such a process forward. As Kennan noted, "what was so conceived as an instrument became, little by little, an end itself. What was supposed to have been the servant of policy became its determinant instead." In the final analysis, the German question in some senses was resolved but at the same time was also left tragically untouched.[22]

Second, the establishment of the two German states legitimized the presence of Soviet troops in Eastern Europe. Once again, Kennan reflected on this problem with prescience in his memoirs:

So long as the dominant Soviet influence over Eastern Europe remains firm, [to rearm Western Germany as a member of NATO is] apparently adequate to the situation. But if some day there should be an insistent demand on the part of the Eastern European countries for some sort of integration into the European community generally, and if the nature of their relations with the Soviet Union is at that time such as to permit this to happen peacefully, then the limitations of the arrangements concluded in 1949 and 1954 will at once become apparent, and people will have to occupy themselves seriously once again with the logic, if not the detailed provisions, of "Plan A" [Kennan's 1948 proposal for the reunification of Germany on realistic terms acceptable to the Soviets as well as to the Germans and the Americans].[23]

As John Lewis Gaddis notes, "the price of administrative effectiveness can be strategic shortsightedness." The Truman administration's conduct of foreign and security policy, which included implementation of the strategy of containment, failed to maintain proper subordination of means to ends. Indeed, in its determined effort to restore Western economic and military strength, the Truman administration lost sight of the objective it purported to serve: ending the Cold War.[24] The price of this failure was to be paid in the future, when the time was ripe for real rapprochement between East and West.

As the prospects for West Germany's formal integration into NATO grew more real, Stalin began to maneuver diplomatically in the early 1950s. The Soviet Union was obviously ready to negotiate, perhaps even seriously, on a united, non-communist Germany, in return for increased reparations, the continued demilitarization of Germany and Western recognition of Poland's postwar borders— a deal which, as Adam Ulam states, would have been in the West's interests, too. But time and again the West reacted negatively to Soviet offers to consider the reunification of Germany on "neutral terms." For example, on May 10, 1952, when the Soviets offered to discuss terms for a neutral and unified Germany, presenting the possibility of a peaceful revision of the initial partition of Europe, the West reacted with remarkable indifference. At this stage, the

Western allies did not deem it proper even to explore such a notion with the Soviet Union.[25]

But Stalin's maneuvers could not halt the process. In this way the West in effect cemented the postwar division of Germany and Europe. Later, Western unresponsiveness to incidents such as the civil disturbances in East Berlin and Plzen, Czechoslovakia, in 1953 and the Hungarian revolution of 1956 confirmed the West's implicit intention to tolerate the division of Europe to avoid the possibility of military confrontation with the Soviets. Actually, rather than "tolerate," the term "prefer" more appropriately described both Western and Eastern attitudes toward the division of Europe in the 1950s. After the June 1953 uprising in East Berlin, which de facto committed the Soviet Union to granting approval to the German Democratic Republic (GDR) and its communist regime, and made it easier for the Federal Republic of Germany (FRG) to join NATO in May 1955, Soviet support for German reunification was withdrawn for all practical purposes. From that point on Moscow openly shifted to a two-state policy, and its diplomacy, as F. Stephen Larrabee puts it, followed a two-track course aimed at 1) stabilizing the GDR and integrating it more tightly into the Eastern bloc, and 2) securing Western, particularly West German, recognition of the postwar status quo.[26]

During Konrad Adenauer's term as West German Federal Chancellor (1949–1963), the FRG based its foreign policy on two principles: 1) full-scale economic, political and military (except nuclear) participation in the Western integration, and 2) eventual reunification, to be achieved through an aggressive policy aimed at the GDR. Since it refused to accept the division of Germany, the FRG did not recognize the GDR as a legitimate state and continued to claim to be the sole representative of the German people. To isolate the GDR internationally, the FRG proclaimed in 1956 what came to be known as the Hallstein Doctrine, which demanded that diplomatic relations be broken with any country that recognized the GDR. This doctrine excluded the Soviet Union, however; Bonn had established diplomatic relations with Moscow in 1955. In actual fact, however, the Hallstein Doctrine left Bonn's room for maneuver extremely limited.

At the same time, Bonn's terms for reunification remained extremely "Western." When Kennan proposed the disengagement of superpower forces from Germany as part of a scheme for reestablishing a united, though neutral, Germany in his 1957 BBC Reith

Lecture, he was bluntly rejected in Western capitals, particularly
Bonn. Kennan's purpose was to warn against the nuclearization of
the military confrontation in Central Europe, and he sincerely
thought that eradication of the division of Europe and of Germany
was the actual policy goal of the United States and its allies. The
Adenauer government, however, considered that this kind of proposal discriminated against the FRG vis-à-vis its allies, threatening the
security and the past policy of Western integration.[27] Nevertheless,
Kennan's suggestion was largely in compliance with several proposals elaborated by the West German opposition party, the Social
Democratic party (SPD), and the British Labour party, in particular
in the late 1950s. The most meaningful of these proposals was put
forth by the leaders of the latter party, Denis Healey and Hugh
Gaitskell, who focused on the establishment of a "neutral belt"
between the two alliance systems that would encompass Germany,
Poland, Czechoslovakia, Hungary and the other states to the north
and south of the zone. Ideas such as these were aimed at defusing the
military confrontation in Central Europe, thus enabling people living
in this area to attain an independent national existence and incorporating Germany into an East–West accord.[28]

By the end of the 1950s the time had passed for working out an
international agreement on the German question. The two German
states constituted a reality that was already incorporated into the
postwar security system of Europe. All possible options for solving
the German question had to be placed within a plan for addressing
European security concerns overall. Although West Germans of all
political stripes were eager to strive for reunification, in the realm of
international diplomacy priority was placed on military over political
security, that is, on framing the German question in terms that
would have endangered alliance unity. Yet rather soon this policy
threatened to isolate the FRG internationally.[29]

THE FINAL BATTLE FOR CONTROL OF THE CENTER OF EUROPE

Germany's geographic location at the heart of Europe accounts for
specific political and permanent realities. European relations have
always constituted in part a battle for control of the center, and
Germany has usually been either too weak or too strong to serve as a
stabilizing factor in the European concert of powers.

The Nazi era (1933–1945) halted the organic development of Germany. Initially most Germans viewed Hitler not as a criminal dictator but as a leader of national renewal, who slew the Hydra of the multiparty state and, astride its corpse, conjured up the vision of a thousand-year Reich, which lay beyond the wrangling of parties and the politics of special interests.[30] One of the paradoxes of World War II was that, as mentioned above, the sense of German national unity reached its peak in the ruinous aftermath of the war. The Germans, however, lost control over their own fate; as Helga Haftendorn states, the founding of the FRG was not an act of free will on the part of the Germans, but a decision of the Western allies and a consequence of the Cold War.[31] The dismemberment of Germany after World War II was a product of the war of aggression unleashed by Hitler and the resulting need for security and self-assertion on the part of his wartime adversaries, amplified by the political, economic, and ideological struggle developing between East and West.

Although the causes of the German "national problem" lie deep in history, the founding of two German states preserved a sense of this problem even as it was transferred to the international arena as a new "German question."[32] In the postwar period the West Germans reduced their concept of nation to a moral postulate and a legal claim, whereas the communists in East Germany tried to give the "nation" an ideological foundation.[33] At the same time, however, historically unifying—organic—features gained a new impetus in both states.

After the founding of the two German states in 1949, the only real option for restoring German unity was a sort of agreement among the four powers, under which the Soviet Union would allow the GDR to leave its sphere of influence and move toward reunification by means of an *Anschluss* with the FRG. This development excluded any "neutral" option for a reunified Germany. A politically solid and economically flourishing West German state would exercise a "magnetic influence" on the people of East Germany, thus accelerating this process and above all making it increasingly costly for Moscow to maintain a communist regime against the will of the people. It could be argued that the FRG's "economic miracle" has turned out to be a West German version of the "policy of strength" originally formulated by U.S. Secretary of State John Foster Dulles in the early 1950s. But both superpowers, although introducing concepts and modalities designed to overcome the division of

Germany, ultimately maintained the partition, thus safeguarding their strategic interests in Europe rather than pressing too hard for change in the political and territorial status quo.[34]

The incorporation of the FRG into NATO and the GDR into the Warsaw Pact meant that by 1955 the formation of the postwar European structures was essentially completed. Two main results of the formative process were the destruction of Europe as an independent political force and the emergence of the United States and the Soviet Union as the dominant global—and European — powers. The political and military presence of these two powers in Europe, along with the partition of the continent and the inclusion of the two parts of Germany in opposing hegemonic spheres, became in fact the decisive structural features of postwar Europe.[35]

Even as they were completing the division of Europe into separate blocs, the superpowers recognized that the actual conflict—over the domination of Central Europe—could not be settled. Thus even while ideological competition persisted and the arms race intensi-fied, the four powers began to strive for a modus vivendi regarding this other outstanding controversy. An initial result of their endea-vors was the Austrian State Treaty, which granted Austria neutral status and enabled it to pursue an independent policy line in international affairs, but banned union with Germany. Any settle-ment of the German question was postponed at this juncture, however, because both superpowers preferred to keep intact their established spheres of influence in Europe.[36]

In forums of international diplomacy, such as the four-power Geneva summit in 1955, top priority was clearly given to military over political security. However, the much acclaimed "spirit of Geneva" also demonstrated that, despite the persistence of the fundamental conflict between East and West, there existed a partial identity of interests among the great powers and a desire on both sides for detente in international relations. In the eyes of Bonn, however, the relaxation of tensions emanating from the Geneva summit entailed dangers that threatened to jeopardize what had already been achieved. For one thing, the West German government feared an accord among the victorious powers of World War II at its expense. Thus Adenauer's trip to Moscow in September 1955 was designed in part to give the West German government direct access to the Soviet leadership, even if this act of emancipation also signified yet another step toward acceptance of the postwar status quo.[37] The worst-case scenario from Bonn's point of view would be "singularization" or "isolation" of the FRG. Although Bonn had largely sacrificed its national interests in favor of NATO interests, it did not entirely trust its new allies. Membership in NATO may have guaranteed military security for the West Germans, but this would not necessarily matter if reunification became a realistic and even necessary option.

The battle for control of Central Europe has also been a function of the evolution of Soviet thinking about international relations. At the 20th Party Congress in 1956 the Soviet Union to a large extent abandoned its strategy of world revolution and declared as its basic political principle the doctrine of peaceful coexistence, which in a certain sense amounted to a strategy of war prevention. The principle of peaceful coexistence was a major outcome of the Soviets' reevaluation of the influence of nuclear weapons on the conduct of international relations. Over the long term, peaceful coexistence came to imply a mutual respect for each side's sphere of influence and the political status quo in postwar Europe. In the future the Soviet Union would be amenable to changes in its security policy only on the basis of the political status quo—unless the latter could be altered to Soviet advantage. This was precisely what, as Helga Haftendorn puts it, the Soviet Union "tried to do from late 1958 on, with the aid of the recurrent Berlin crisis, once the Soviet willingness earlier in 1955–58 had failed to have the desired effect."[38]

Although the Soviet Union basically rejected the policy of world revolution in 1956, it started to practice an aggressive "nuclear diplomacy" to achieve political advantage, particularly in Europe. This diplomacy in fact frightened many in the West and caused dissension within NATO. Western public opinion gradually began to favor unilateral denuclearization, and "better red than dead" was a popular slogan in many West European countries in the late 1950s. Fully aware of the fears of ordinary people in the West about the threat of nuclear war, the Soviet Union launched a diplomatic campaign to transform West Berlin into a "free city." This campaign was also propagated as an effort to overcome the division of Germany through "reunification in peace and freedom." The aim of this kind of propaganda was to cause disintegration in West German and West European domestic politics: to strengthen the leftist parties, which had been more "soft" vis-à-vis the Soviet Union. In November 1958, Nikita Khrushchev pronounced his de facto ultimatum that the time had come for the occupying powers to withdraw from Berlin.[39] On January 10, 1959, Moscow put forward a draft peace treaty with the two German states, combined with a proposal to handle the issue at a summit conference with the states involved. Finally, on February 17, 1959, Khrushchev threatened to conclude a separate peace treaty with the GDR and transfer to it all rights and obligations regarding Berlin.

Khrushchev's goal was to eliminate the Western presence from Berlin. He had described this presence as a "bone in Russia's throat," and it undoubtedly did represent an acute and constant danger, threatening, in fact, Soviet control over East Germany and ultimately over all of Eastern Europe.[40] If successful, Moscow would greatly strengthen its geopolitical position at the heart of Europe and, at the same time, cement the Yalta legacy. Furthermore, the Soviet Union would have been able to demonstrate superior strength vis-à-vis the United States by making Europe its (nuclear) hostage.

The West experienced great difficulties in reaching a united position in the early weeks and months of the crisis. In both Bonn and other Western capitals, various options were considered for finding a "compromise formula" that would meet the Soviets' demands without risking a nuclear exchange. The West Germans often considered themselves disengaged from their own crisis, mainly because Washington and especially London expressed their readiness to negotiate a deal with the Soviets over the heads of the West Germans. Only France was determined to reject any concessions, albeit less for objective reasons than because it had no interest in an East–West rapprochement that could result in the restoration of Germany's national unity. As the crisis continued, the West did not, in fact, express any real willingness to retreat, and the Soviet Union for its part had to face certain realities of the nuclear age—namely, that in situations like the Berlin crisis, in which neither side is willing to risk the ultimate showdown, the defender of the status quo has a definite advantage over the challenger. It is the challenger, not the defender, who proposes to take the steps that will lead to a nuclear showdown. It soon became clear, however, that Moscow was determined to achieve its goal only by using the threat of war, not its realization, which meant that time and again Moscow had to modify its ultimatums.[41]

In 1960–1961, however, the Soviet Union stuck to its original position, which effectively maintained a high degree of tension in East–West relations.[42] Khrushchev was determined that the Soviet Union's new military strength should provide a historic opportunity to consolidate the postwar spheres of control, and in the subsequent months no common ground was ever reached between East and West over Berlin. After the developments in Berlin, the U.S.– Soviet confrontation over Cuba presented a double crisis. The installation of Soviet missiles on this Caribbean island was surely designed to bolster the thesis of a global East–West balance of power, which would obviate the use of nuclear power in a limited regional conflict. Undoubtedly this step also gave the Soviet Union added leverage over the United States to induce a U.S. compromise on Berlin and Germany. These Soviet attempts to alter the international balance of power triggered the crises over Berlin and Cuba. The postwar international system had reached a turning point, however; the Cuban and Berlin crises revealed that any forcible change in the status quo would entail the danger of the aggressor's own annihilation.[43]

Although the Soviet Union's aggressive nuclear diplomacy in Europe was a major failure, Western passivity during the construction of the Berlin Wall can be considered the West's de facto recognition of the postwar status quo entailed by the existence of two German states. Nevertheless, the Soviet Union still had to change its tactics in the international arena. Moscow did not give up its original goal of strengthening its geostrategic position in Europe and around the world, but from this point on it put more emphasis on gradualism and the maintenance of stability than on dramatic systemic change. In Europe, the USSR began campaigning for a European security conference. For the Western alliance the Berlin and Cuban crises were obvious setbacks to the cause of unity. Thereafter the difference of interests between the United States and the FRG in particular over the question of overcoming or maintaining the status quo led to a serious crisis of confidence in German–American (as well as Franco-American) relations. This development was reflected in West German domestic politics as a conflict between so-called Gaullists and Atlanticists. The first concurred with the views of President de Gaulle of France, who never really trusted the United States in defending European security interests against the Soviet Union. The Atlanticists—such as Adenauer—considered that a transatlantic relationship balanced the Soviet threat. The United States unintentionally began to push some opinion leaders in the FRG along the path of Ostpolitik, which later would produce a major headache for Washington.

The Berlin and Cuban crises ultimately confirmed the latent stability of the East–West structure then coming into existence.

Both East and West had to start the long process that, as Allen Lynch reasons, "by promoting stability over system change would yield detente and the post-Cold War era."[44] Europe would no longer be a source of East–West military conflict; in the future, the superpower rivalry would be fought in ever more distant regions of the Third World. Nevertheless, Europe remained heavily armed, and Eastern Europe occupied by Soviet troops, although overall stability was greatly strengthened in the coming era of detente.

2 The Rise of Detente

The Berlin and Cuban crises constituted a turning point in postwar European history. It soon became widely recognized, especially in the capitals of the two superpowers, that in the age of nuclear and missile technology, war could no longer be an acceptable means of managing relations among European states. Furthermore, it was understood that a relationship of "negative interdependence" between the East and West was a tragic fact of life in the nuclear age. One repercussion of this new knowledge was the more or less hidden acceptance of a new order of priorities in European politics: security superseded justice, at least in the immediate aftermath of the Cuban and Berlin crises.

Yet it was also widely recognized that in the long run the division of Europe would constitute a permanent source of conflict. As President Urho Kekkonen of Finland stated in 1962:

> It is the fervent hope of the Finnish people that barriers be lowered all over Europe and that progress be made along the road of European unity, for the good of Europe and thus humanity as a whole.[1]

Finland was dragged into the superpower conflict in 1961– 1962, when Moscow sent Helsinki a note requesting immediate military consultations and even considered deploying nuclear weapons or air defense equipment on Finnish territory as part of the superpower nuclear rivalry. President Kekkonen managed, however, to convince Khrushchev that any increase in the Soviet military presence in Scandinavia would trigger a Western counterreaction and could increase tension in this otherwise peaceful area of Europe.

Finland's dilemma was only a minor incident in the larger drama, but it provided a good example of the kind of political interdependence that had developed in a divided Europe. The Berlin and Cuban crises convinced the smaller and medium-sized European countries that they, too, should have their voices heard in security matters in which they were intimately involved. The only possibility for them to achieve this aim would be in the creation of a structure of collective security.[2]

But the process of development of a European collective security arrangement was largely triggered by the big powers themselves. Although East–West confrontation had gradually gained momentum since it was set into motion in 1945–1946, experiencing only temporary pauses in the mid-1950s as a result of the "spirit of Geneva," the Cuban and Berlin crises definitively broke off the spiral of crises. A more controlled relationship was now sought by all participants in the East–West system, not just by the smaller and medium-sized states. Yet the most important diplomatic initiatives were first taken by the big powers. The rise of detente was to constitute a rehearsal for the big powers of the "all-European concert" of the late 1960s and early 1970s.

According to Kenneth Dyson, detente "stresses the need for a common code of behavior in East–West relations, for the revival of a constitutional tradition of diplomacy."[3] The concept is subject to an array of interpretations, however, which has made it very difficult to agree upon any specific policy recommendations. Thus the history of detente is "a story of intelligence contradictions."[4] Indeed, the process can be described as a modest formula for Cold War rivalry, which is often full of deception and ideological warfare. Accordingly, the West was attacked for using detente to bring about the internal erosion of the socialist camp, while the East was accused of seeking military superiority behind the camouflage of rhetoric about a common European security pact. In the Soviet vocabulary, the term "common" in connection with European politics would in fact come to mean "Soviet" or "Soviet-minded." Criticism of the results of the policy of detente led many people, mostly in the United States, to reject the concept entirely. However, as a conceptual umbrella, detente typified the essence of East–West relations after the Cuban and Berlin crises until the end of the 1970s. The rise of detente in itself constitutes an identifiable period, which is most fruitfully analyzed separately from the heyday of detente in the early 1970s.

Although the concept of detente will always remain somewhat ambiguous, it describes a particular feature of international and East–West relations: the turning away from a sense of international tension toward its reduction or relaxation. This turn of events found expression in an array of tendencies toward increasing cooperation. These tendencies were, as Harto Hakovirta states, "the basic precondition for the take-off and progress of more far-reaching detente, which manifests itself in concrete efforts towards the prevention of tensions and the promotion of cooperative international relations."[5] Some time in the mid-1960s the process of detente began in earnest as a series of initiatives for strengthening European diplomacy and cooperation in security issues.

It is also important to put the phenomenon of detente in the right context in West–West relations. Although the United States had been ready to pursue a policy of rapprochement with the Soviet Union since the end of the Cuban and Berlin crises for various reasons, not just because of nuclear arguments, ultimately detente became a European phenomenon. Indeed, it triggered a more genuinely European phase in the postwar history of East–West relations. In particular, the U.S. refusal to block the construction of the Berlin Wall in 1961 provided convincing proof to West Germans like West Berlin Mayor Willy Brandt that the Western powers simply did not share West German enthusiasm for reunification and that any amelioration of the conditions of Germans in the East would have to depend on a more independent West German diplomacy. Indeed, the lessons of the Berlin crisis laid the foundation for Ostpolitik, which, if it were to be successful, would need the international climate and structure provided by detente.[6]

Detente did not, however, stop the arms race or East–West competition. On the contrary, it more or less "legitimized" efforts to strengthen military preparedness. Yet detente also provided a strategy for communicating about all issues related to East–West relations. Over the long term, the policy of detente expanded in two primary dimensions: in inner-German relations and on the all-European level.[7] In addition, detente gave rise to a debate on the future of Europe and thus provided a reasonable concept with which to start defining a new security arrangement beyond bipolarity.

SOVIET-LED CAMPAIGNS FOR A COLLECTIVE SECURITY ARRANGEMENT

Since the time of Peter the Great, Russia (and later, the Soviet Union) has, with only a few short breaks, always worked at strengthening its "European profile." Russia managed to play an important diplomatic role in the Concert of Europe, most particularly at the Congress of Vienna in 1815. Tsar Alexander I drafted the Holy Alliance that envisaged a new system of international order based on peaceful cooperation; however, it was rejected by other participants in the Congress of Vienna as a piece of "sublime mysticism and nonsense." Since then, Russian tsars and their Soviet successors have usually met with great difficulty in convincing other European leaders of the basic sincerity of their motives in European politics. Despite this obstacle, Russians and Soviets have had a more or less permanent interest in participating in efforts to "reorganize Europe." The Soviets have elaborated various kinds of pan-European models for Europe, mainly in order to ward off the emergence of a "united Europe" which might exclude Soviet participation. After World War II, Moscow pursued this effort for years in an attempt to push the United States out of the sphere of European politics.[8]

All Soviet initiatives regarding the development of a new European security system have postulated certain specific features of that system. After the division of Europe was established in the mid-1950s, the Soviet government rushed to international forums with proposals intended to neutralize Germany and, by extension, hinder the establishment of a "Western Europe" containing Germany. During the Berlin four-power conference of foreign ministers in 1954 the Soviet delegation submitted the draft of a "General European Treaty of Collective Security in Europe," to be signed by all European powers, including, as equal participants, the two German states, "pending the creation of a united, peace-loving and democratic German state." In 1955, Soviet Prime Minister Nikolai Bulganin returned to this theme at the four-power Geneva summit, proposing once more a treaty on European security that also advocated disarmament and resolution of the "German question." Under his plan, the conclusion of a nonaggression pact, which would include the reunification of Germany and the peaceful solution of disputes, would be followed by the "dissolution of blocs" or East-West alliance systems and their replacement by an all-European security system. Withdrawal of foreign troops from Europe was an absolute prerequisite of this scheme, which was laid out in the Soviet draft of an "All-European Treaty on Collective Security," submitted to a meeting of foreign ministers in late 1955.

When the "spirit of Geneva" waned, mainly as a result of the 1956 Suez crisis and the Soviet military crackdown on the Hungarian popular revolution that same year, prospects for any kind of collective security effort in Europe dimmed. Yet the Soviet Union did not abandon its efforts to find the ways and means to strengthen security and its own influence in Central Europe. In October 1957, Polish Foreign Minister Adam Rapacki introduced a plan that was primarily aimed at gaining international recognition of the Polish–

German border along the Oder–Neisse line and of the GDR as a
sovereign state, as well as obtaining international support for the
establishment of a nuclear-free zone in Central Europe. The Rapacki
Plan would have effectively foreclosed the FRG's nuclear option,
which had, of course, been a main goal of the Soviet Union since the
FRG joined NATO in 1955. A more elaborate plan was put forward
by Poland in 1964, since the original formula had met with strong
reservations in the West and the international climate had proven
unfavorable. The revised version was introduced after Khrushchev's
dismissal, during an early stage of detente. The 1964 Rapacki Plan
included the basic concept of an all-European security system, and
provided for and acknowledged both Soviet *and* U.S. participation.
The Political Consultative Committee of the Warsaw Pact adopted
the Polish resolution in January 1965 and issued its own communi-
qué pressing for the "convening of a conference of European states
to discuss measures to ensure collective security in Europe." This
document paved the way for the creation of additional documents
between 1966 and 1969 that further elaborated the theme of
"European security" by concentrating on such issues as the dissolution of the two military alliances, the importance to both East and
West of all-European nonmilitary cooperation, the central role of the
German question and the territorial status quo, the interpretation of
national sovereignty, and the role of an all-European security
conference.[9]

Soviet or Soviet-sponsored proposals for establishing a European
security system, which was also aimed at dismantling the continent's
division, remained at the forefront of diplomatic initiatives in East–
West relations for much of the 1960s. This development came in
large part as a result of the acceleration of the U.S.–Soviet arms
race, which was strongly experienced in Europe, as well as because of
the Vietnam war. As the United States gradually became caught up
in the Vietnam war, it needed to develop a less hostile relationship
with the Soviet Union. In any case, both superpowers came to
recognize that mutual interest in a revised East–West political
framework would help contain and manage crises and could thus
help prevent further escalation of the arms race. By 1967, U.S.
leaders were prepared for political actions of this sort. In a speech
in Montreal in 1967, U.S. Defense Secretary Robert McNamara
suggested that "bridges" had to be built to Moscow and even to
Beijing in order to stop the arms buildup. At a hastily planned
summit conference in Glassboro, New Jersey, in 1967, U.S. President

Lyndon Johnson and Soviet Premier Alexei Kosygin signed a historic treaty to halt the proliferation of nuclear weapons to third countries. Although the Glassboro summit also revealed some fundamental disagreements between the two superpowers, it constituted a turning point in their postwar relations. Undoubtedly the conference encouraged a climate of cooperation within the East–West system.[10]

Although the Soviet concept of a European security system was, as mentioned above, developed further by the Warsaw Pact countries, it nevertheless remained rather vague—no doubt deliberately so. No priorities were expressed, nor was any time limit proposed for realizing the program. From the Western point of view, the concept included a striking weakness in that it failed to provide any framework for an overall postwar security arrangement. The United States would be virtually excluded. At Glassboro the Soviets managed to extract a U.S. guarantee that the FRG would remain outside the "nuclear club." The process of establishing a European security system was moving forward, and, if realized in its "advanced" formula, it would strategically "decouple" Western Europe and the United States.[11]

In 1967 and early 1968 the Soviet Union intensified its campaign toward "strengthening peace" in Europe. Sensing increasing problems of unity in the Euroatlantic security community—the result, inter alia, of the Cuban and Berlin crises, the 1966 French withdrawal from NATO's integrated military command, and the heated debate over the role of nuclear weapons in NATO's strategy— Moscow focused its efforts on the grassroots level in Western Europe. The Soviet Union tried to use the idea of a security conference to expand its ideological and political influence throughout Europe,[12] and indeed, public sentiment gradually grew more receptive to Soviet initiatives, in part because of the failure to end the Vietnam war. In addition, many West European domestic structures were politically radicalized as a reflection of the general sentiments of the 1960s.

The Soviet-led Warsaw Pact invasion of Czechoslovakia in 1968 was the turning point in Soviet diplomatic and ideological "expansionism" in Western Europe. Although the emergence of the Brezhnev Doctrine ultimately did not hinder the development of a European security conference, the main responsibility for determining its nature and realization was to a large extent transferred to the West. The need to overcome the outstanding political problems of World War II was not merely a Soviet camouflage but had, in fact, long been a serious concern for all Europeans. Now the time was ripe for an all-European conference on "realistic terms."

After a brief pause occasioned by the Czechoslovakian crisis, the Warsaw Pact issued a new security conference proposal from Budapest on March 17, 1969. The "Budapest Appeal" dropped much of the hostile language of the earlier initiatives and called for a meeting "in the immediate future" of representatives of all European states to establish procedures and an agenda for the conference. Now the Soviet bloc was ready to move forward through diplomatic means and on much more realistic terms.[13] The idea of a European security conference (ESC) was formulated in the East–West dialogue emerging at both the informal and the inter-alliance level after the process of rapprochement began in 1966. Encouraged by this development, representatives of the NATO countries, meeting in Washington in April 1969, let it be known that they were now ready for serious negotiations with the Soviet Union and other European countries. The government of Finland rapidly seized the initiative and on May 6, 1969, expressed its willingness to host such a conference.

Although the door was now open for an all-European security conference, its agenda and parameters remained unresolved, and there was a lengthy process of negotiation before agreement was finally reached in 1973. For their part, the Warsaw Pact countries laid down their negotiating position in October 1969 with a proposal consisting of two brief but lucidly formulated items for the agenda:

1. ensuring European security and renunciation of the use of force or the threat of its use in mutual relations among the states of Europe; and
2. expanding trade, economic, scientific and technical relations on the principle of equal rights, aimed at the development of political cooperation among European states.

Although the Warsaw Pact proposal contained certain elements crucial to the later agenda of the Helsinki process, it only focused on those areas of greatest concern to the Soviet Union and its allies. The first paragraph of the proposal was aimed at recognition of the postwar territorial status quo, which had been the main goal of the Soviet campaign in convening the ESC in the first place. In addition, the lack of sophisticated technology was already beginning to pose a problem to the USSR and Eastern Europe.

Yet a common ground for negotiations between the East and the West was finally reached. The Soviet Union had, as it liked to point out, won the first round of bargaining. However, it had to prepare for another round, which would surely entail many fundamental concessions if the Soviet Union were to continue to champion the idea of the ESC. Detente was to embrace more than simple rapprochement among states. Indeed, "the Iron Curtain would have to become permeable," as one Western observer put it.[14]

THE WESTERN PILLARS OF DETENTE

The emergence of a genuine policy of detente in the 1960s was not the result of a Soviet-led campaign for a European security system, but of a much more complex process of East–West interaction. This interaction was evident not only at the level of superpower rapprochement, but perhaps even more strikingly at the subregional level, in terms of inter-German relations as well as Franco-Soviet rapprochement.

In the postwar process of restoring Europe and establishing normal and peaceful relations among its states, the emergence of detente was without a doubt the crucial turning point. Within the framework of detente, West German Ostpolitik played an important, perhaps quite central, role. In retrospect, the policy of detente demonstrates a triumph of traditional diplomacy, in which questions of gains and losses are always relative—and every gain contains at least one major paradox.

As mentioned above, detente developed in the aftermath of the Berlin and Cuban crises. In one respect, it is clear that Khrushchev's Cuban gamble was related to his desire to obtain political leverage over the German problem through a publicized shift in the strategic balance.[15] Although this assessment may be a bit simplistic, a consensus seems to have emerged in both Europe and the United States that these two crises were interrelated.[16] This in turn led to a general belief in West European capitals that disputes between East and West should be settled peacefully and gradually rather than by the use or threat of force. A similar conclusion was reached in Washington, but it also included the conviction that the division of Europe was the price that had to be paid for the maintenance of

stability and peace. One authoritative observer has summarized the
U.S. view in that period as follows:

> The only sensible course was to accept the division as an enforced
> reality, which only war could undo, and encourage increased
> contacts with the Eastern zone to better the lot and maintain the
> hopes of those denied their political rights by the Soviet system.
> ... No agreement remotely satisfactory was possible, none was
> really even necessary, since the situation was finally stable, if
> admittedly imperfect.[17]

The U.S. grand vision of detente also included wishful thinking
along liberal lines. The hope was that detente might liberalize Soviet
security internally and induce Moscow to be less aggressive externally. Greater economic interdependence might inhibit the Soviets
from disturbing the global system, lest their own prosperity be
adversely affected. These ideas found support in the analyses of
liberal as well as pragmatic thinkers in the Kennedy, Johnson and
Nixon administrations.[18] Yet the most divisive aspect of the
American vision of detente in comparison with the West European
version lay in its basic approach, which put greater emphasis on the
responsibility of the superpowers in maintaining world order. In
effect, this meant the pursuit of Realpolitik on superpower terms. As
David Calleo points out, the "bilateral focus [of the U.S. conception
of detente] recalled the first phase of America's postwar diplomacy,
with Roosevelt's dream of incorporating the Soviets into the Pax
Americana."[19] In retrospect, this vision has not been completely off
base. Yet in the 1960s it caused a deep division in the ranks of the
Atlantic alliance.

From the outset, Western Europe viewed detente from a different
diplomatic perspective. While welcoming decreased tension between
the two leading powers, it firmly resisted the notion of a U.S.
monopoly over Western diplomacy. The West Germans considered
themselves to have been betrayed by the United States. Moreover,
most West Europeans—with France in the lead—vehemently refused
to permit the United States to negotiate any settlement of European
issues remaining from World War II on their behalf. The deepening
division within NATO now involved two main issues: differences
over military strategy and over relations with the Soviets. The latter
issue was to become a more serious problem later on, until,
paradoxically, it started binding the United States more firmly to

the policy of detente as West German Ostpolitik produced concrete results.

In the mid-1960s the President of France, Charles de Gaulle, took the lead in challenging U.S.—and, implicitly, Soviet— hegemony by promoting detente as a process for shaping a "new Europe." De Gaulle challenged acceptance of the division of Europe and Germany as a permanent reality and argued that a completely new, more autonomous continental system was the only possible context for realizing some form of German unity. In his view, Western Europe should maintain its military alliance with the United States as a needed counterweight to Soviet militarism, on the one hand, while on the other it should seek closer relations with the USSR[20] because Soviet cooperation was also essential to resolving Europe's old German problem. According to de Gaulle, Germany ought to be unified, but tied into the security arrangements among all European states. These French efforts to loosen up the European political environment came at a time when the leadership of the Soviet Union was less imaginative, less theatrical and perhaps not even as confidently installed in power as Khrushchev had been. They also coincided with the increasing preoccupation of the superpowers with their respective Asian problems.[21]

De Gaulle's diplomacy—which has often been interpreted as an anti-U.S. policy—was received with sympathy in the FRG, in particular by Chancellor Konrad Adenauer, who was by now receptive to de Gaulle's larger views and believed his policies were useful to German interests. However, a major power struggle broke out in the FRG that divided the parties between the "Gaullists" and the "Atlanticists." By 1966, the German Gaullists managed to gain power under the able leadership of Willy Brandt, who himself became minister of foreign affairs in the so-called Grand Coalition of the Christian Democrats, Bavarian Christian Social Union and Social Democrats.[22]

Consequently, the viability of Western unity became even more inextricably tied to the German question. Although de Gaulle sparked a rebellion in the alliance when he pulled France out of the NATO military command in 1966 and flirted openly with the Soviet Union against the will of the United States, his actions did not pose a challenge to the vital interests of the United States. In certain ways de Gaulle's "Europeanism," which found expression in his repeated calls to Europe to stand on its own two feet, was in the interests of the U.S., too. A unified Europe played a crucial role in the U.S.

long-term strategy of containment. By definition a united Europe included an integrated FRG, which, in turn, would have to be predicated on a solution to the German question. De Gaulle's resentment of superpower hegemony in Europe contained a clear message for Moscow as well as Washington. His definition of Europe as a geographic area stretching from the Atlantic Ocean to the Ural Mountains remained somewhat vague, and in Washington it was considered primarily a propaganda tool for molding East European public opinion to be more favorably inclined toward West European integration.[23]

Although the United States pushed detente forward in the early 1960s, the situation changed dramatically in the course of the decade. As a result of West German Ostpolitik—and, indeed, much less as a result of de Gaulle's diplomacy—the United States started to speak out vigorously for unity in the Atlantic alliance. In practice, U.S. rhetoric narrowed down increasingly to one substantial concern: West German unilateralism vis-à-vis Eastern Europe and the Soviet Union. Henry Kissinger, who assumed his position as de facto designer of U.S. foreign policy in early 1969, expressed his deep worry over the course of events in Europe. For example, he considered Egon Bahr, Willy Brandt's alter ego and an Ostpolitik specialist, to be "above all a German nationalist who wanted to exploit Germany's central position to bargain with both sides."[24] The containment of Germany, no longer just of the Soviet Union, would come to play a major role in U.S. participation in detente in the future. Consequently, the process of agreeing upon a Western position was to become more difficult. Indeed, at the end of the 1960s at least three Western positions on detente existed—American, West German and French—that had to be incorporated into a united position before the alliance could make any credible response to proposals introduced by the Soviet Union and the Warsaw Pact for shaping a "new Europe."

The first Western strategy for dealing with the rapidly changing European security problem was set forth in the so-called Harmel Report of 1967, which argued that "military security and a policy of detente are not contradictory but complementary." The report assimilated ideas that had previously been developed by three of NATO's member states: the suggestion first raised by U.S. President Lyndon B. Johnson of "building bridges" between East and West; de Gaulle's notion of "detente–cooperation–entente"; and Willy Brandt's scheme for a "European order of peace." The nuances of these basic concepts indicated that *only the West Germans genuinely sought the dismantling of the division of Europe.* Nevertheless, the Harmel Report constituted what was essentially a united Western response, though only in general terms, to the detente initiatives of the Warsaw Pact.

The Harmel Report had tremendous implications for the future of both West–West and East–West interaction. The solution it presented for avoiding potential disintegration within the Euroatlantic security community embodied detente and represented a cooperative approach to East–West relations. The report constituted a major step toward more collective management of European relations as well as East–West relations in general.[25]

It has been argued that the Harmel Report established the Euroatlantic security community as a two-pillared structure, with deterrence and defense constituting one pillar, and negotiations and detente the other. But it could also be argued that the Harmel Report acknowledged the differentiation of security interests within the alliance. Although it presented a basic strategy, the report did not propose policies for any of the concrete problems. Instead, it granted considerable room for maneuver to each of NATO's member states. Indeed, the Harmel Report represents the end of the era of U.S. dominance in the Euroatlantic security community and essentially confirms the division of NATO into two pillars.[26]

In the late 1960s, West German Ostpolitik and its many achievements "singularized" the FRG within the Euroatlantic security community. De Gaulle's successor, Georges Pompidou, grew worried that Ostpolitik might ultimately lead to the neutralization and reunification of Germany. France rapidly compensated for its failure to deepen cooperation with the FRG by seeking better relations with the United Kingdom. As for the prospects for a European security conference, such a development created new frictions within the Western camp. On the one hand, the German-led states, including the smaller NATO states and the neutrals, constituted a pro-Ostpolitik front. On the other hand, the remaining Atlanticists plus a deviating France constituted a more cautious front of "detentists." In the end, the first concrete steps toward an all-European security arrangement were taken with an eye on managing the complex adjustment of interests between the alliances, the neutrals and any disputing "factions" within the alliances. The ESC process proved increasingly to be a metaphor for harmonizing the policy of detente, and it captured hopes for both change in and maintenance of the status quo in terms of traditional power politics. But no real progress would have been possible without Ostpolitik and a temporary settlement of the German question.

TEMPORARY SETTLEMENT OF THE GERMAN QUESTION

The success of Ostpolitik demonstrates the irony of history: when the policy did not exist it was advocated by almost everyone, but when it was finally realized Ostpolitik became the object of widespread fear and suspicion. For the FRG, Ostpolitik was the last rather than first option for overcoming the outstanding political problems of World War II. For the GDR, Ostpolitik initially posed a danger, particularly because it threatened to cement West Berlin's ties to the FRG. But the settlement of the legal and political status of Berlin turned out to be the key to inter-German rapprochement and, subsequently, to further progress in detente in general. After the new West German government led by Chancellor Willy Brandt finally expressed its willingness to recognize the existence of two German states, genuine progress in European detente began to take off in 1969.[27]

In the mid-1950s, the GDR became the advocate of the theory of "two states—one nation," and the East German government began to press for legitimization of the division of Germany and establishment of "normal" diplomatic relations between the two German states. Meanwhile, West German strategists of Ostpolitik recognized that the German problem was not an isolated one, but was deeply rooted in the East–West conflict. This led Brandt to pursue the issue more vigorously with Moscow than with East Berlin. His tactics worked, and the Kremlin, wishing to reach a quick agreement that could pave the way for a conference on European security and cooperation, which would in turn legitimize the political division of Europe, urged the GDR to go along with Ostpolitik. This goal, however, could only be achieved by the replacement of Walter Ulbricht, the aging leader of the GDR, by a more flexible player who would choose a course of rapprochement with the FRG. According to Richard Lowenthal, the new East German leader, Erich Honecker, was willing to pay "the price of increased Western influence within the GDR in exchange for the international recognition and the increased legitimacy which the agreements with the FRG permitted."[28] Indeed, for the GDR, the emerging inter-German relationship posed a threat of "reassociation," on the one hand, but also presented an opportunity to perform as a loyal member of the Warsaw Treaty Organization, on the other.

In the long run, the rather complex treaty arrangement among the four powers over the status of Berlin, as set forth in the Quadripartite Agreement (1971) and the Basic Treaty between the two German states (1972), was a starting point for further strengthening and deepening inner-German relations. These treaty arrangements also removed the final obstacles to setting the CSCE process into motion.[29] Although the German problem was only temporarily settled, this kind of interim arrangement provided a workable structure for German relations and eventually constituted a framework for the Europeanization of detente. Thus a linkage was established between the policy of detente and finding a solution to the German problem on "German terms." West German Chancellor Kurt Georg Kiesinger had already predicted the significance of this kind of linkage at the dawn of Ostpolitik in 1967:

> Germany, a reunified Germany, would be of critically large size. It is too big not to have an effect on the balance of power, and too small to be able itself to hold the balance with the power round about it . . . . For this reason, one can see the separate halves of Germany growing together only if this is firmly anchored in the process of overcoming the East–West conflict in Europe.[30]

Kiesinger went on to conclude that the most fruitful policy would be to promote inter-German detente at all levels. This prediction anticipates the basic framework for various processes of detente, which in coming years would not be limited to inter-German relations, thus testifying to the importance of the German states in the overall European security order.

In retrospect, it is obvious that detente was not a necessary precondition for implementing Ostpolitik. Undoubtedly European detente did not harm Ostpolitik either. For the United States, detente was primarily of use in promoting its interests vis-a-vis the Soviet Union, and its essence was crisis management and "bridge-building" rather than any kind of reassociation or reunification of a divided Europe or Germany. For the West Germans, however, especially for the architects of Ostpolitik, detente primarily served the FRG's interests vis-a-vis the GDR. In their view, the purpose of detente was the promotion of reassociation and reunification. Brandt once said that "the German question was not the key to an understanding of the worldwide conflict between East and West."[31] Thus Ostpolitik was built upon a realization that reunification was no longer a realistic aim, even though it remained a long-term goal "as a process of change through contact."[32] From the U.S. point of view, however, even this kind of approach seemed a bit too much. Although the "normalization" of inter-German relations was still in compliance with the U.S. understanding of detente, the de facto "Germanization" of detente was not.

In fact, the growing dispute between the original architects of Ostpolitik and the United States, joined to a certain extent by the European Atlanticists, set off a major domestic debate in the FRG. The concept of "Finlandization," which was initially introduced to Germany and world politics in the autumn of 1969 by Walter Hallstein, then a retired Christian Democrat, was at the center of this debate. The term first caught the public's attention when Franz-Josef Strauss, the leader of the Christian Social Union (CSU), stated in a television interview in late 1969 that Moscow aimed at the permanent division of Germany, undiminished Soviet control of the GDR and the Finlandization of the FRG. In Strauss's use of the term, Finlandization included the neutralization of the FRG, the dissolution of NATO and the termination of all ambitions to reunite Europe. Thereupon followed a lively press debate in both the FRG and Finland, where Strauss's comments were fiercely condemned. In the FRG most newspapers criticized Strauss, and Chancellor Brandt even apologized for Strauss's statement. On January 31, 1970, the federal government officially denounced the statement as an act liable to harm Finno-German relations.[33]

There was a clear link between Strauss's use of the term Finlandization and Willy Brandt's Ostpolitik. Strauss considered West German "bilateralism" a threat to Western integration and a result of efforts by the Soviet Union to neutralize the FRG even as it was strengthening its control over the GDR. With his reference to Finlandization, Strauss triggered a chain reaction throughout Western Europe and the United States. He had created a convenient threat image in the concept of Finlandization, which was soon inserted into the larger framework of European politics. In the autumn of 1971 Professor Raymond Aron, a highly respected French scholar, wrote in *Le Figaro* that Finlandization was part of "the new European arrangement" that he opposed. Aron criticized the CSCE venture in the following words:

I admit I see more harm brought about by it than good. The dissymmetry will remain the same. The Soviet Union will strive—through the CSCE as well—towards its old goals: maintaining discipline in its own sphere of interest, reducing the American presence on the Old Continent, and settling matters separately with each West European country, not in order to prepare a military attack, but to assure itself of a certain veto and tutelage in respect to Western Europe. The term "Finlandization" is a vague expression of Moscow's ultimate goal.[34]

Aron's use of the term Finlandization shows how easily it played upon Western fears about the development of Ostpolitik. It was widely thought that after the FRG was neutralized, the rest of the countries of Western Europe would follow suit, one by one. Accordingly, the CSCE process was now widely regarded in the West as a Soviet achievement primarily aimed at splitting NATO. Rightly or wrongly, a threat image based on Ostpolitik was implanted in the West, and from then on it became evident that West German bilateralism was on the decline. Europe would need a completely new setting to further promote Ostpolitik. Ultimately, many of the original principles of Ostpolitik were achieved or expounded within the general East–West process of change, which in a certain sense began to follow its own logic in the 1970s and even more dramatically in the 1980s, when history followed its own course, ignoring the advice of scholars and analysts alike.

Treaty arrangements based on Ostpolitik such as the Basic Treaty, had to be approved by the West German political process as well as, to a certain extent, by the Western allies of the FRG. The core problem was whether or not inter-German arrangements de jure constituted a solution to the German question. In 1972 Erich Honecker, the leader of the GDR, declared that history had rendered its verdict. On German soil two German states had emerged with different social systems; yet despite these irreconcilable social differences, the two states could peacefully coexist and have normal relations with each other within the context of a divided Germany and Europe. Furthermore, the ideological antagonism between the two states made demarcation, rather than reconciliation or convergence, the order of the day.[35] In contrast, the Bonn government maintained that the Basic Treaty and other arrangements had in no way altered the legal situation of Germany. The German question would remain open until it was possible for the

German people to regain their unity through peaceful self-determination. As West German Foreign Minister Walter Scheel put it: "The treaty is a treaty for the people and for the future of Germany. We want to strengthen the bonds between the two parts of Germany and we want to make possible again contacts between the people."[36]

Obviously, the Bonn government had to recognize the de facto emergence of two German states on German soil with different social systems and alliance structures. At the same time, however, in order to avoid a challenge on constitutional grounds and parliamentary rejection of the treaty arrangements, it had to keep open the de jure German question through a number of compromise formulations. Ostpolitik had already become the object of domestic infighting by the end of the 1960s. Yet while the policy was being developed and put into practice between 1969 and 1973, West German popular support for Ostpolitik grew dramatically. West German opinion polls showed that in 1972 two-thirds of the respondents favored Ostpolitik.[37] Even though the opposition parties, the Christian Democratic Union (CDU) and the CSU, voted against the major treaty arrangements related to Ostpolitik, the West German parliament gave its approval, although not without political crises in 1972–1975.[38]

In the final analysis, the FRG's allies, though expressing occasional doubts about its excesses, were generally supportive of Ostpolitik. Indeed, without this support the FRG could not have proceeded with Ostpolitik at all. Brandt made clear that its foundation was in the Western alliance. As he stated in 1971:

The FRG conducts its Ostpolitik not as a wanderer between the two worlds, but from a position firmly established in Western cooperation. Atlantic alliance and West European partnership are for us prerequisites for the success of conciliation with the East.[39]

In the West European perspective, Brandt's Ostpolitik had to be coordinated with NATO and especially the United States.[40] Yet the United States accepted Ostpolitik only selectively. As Henry Kissinger frankly stated in his memoirs, Brandt's recognition of the division of "his country was a courageous recognition of reality. For German unification was not achievable without a collapse of Soviet power, something that Bonn was in no position to promote." Kissinger expressed his support for that part of Ostpolitik, but he was extremely dubious of the policy's other goals, especially if defined as gradual unification through increasing interaction between the two German states. Kissinger was of the opinion that in such a process the GDR had more to gain and, indeed, would convince Western Europe to tilt strategically toward the East. However, Kissinger was also concerned—perhaps even more strongly—with the role of Western Europe in NATO's overall strategy. "What concerned us was a tendency to avoid controversies outside of Europe; a creeping dissociation from Western Europe; and a more cautious approach to Soviet challenges that tended to drain the Western response of meaning."[41] This process, if it progressed further, would in Kissinger's view divide Europe from the United States.

The Euro-American—that is, German–American—dispute included ideological aspects as well. The U.S. administration deeply feared the possibility of Soviet ideological infiltration into Western Europe. For example, Kissinger believed that the phenomenon of "Eurocommunism" could endanger Western security. "All of Europe will be Marxist within a decade," he reportedly declared in 1976.[42] Even this most brilliant observer of international affairs was sometimes unable to grasp the basic essence of historical processes: within a decade, Europe had become almost entirely anti-communist. The Americans were, however, wounded by the fact that the Vietnam war had alienated Western Europe from the United States. In any case, the Nixon administration overestimated the danger of the Soviet Union's ideological attraction for Europe. In the final analysis, the real problem with Ostpolitik for the United States was the prospect of the reunification of Germany. This obliged the United States to commit itself more firmly to the policy of detente for reasons of "European unity."[43] The initial CSCE process[44] provided an opportunity to combine Ostpolitik and detente. For one thing, the multilateral approach would shield the FRG from its allies' accusations that Bonn was risking the continuation and cohesion of NATO for the sake of transient success. But beyond protecting its image among its allies, the Brandt government also considered the CSCE a suitable framework for a "European peace order," one of the major goals of Ostpolitik. The preparatory phase of the CSCE had already produced a satisfactory settlement of the German question that included West Berlin. Now the CSCE could improve East–West relations to such a degree that the division of Europe and Germany could be dismantled at some point in the future. But here again, the FRG became engaged in a dispute with the United States. Washington did not want to pay much attention to the CSCE and was prepared to participate in its proceedings primarily for the sake of "Western unity"—one could say, in fact, to "contain" the FRG. From the U.S. point of view, the CSCE provided a means to control the policy of detente as well as Ostpolitik. But from the West German point of view, it was only in a multilateral context such as the CSCE that "the FRG [could] hope to continue a limited detente and Ostpolitik without coming into conflict with its security interests, which implied as undisturbed a relationship with the U.S. as possible."[45] For the FRG, the first phase of Ostpolitik during the period of 1969–1973 had brought many positive results, though not a solution to the German question. For the rest of Europe and the United States, however, the temporary settlement of the German question constituted an acceptable long-term solution.

Part II
Change in Europe

PART II
CHANGE IN EUROPE

The postwar European status quo cannot be equated with a stable peace. Although a high degree of military stability has occurred, political stability has been rather low. Thus Europe as a whole has not met the criteria of a "security community" if a minimum condition of such a community is the expectation shared by its members that their conflicts will be resolved peacefully.[1] For the overall change in Europe did not primarily touch on either political or military aspects of security but on a number of systemic factors. The life in civil societies and the process of economic integration began to set their parameters for the credibility of the bipolar security arrangement. In the longer term the bipolarity could no longer hinder the political change. This began to shake the postwar status quo.

An international system is established for the same reason that any social or political system is created: actors enter into social relations and create social structures in order to advance particular sets of interests, such as political and economic goals. Over time, however, the interests of individual actors and the balance of power among the actors undergo change as a result of economic, technological and various other developments. Some participants benefit more from such change and thus try to alter the system. The new system that results will reflect a different distribution of power and the interests of the new dominant power. Thus, as Robert Gilpin states, "a precondition for political change lies in disjuncture between the existing social system and the distribution of power toward those actors who would benefit most from a change in the system."[2] The pressure for change in the European system was not being exerted primarily by dissatisfied powers aiming at, for example, territorial modifications; rather, it was increasingly evident that it stemmed primarily from certain systemic and domestic factors. The international system is always subject to change, especially by deep transformations in the foundations of world power that in time make their way to the surface.[3] Although the factors currently stimulating change in the European security order can be identified, it is clear that the most desirable security order will not emerge automatically from some kind of systemic process.

The bipolar structure of Europe has largely overshadowed its substructures. First, there is the Eurasian security system with the

WTO as its political–military denominator, which accounts for six smaller countries and one of the superpowers. This system was created largely by coercion and sought cohesion by advancing the vital political–military security interests of its member states. The WTO, however, has not managed to find unity in terms of its members' political, economic or cultural interests. Second, there is the Euroatlantic security system, NATO and its 16 member states, which has also created cohesion on the basis of its most vital political–military security interests. However, NATO was founded by consent; thus the two military alliances may balance each other in terms of military capacities but are not symmetrical regarding their legitimacy. In political terms, NATO is a much more united alliance than the WTO. Third, the neutral and nonaligned (NNA) nations of Europe constitute a kind of mediating level "between" the alliances. The role of the NNA states has become more visible and important since the heyday of the Cold War.

Although postwar European stability was by and large maintained within the context of the political status quo, superpower rivalry did not cease. On the contrary, the United States and the Soviet Union increasingly sought security through military means. In the late 1970s and the early 1980s, when the two superpowers tried to create "absolute" security primarily through strengthening their strategic positions, detente in its original meaning collapsed. Specifically, by overemphasizing the military elements of security and the militarization of security, the arms buildup was no longer interpreted as the consequence of a multidimensional East–West conflict, but rather as the conflict itself.[4] But military defense is only one component of security, a fact that has been acutely realized in Europe, both in the East and the West. At the peak of the "new Cold War" in the early 1980s, the Europeanization of detente gained strong support in Europe, most particularly in the two German states. During this period the gap widened between the strategic interests of the superpowers and the more regionally oriented interests of their European allies. In addition, domestic sociopolitical changes in Eastern Europe and the process of integration then gathering force in Western Europe contributed to the erosion of the division of the continent.

Indeed, especially since the late 1960s, postwar developments have not conformed to the rules of hostility reflected in Europe's bipolarity. The "European plant" has begun to sprout and even the mightiest artificial structures are shaking. The systemic and political processes of change influencing the East–West system can be characterized as "European" in their essence, for it is the policy of detente and its concrete results, including Ostpolitik, the CSCE and superpower arms control negotiations, that have provided the political framework for such change. Originally detente was also based on the assumption that the European territorial and political status quo would remain a more or less permanent solution, and that all states participating in CSCE activities benefited more from the stability of the status quo than they would from efforts to remove it. This attitude reflects the needs of the superpowers in particular. But as the following chapters demonstrate, this sort of structural "metastability" did not provide a permanent framework for European security. Between 1969 and 1989–90 a new kind of structure emerged beneath the surface of the status quo. Part II of this book deals with these primarily Eurocentric processes of change. This part does not follow, however, a rigorously chronological order; its focus is in any case on the premises of the revolutionary year of 1989, which means that Part II covers partly that revolution but not necessarily its ramifications, which I attempt to analyze in Part III.

3 The Europeanization of the East–West System

With respect to the original East–West structure described above, the era of detente did not lead to its real change. However, some important developments did take place that blurred the division of Europe. First, interbloc communication increased through tourism, mass communication and, to a certain extent, trade. Second, ideological confrontation ceased, despite the attempts of the socialist states and also the Reagan administration to maintain it until the mid-1980s. Although the East–West military balance remained unchanged and the level of confrontation even worsened because of the arms buildup, the policy of detente and a number of systemic processes still managed to shake some of the pillars of the traditional East–West structure.

The East–West bipolarity above all reflected the confrontation between the two superpowers. The United States and the Soviet Union managed to establish themselves as the dominant power centers in a class by themselves, and most of the states of Europe aligned themselves with either one or the other in the aftermath of World War II. Ideological confrontation was a prominent component of the superpower rivalry, and one can assume that the cessation of ideological rivalry in Europe is partly due to the diminishing role of the superpowers there.[1] Of course, the roles of the superpowers within Europe have not been symmetrical. Moreover, the superpowers increasingly became rivals on a global scale, while the European states retained their primarily "Eurocentric" interests. Most Europeans are increasingly recognizing two basic interests: first, they consider themselves citizens of their original homelands, defined, for example, by language and birthplace; and second, they increasingly consider themselves as sharing a common European heritage and the same threat perceptions.

Characterizing an international system is always an extremely difficult task. Most often the system is characterized by a variety of basic features, and in attempting to periodize its history observers must give particular emphasis to only certain features. Thus, while the postwar European system has been a product of an "age of ideology," most observers would argue that since the early 1970s the phenomenon of interdependence has become the most important factor for explaining the rapidly growing rates of transaction among societies. "The development of closer and multidimensional contacts between societies thus constitutes one of the fundamental forms of system change in the twentieth century."[2] In Europe, this development has been very concrete and has had political ramifications as well.

The phenomena of change in Europe have largely occurred without regard to the ups and downs of superpower relations. They are manifested in the CSCE process and in the development of interdependence among states, as well as in the "minds of the people." In sum, the Europeans—in particular in East Central Europe and the Soviet Union—are redefining their societies' political priorities. This evolution has strengthened the dominance of pragmatism over ideology and national interests over bloc interests. The struggle between Marxist and liberal thinking is also coming to an end in Europe, in favor of the latter. In particular, the phenomenon of interdependence finds its most meaningful expression in Europe at the subregional level, although some developments are also taking place at the all-European level. In short, as a result of interdependence, a rather dynamic picture is emerging, "that of significant degree of geopolitical fragility with a potential for evolution unprecedented since the emergence of the postwar order in Europe," as François Heisbourg has stated.[3]

THE EVOLUTION OF THE CSCE STRUCTURE

Even as the heads of state of 35 nations signed the CSCE Final Act in Helsinki in the summer of 1975, the spirit of detente was already fading away. Detente had reached its peak in the superpower summits of 1972, 1973 and 1974; as Walter Lafeber writes, "these meetings opened the first important era of U.S.–USSR detente."[4] The development of new international conflicts soon after the 1974 summit, though occurring outside Europe, created new tensions in the general atmosphere of international politics. Both superpowers were determined to resist each other's policy goals in the developing world: the East–West rivalry had finally been pushed beyond the European stage. As Henry Kissinger declared in 1976, "the peace of the world will be threatened, when it is threatened, not primarily by strategic forces [of the superpowers] but by geopolitical changes, and to resist those geopolitical changes we must be able to resist regionally."[5] This basic fear did not disappear when the superpower leaders signed the Basic Principles agreement at the 1972 summit, which committed them to respect the global status quo. Thus the CSCE Final Act was to confirm the postwar status quo in Europe.

Most Europeans expected that the implementation of the Helsinki Final Act would further strengthen detente, however. The FRG, the NNA countries and the smaller member states of the two alliances were the most eager advocates of the CSCE process. As mentioned above, the United States was primarily interested in the CSCE vis-a-vis relations with the Soviet Union and the task of "containing" the FRG. The United Kingdom and France were also skeptical about East–West detente in general as it had evolved during the 1970s. Indeed, the CSCE process had stirred up fears in Western Europe and the United States about the real motives behind the Soviet peace campaigns. The U.S. journal *Foreign Affairs* expressed these fears in its editorial of April 1972, which related them to the threat of the Finlandization of Western Europe:

> The term alludes to a process whereby the Soviet Union acting in the context of its strategic–military superiority in Europe and subtly mixing threat with blandishment would gradually establish hegemony over all of Europe.[6]

Undoubtedly these words reflect a highly militarized view of security, which considered that the strategic-military position of the Soviet Union would automatically benefit Moscow politically. In reality, however, this Soviet strategy of "softening" the minds of the West through the CSCE while continuing the military buildup proved to be a trap for the Soviet Union over the longer term. In the 1970s, however, such an outcome was not evident and, in any case, the CSCE divided Western opinion from the outset. In the final analysis, the CSCE offered only limited advantages to countries to the west of the FRG, while providing the prospect for change to countries east of that same line. For the neutral and nonaligned countries, the CSCE was primarily a forum in which their voices could finally be heard regarding decisions on issues related to European security. In essence, the Final Act recognized the existence in Europe of a world outside the blocs.

Yet the CSCE process developed gradually and not without contradictory wishes. The CSCE addressed some of the most important goals set forth in the foreign policy agenda of the Kennedy administration. In June 1963, U.S. President John F. Kennedy had called upon the Soviet Union and the United States to break the "cycle in which suspicion on one side breeds suspicion on the other, and new weapons beget counterweapons."[7] One of the Final Act's three issue-areas, or "baskets," provided that force would not be used to redraw frontiers, an agreement the Soviets had wanted to reach with the United States ever since the Red Army staked out new European boundaries between 1944 and 1948. In return, however, the Soviets had to agree to recognize the right of people to enjoy basic human freedoms, including the freedom to cross national borders. But when "Helsinki Watch" groups appeared in the Soviet Union to ensure that these rights were respected, their members were brutally beaten and imprisoned. Indeed, the Helsinki baskets that seemed to offer the most hope for detente turned out to be, as Walter Lafeber states, "another reason to believe that detente was dying, if not dead."[8] Thus the whole issue of detente was subjected to harsh criticism in the United States during the presidential election campaign of 1976.

Nevertheless, the CSCE proved to be one of the new structures of cooperation that may have altered the course of modern history. The CSCE introduced a broader concept of security and touched upon the everyday lives of ordinary people throughout Europe. In the long run, the true essence of detente gained more ground in Europe through the CSCE process. In practical terms, the CSCE aimed at improving relations between Eastern and Western Europe, in addition to building confidence through increased East–West trade, more frequent contacts across borders and guarantees protecting human rights. At the same time, however, the Helsinki Accords of 1975 ratified the territorial status quo, thus fulfilling a major Soviet goal, and affirmed the principle of noninterference in the internal affairs of the signatories.

The CSCE provided a framework for various systemic changes[9] in both Eastern and Western Europe in the hopes of benefiting the whole of Europe. The conference and its three follow-up meetings and related expert meetings constituted an essential tool for furthering the original goals of detente, and have pointed the way to new opportunities for cooperation. In the words of U.S. Senator Joseph R. Biden, "This CSCE diplomacy has worked. Indeed, its promotion of human rights laid the groundwork for the revolution of 1989."[10]

To a certain extent the CSCE initiated a restructuring of the political map of Europe, since it inter alia involved five political "entities" that have mainly evolved since the outset of the process: Western Europe, the neutral and nonaligned nations, the United States, Eastern Europe and the Soviet Union. The CSCE process represents an interplay among all five "entities," while the *core* of systemic transformation in Europe involves a bridging of the gap between Eastern and Western Europe. In its final stage, the CSCE has pan-European goals,[11] and it has started a process that encourages the intensification of a policy of system-opening cooperation. This process is an unusual, if not unique, phenomenon in contemporary world politics. For one thing, time and again the CSCE has regained its strength not through institutionalization, but by being a forum for open dialogue, cooperation and even confrontation among the 35 participating states.

With equal weight the following features can be said to contribute to the historical value of the CSCE: 1) the CSCE can be considered the *charter* of the European peace order; 2) it is the only realistic process for overcoming the division of Europe, provided the principles of the three baskets are consistently implemented; 3) in the wake of perestroika and glasnost, the CSCE gives Europeans the chance to understand themselves as a learning community; 4) the CSCE could serve as the cornerstone for a "common European home," with its principles providing basic rules of the household; and 5) it has improved the historically problematic attitudes of Western Europe toward the Soviet Union and, perhaps even more, Soviet attitudes toward the West. In sum, the CSCE has strengthened a pan-European—or all-European—security order. However, it would be unrealistic to assume that the CSCE as such could be the driving force of change in Europe; rather, it primarily tries to control and coordinate the processes of change.[12]

To comprehend the possibilities as well as limits of the CSCE process, one must evaluate it in more theoretical terms. By definition, the CSCE prefers multilateral and self-restrained approaches to problems, rather than more common unilateral and less restrained ones. It is assumed that member states do not play the game as hard as they could; they do not take advantage of the short-term vulnerabilities of other member states. In short, states cooperate in the expectation that the others will do the same.

The bipolar security system is based on the assumption that states are restrained only externally, by the actions of others or by

anticipating what other states might do if one acts against their
interests. The CSCE was a move away from this balance-of-power
system of balancing power toward a European concert.[13]

To draw any conclusion as to whether the CSCE has been a step
in the right direction would be premature and extremely subjective.
Nevertheless, the CSCE has provided a useful means of maintaining
stability in Europe. The process has survived chills between the
superpowers, the causes of which did not arise in Europe but mainly
in the Third World. As a consequence, the CSCE has strengthened
the image of the Europeanization of detente, thus deepening the
division not only between Western Europe and the United States,
but to a certain degree between Eastern Europe and the Soviet
Union as well (for a fuller discussion of what constitutes "Europe,"
see below, p. 63, note 1). At the same time, barriers in East Central
Europe have been lowering, at least on the level of human contacts.
As Eric G. Frey puts it:

> Most important has been the effect of detente on the psychology of
> the continent. A decade of relaxation of tensions had changed
> Europe from a tension-ridden region to one of the most stable
> regions in the world. Once detente failed on a global basis,
> European leaders came to share the Soviet goal of making detente
> divisible so that it could be maintained on the European con-
> tinent.[14]

The Eurocentric dynamism of the CSCE process has been further
strengthened by the prospect of a less ideological Soviet foreign
policy. Indeed, the "new thinking" in the Soviet Union has to a large
extent changed the East–West conflict from an ideological to a
purely political one. A central purpose of the Helsinki Accords was
to mark the end of ideological crusades in East–West relations. The
participating states have put top priority on their common interests
rather than on those that divide them. Nevertheless, the CSCE
provisions do not eliminate the sources of conflict; instead they
provide instruments to resolve conflict through peaceful means,
political consultation and cooperation.

This increase of pragmatism in Europe fostered European self-
awareness and a Europeanization of East–West interaction.[15] Whether or not this development was a result of the CSCE process can be
assessed only at a later date. What is certain, however, is that the
CSCE has become an integral and somewhat permanent component
of systemic transformation in Europe. In the long run, it will be up

to the political will and statecraft of the CSCE "entities" to deepen the process of change. The CSCE as such does not constitute a political "entity" or a collective security system for settling outstanding political conflicts, but it is gradually becoming more of a symbol of a changing world order—at least at the regional level—that engages sovereign rather than hegemonic entities in new kinds of interplay.[16]

In particular, the CSCE process has strengthened the position and role of the NNA states and smaller alliance members. To the extent that these states have been the most outspoken advocates of the territorial status quo, their views have often concurred with those of the superpowers.[17] However, their satisfaction with the territorial status quo should not be confused with a goal of freezing the political status quo. The Helsinki Accords do not in fact offer any protection to the political status quo itself. On the contrary, the CSCE can be considered primarily a vehicle for promoting political change in a peaceful manner. One of the tests of the CSCE lies precisely in this challenge of constructively channeling the political and human needs of Europe to reflect the main concerns of the continent's people. If it cannot, then it fails to achieve its noble goals as set forth in the Helsinki Final Act.[18]

The CSCE is not and was never meant to be a panacea for concerns regarding European security and cooperation. The process is primarily related to the overall East–West relationship. By definition, the CSCE was based on an all-European approach; this could be due in part to the emphasis on military and confidence-building issues, the parameters of which are by definition Eurocentric.[19]

The CSCE process has also failed to a large degree in a number of areas, such as the promotion of East–West trade. Innovations are needed to develop future systemic economic transformations. Economic bipolarization seems to be deeply rooted, and the economic division of Europe has in fact been deepening in the CSCE era. Yet without the CSCE, this division would probably have become at least a bit deeper than it already is.[20]

As a diplomatic exercise the CSCE is *sui generis*. The Final Act, or Helsinki Accords, have been interpreted in a variety of often contradictory ways. Each party has tried to convince the others of an interpretation that suited it best. K. J. Holsti once called the Final Act "a source of conflict" that, because of its ambiguity and vulnerability to differing interpretations, "has, if anything, increased East–West conflict."[21] After a number of successes, such as the

Madrid Follow-up Concluding Document of 1983 and the Stockholm Concluding Document on Confidence- and Security-Building Measures and Disarmament of 1986, the Final Act has increasingly proved to be a source of East–West rapprochement, above all in military matters. Yet the Helsinki Accords, like East–West discourse in general (a paramount example is the Yalta declaration), have a history of being subjected to conflicting interpretations and misunderstandings. Although the root cause of the East–West rivalry lies in competing interests, misperceptions and enemy images can, as Daniel Frei puts it, "intensify the conflict."[22] Undoubtedly, then, the CSCE is a source of both conflict and agreement. In the end, however, the CSCE should be a forum within which misperception can be replaced by accurate perception and mistrust can be replaced by confidence. With justification one may state that the CSCE is, in this respect, on the right track.

In the 1980s both East and West came to accept a similar interpretation of the Helsinki Final Act: they regard it as a comprehensive concept. Within this concept, however, the CSCE structure seemed divided into two tiers in practice. The hard core of European security issues, i.e., immediate security matters, follow their own dynamic, whereas other less sensitive areas of cooperation proceed at a slower pace. One can find two obvious reasons for this "separation of European orders." First, the security of Europe is not a European matter as such, but primarily a superpower issue with repercussions in non-European spheres. Second, the so-called Madrid mandate regards confidence- and security-building measures as "a substantial and integral part" of the CSCE. It has been estimated that "this linkage may hamper progress in areas where national security areas are not as visible and obvious."[23]

Although the CSCE has become a two-track exercise in which the hard core of European security matters are dealt with directly by the military alliances, the process has gained new energy in other areas. At the end of the 1980s interest in the CSCE grew rapidly. Plenty of proposals were introduced on how a new Helsinki II Treaty could guide Europe's revolution.

THE EMERGENCE OF COMPLEX INTERDEPENDENCE

One of the major changes in recent international politics relates to the concept and role of power. It is now more evident than ever before that power politics—which will remain a crucial feature in any future international system—is in a state of transition. Power is increasingly defined by production, innovation, education, trade and national cohesion. Military preparedness is no longer the single most important power factor; already by the early 1960s a "military stalemate" resulting from the strategy of nuclear deterrence was widely acknowledged. It has been stressed that both superpowers need to end their adversarial relationship in order to salvage their economies—though, of course, this problem is much more alarming in the Soviet Union. Yet in the long run the terms for defining the strategic balance will have to be reconsidered as well.[24]

Interdependence can be regarded as that quality of a system that embraces the interconnection among all our problems, our collective well-being and our survival. A sense of interdependence leads us to ponder collective security solutions instead of unilateral actions; it also leads us to reject the traditional zero-sum game. In the final analysis, gains and losses are shared; one part of the European continent cannot flourish at the expense of others. By the same token, however, the centrifugal forces of national aspiration are growing more powerful than the centripetal forces of transnationalism. Thus the two trends of integration and disintegration or fragmentation coincide, and the latter in some cases is the consequence of, or a reaction to, "too much" interdependence or integration. In Holsti's view, both trends represent different types of systemic change.[25]

In the early 1990s the European situation can very accurately be described as a reflection of both the processes of integration (e.g., the impending establishment of the European Community's single market in 1992) and disintegration or differentiation (e.g., Gorbachev's perestroika and its implications for Eastern Europe). In addition, there are ongoing processes which are increasing interdependence at the all-European level (e.g., the CSCE process) and at the subregional level (e.g., unification of the two German states and ecological issues). Nationalistic movements and sentiments, especially in some of the Soviet republics, sow further confusion when one tries to formulate a general outlook on the situation.

Moreover, certain technological developments of the postwar world, especially the development of nuclear weapons and their delivery systems, have made even the superpowers mutually interdependent (that is, militarily vulnerable) to a degree never before experienced by great powers. Additionally, NATO and the Warsaw

Pact have each expanded their web of military-strategic interdependence to include states formally allied and supposedly protected by the superpowers. As is commonly recognized, military interdependence in Europe has been an extremely sensitive question for the members of the alliances, especially since the mid-1980s. Thus interdependence in the field of military security can more accurately be labeled an obstacle to change than a factor in support of its improvement.[26]

One circumstance accelerating interdependence in Europe is, of course, the changing attitudes of the Soviet Union toward the international community. As it approaches the 21st century, the Soviet Union wants to be an integral part of the economically functioning world community. As Oleg Bogomolov has stated:

> Now countries are so interdependent on each other for their development that we have quite a different image of the solution of international questions. The worsening of the situation in Europe will not at all help the development of the socialist part of Europe; on the contrary, the better things are going in the European world economy, the higher the stability and the better the prospects for our development.[27]

The "European world economy" forms the major framework for the Soviet economy, and the Soviet Union wants to improve the interrelation of its economy with the economies of the rest of Europe. Although this incipient interdependence is still rather weak, it seems to be moving inexorably toward the interdependence of all European states. The process was slowed, however, by continuing political–military confrontation characterized by "adversarial interdependence," or a mixture of confrontation and cooperation over a wide range of issues. Nevertheless, threat images on both sides of the dividing line are rapidly fading in the beginning of the 1990s.[28]

At the end of the 1940s, Europe was divided into two economic camps. In the context of East–West rivalry, however, particularly as defined in Cold War terms, economic competition has played only a marginal role. Charles Yost emphasizes that for many years the East–West economic contest took place only in a symbolic sense.[29] By the 1980s this contest—if it ever existed—was already over: the West was far ahead, no matter which yardstick was used to measure the difference.

Since the Cold War began to wane it has been widely hoped in both East and West that politics would play only a minor role in the development of East–West economic relations. The avowed goal was to develop a structure that would mobilize the untapped potential of commercial exchange. At the same time, active steps were taken to overcome the political obstacles that blocked good neighborliness and stability. Despite these efforts, no real "autonomy" has ever been created for economic relations in the East–West system. A commercial detente has never really caught on. Instead, economic relations developed into "economic warfare," a strategy based on the assumption that "a prosperous bear has a bigger punch, not a bigger paunch."[30] In the final analysis, this policy of economic warfare has meant minimal trade between the West and the Soviet Union and its allies.

In the postwar period "business as usual" between East and West has not meant very much business. Profound differences in economic systems have hampered exchanges between capitalist and communist countries, even during the period of detente. The population of the WTO countries is about two-thirds that of the NATO countries, and probably produces less than half of the level of total output of the NATO countries. The Western economies are in an obvious and important sense stronger than those of the East. In the late 1980s this gap widened further.[31]

For the West, economic relations with the Soviet Union and Eastern Europe are not of crucial statistical importance. For almost all Western states, in the mid-1980s trade with the CMEA (Council for Mutual Economic Assistance) countries was less than 5% of their total trade volume.

The main and most important exception to this figure among the NATO countries has been the FRG. The FRG has had a special trading relationship with the GDR; in the mid-1980s, about a quarter of West German East–West trade and almost 2% of total West German trade was conducted with the GDR. In 1985 the FRG conducted about 6% of its total trade with the CMEA countries, which was equivalent to about 1.7% of its GNP. This is not a politically insignificant proportion, and its political significance is greatly increased by the division of Germany and the FRG's central position in East–West relations as a whole.[32]

In itself, East–West trade has had relatively little economic importance for the West. However, from the European political point of view, East–West trade does matter. Aside from the special German factor, the West European share of East–West trade was 82% between 1982 and 1984, while the share of the United States

and Canada was 8% and Japan's share was also 8%. East–West
trade relations are heavily "Eurocentric" and will most probably
remain so in the foreseeable future.[33]

Regarding the security implications of East–West economic ties,
East–West trade has been the object of some disputes between the
United States and its European allies. As Angela E. Stent puts it:

> Although East–West economic relations remain primarily an East-
> West issue, they have recently become more of a West-West
> problem. Contrasting U.S. and European views on East–West
> trade reflect far deeper transatlantic differences over how to
> interpret and respond to the Soviet challenge.[34]

These disputes also reflect differences between the U.S. and West
European definitions of security and contrasting U.S. and European
views of the linkage between politics and economics. The United
States has traditionally viewed East–West economic relations as
essentially political, disproportionally beneficial to the Soviet Union, and even morally questionable. Europeans, in contrast, view
East–West commercial ties as a normal, even desirable element in
their relations with the CMEA countries, both for economic and
political reasons. It must be emphasized that the European economies are much more dependent on trade than the U.S. economy, and
in times of high unemployment East–West trade appeared to be a
guarantee of additional export markets.[35]

For the CMEA countries, East–West economic relations have been
much more important, even if measured in terms of the officially
reported trade flows. The dependence of the CMEA economies on
Western trade has become especially evident in such strategically
important areas as food supplies and technology imports. In any
event, Soviet dependence on trade with the West is much greater
than the Western need for trade with the USSR, and East European
dependence on Western machinery is even greater than that of the
Soviet Union, though it has recently been held to low levels. This
situation reflects the failure of past attempts at import-led growth
(via technology imports) in several East European countries. In
general terms, East–West economic relations are at a crossroads or,
in the words of Laszlo Lang, these "relations are at structural
deadlock."[36]

What, then, should be the longer-term strategy for East–West
economic relations in order to develop a more stable security
structure in Europe? It can be assumed that as long as the military

alliances and their conflicting rationales continue to exist, a certain degree of "economic warfare" will remain in force. For instance, the so-called COCOM coordination among the NATO countries (minus Iceland and plus Japan) will be maintained—although in ever more precisely defined areas—because of important strategic considerations. Although COCOM, the Coordinating Committee for Multilateral Export Controls, which oversees high-technology exports, is an area in which U.S. interests often supersede those of Europe—as was the case in the pipeline project in 1982—the European NATO partners do agree with its basic military rationale: that controlling high-technology exports helps to preserve the lead time required to maintain the military balance between NATO and the WTO.[37]

But the West, and in particular Western Europe, cannot escape the fact that the relative dependence of Western economies on trade with CMEA countries will be a security issue in and of itself "if and when," as Frost and Stent explain, "it leads to vulnerability to Soviet pressure." Indeed, the concept of economic security has been debated most heatedly in connection with efforts to increase West European dependence on Soviet energy supplies. Here the question is precisely whether such dependence will make the Western economies more vulnerable to pressure from the Soviet Union.[38]

By the end of the 1980s the political climate became very favorable for increased East–West trade and economic interaction in general. At the same time, stubborn structural problems remained that greatly hampered any real progress. In fact, the economic gap between East and West was still widening.[39] It is obvious that this second time around, political detente will not play an important role in solving East–West trade problems, as was the case during the early 1970s. Of course, political detente will not increase such problems either, and thus East–West trade is less of a West-West issue than ever before. This fact undoubtedly improves possibilities for designing a more dynamic and unified Western strategy in East–West economic issues—a strategy that would primarily entail economic interaction instead of economic warfare.[40]

The question of economic security, as well as economic interdependence and interaction in broader terms, however, must be primarily considered within the framework and conditions of the processes of economic integration. Despite considerable differences, it is understood that balanced economic relations among all European nations are desirable. But as Michael Dobroczynski reasons, "the building of a monolithic European economic organism

Change in Europe

without discrimination remains a hard task requiring tolerance, a task that will take a few decades to accomplish."[41] However, differences between the two sociopolitical systems have largely ruled out any temptation to build an entirely uniform European civilization that would transcend the sociopolitical specificity of individual states. Yet common foundations and elements or parallel goals can and should be sought. The political earthquake in Eastern and Central Europe removed the final obstacles for an all-European economic interaction. This became a real challenge to West European integration in the beginning of the 1990s.

Although the political principles of European economic cooperation were jointly formulated in the Helsinki Final Act, the CSCE structure has not provided concrete models for tackling the challenges posed by, for example, the emergence of "blocs" of integration in Europe. A historical turning point took place, however, in this respect at the CSCE Conference on Economic Cooperation in Europe held in Bonn in March 1990. The concluding document of this conference confirmed, for example, market-based economics as a starting point for economic relations in Europe. It was stated in the concluding document that "the progressive convergence of economic policies among the participating states opened new long-term perspectives for the strengthening of their economic relations."[42] The conference primarily tried to develop ways and means to integrate the reforming states into the international economic system. In concrete terms, the question is whether the CMEA countries can effect the transition from "extensive" to "intensive" economies and begin benefiting from the economic growth and prosperity of Western Europe.[43] The economic division began rapidly losing its military–political premises in Europe in the beginning of the 1990s.

4 The Imperatives of Political Change

This study equates the concept of an organic security order with a specifically European security order. After World War II Winston Churchill was of the opinion that Europe should restore itself as a political "world region." Such a restoration was necessary to create a more stable world order based on "regional pillars," with a "unified Europe" as one of those geographically organic pillars.[1] Churchill's hope concurred with the views of, among others, George F. Kennan, who in his capacity as one of the chief planners of the postwar foreign policy of the United States advocated a strategy of a federated Europe "into which the several parts of Germany could be absorbed."[2] Unfortunately, none of these plans was ever realized. Instead, a divided Europe emerged and the military alliances became the symbol of this failure.

As stated above, the two alliances did not constitute symmetrical substructures within the European bipolar structure, although the hegemonic position of the superpowers within their respective alliances has de facto legitimized the spheres of influence drawn by the dividing line in Europe.[3] The Warsaw Pact has been an instrument for the Soviets to maintain ideological and political control over Eastern Europe: in 1956 in Hungary and in 1968 in Czechoslovakia, the Soviets used military force to crack down on antisocialist uprisings. Although it has frequently been denied that any kind of delimitation of spheres of interest exists in Europe, the vague Western reaction to the implementation of the Brezhnev Doctrine has led many to believe that the superpowers have had a mutual interest in supporting Realpolitik in terms of the division of Europe. At a certain point in the mid-1970s there even seemed to be an interest within the U.S. government in declaring this attitude in doctrinal terms. A member of the Ford administration, Helmut Sonnenfeldt, went so far as to state that the tasks of the United States included, among other things, ensuring that the relationship that developed between the East Europeans and the Soviet Union was an "organic" one. This so-called "Sonnenfeldt Doctrine" was wrongly regarded as an explicit recognition of the Brezhnev

Doctrine.[4] However, one would be justified in claiming that Sonnenfeldt foresaw future developments in Eastern Europe more clearly than many of his colleagues. Indeed, in the 1980s Sonnenfeldt's prophecy seemed to come true: the Brezhnev Doctrine became obsolete and a more organic relationship began to emerge between the Soviet Union and Eastern Europe.

At the end of the 1970s and the beginning of the 1980s, the crisis symptoms in the socialist world increased and the future for it became clouded. The Soviet Union was confronted with "dramatic alterations of the international and internal environment," and it was already feasible for experts to predict that "in the 1980s the Soviet Union will be facing issues and events which may make for incremental changes—conceivably even fundamental changes."[5] Indeed, behind the facade of economic development, stable political systems, accepted party leaders and unassailable Soviet hegemony, a process of destabilization had started.[6] At the same time, world capitalism had sailed through the economic gales of the 1970s and early 1980s with surprisingly little difficulty. It had entered a new technological phase successfully. The socialist community was not able to make it. As Eric Hobsbawm states, "socialism was incapable of moving fully into, let alone generating, the new high-tech economy and was therefore destined to fall ever further behind."[7] In addition, in a society marked by global communications, media, travel and transnational economy, it was no longer possible to insulate socialist populations from information about the non-socialist world, that is, from knowing just how much worse off they were in material terms and in freedom and choice. This economic stagnation led to political destabilization.

Furthermore, ecological catastrophes and popular resistance to nuclear weapons fostered political disintegration, prompting the questioning of the leading roles of the Communist parties; consequently, a final pillar of stability and cohesion was crumbling. As early as 1980 both these factors, economic decline and weakened party rule, caused the rise of the Polish "Solidarnosc" that shocked the Soviet leaders and the whole "socialist community."

THE EROSION OF THE EURASIAN SECURITY SYSTEM

From a historical perspective, Russia has traditionally been a peripheral power of some significance in Europe, a competitor for land and, in the 19th century, an active participant in the European system. After 1945, however, roles were reversed: Europe had to accept a drastically diminished role in a new world order, the agenda of which was set by others, namely the Soviet Union and the U.S. In Eastern Europe[8] the agenda was set solely by the Soviet Union in its role as a new great power.

Nevertheless, in the postwar period Eastern Europe has remained a source of instability and ferment for the Soviet Union, which has been unable to work out a relationship with the region that would allow for organic, peaceful change. The Soviet Union has had two basic goals in Eastern Europe: viability and control. It wants regimes that are economically and politically viable but not alienated from Soviet influence and control. The creation of the Warsaw Pact in 1955, although a logical response to West Germany's entry into NATO, was in large measure a political act designed to help bloc cohesion. In Kennan's view, the WTO helped keep the psychological shadow of the Soviet Union hovering over Eastern Europe. In the Warsaw Pact's early years, the military role of the East European member states remained extremely limited.[9] However, the ultimate goal of the Soviet Union was to establish a socialist commonwealth —a kind of security community—which would be an association of sovereign Soviet allies linked by common defense interests, common economic interests and a common ideology.[10] In essence, the concept of the "socialist commonwealth" or "socialist community" (as described earlier in Chapter 1) meant the adaptation of the Soviet model of "real existing socialism." Ernst Kux states that "this subordination, which constituted the main factor for stability in Eastern Europe, became the cause of instability."[11] The East European economies in the late 1970s were not only saddled with the burdens of the military confrontation with the West, but also with those of the maintenance of a huge Soviet military force on their territories and latterly of the Soviet Union's expansion towards the east and south as well. In addition, they had to bear the increasing costs of Soviet oil, energy and raw materials, and gradually they became dependent on huge western credits. These developments contributed to the social dissatisfaction that emerged in Eastern Europe in the 1980s. In the overall geostrategic picture of Europe, the WTO constituted a Eurasian security system whose members share similar military–strategic interests but increasingly show signs of fragmentation in economic and even political questions. In fact, the whole existence of the WTO was at stake following the revolutions of 1989.

For decades the ideological, as well as geopolitical and strategic, importance of Eastern Europe for the Soviet Union superseded the risks of promoting reform within the bloc. However, the cost in geostrategic terms of the imposition of Soviet control over Eastern Europe after 1945, and especially the Stalinization of the region after 1948, was decreased Soviet influence in Western Europe. In the long run, this created a major dilemma for the Soviet Union as it strove both to influence Western Europe and maintain stability in Eastern Europe. In the Gorbachev era, this dilemma has become even more acute, because the process of restructuring is aimed at improving relations above all with Western Europe.[12] Was the Soviet Union ready to jeopardize its power in Eastern Europe in order to improve its relations with both Western Europe and the United States?

Traditionally, the Soviet Union has viewed Eastern Europe primarily within the context of its overall strategy to influence Western Europe. Eastern Europe has been not only a buffer for the Soviet Union but also a springboard for its diplomatic, political and military efforts to decouple Western Europe from the United States and to increase Soviet influence there. In the West, many East European initiatives, such as the Polish Rapacki and Gomulka Plans of the late 1950s and 1960s for nuclear-weapons-free zones in Europe, have been pigeonholed as Soviet efforts to weaken NATO's defenses without corresponding reductions in the USSR's own military capabilities. East European promotion of "European detente" has traditionally met with similar criticism.[13]

In terms of history, culture, economics and general identity, most of the East European countries differ significantly from the Soviet Union, as well as from each other. In 1989, the dispute between Romania and Hungary over the situation of the Hungarian minority in Romania constituted perhaps the most dangerous interstate problem in Europe. Furthermore, since the mid-1970s, the countries of Eastern Europe have managed to gain more and more room for maneuver vis-à-vis the Soviet Union, even in political and ideological matters. In sum, since Mikhail Gorbachev took power in the Kremlin, the situation has started to change dramatically.

The post-Brezhnev leadership in the Soviet Union has begun a fundamental reevaluation of Soviet security needs in the context of world politics. This process finds expression particularly in efforts to redefine the relationship between economic restructuring—perestroika—and foreign policy. As Foreign Minister Eduard Shevardnadze stated in his address to Soviet diplomatic personnel on June 27, 1987

We must increase the profitability of our foreign policy and try to reach a situation where interrelations among states encumber our economy as little as possible and create a stable psychological atmosphere in which Soviet people can work peacefully.[14]

Shevardnadze went a bit further on July 4, 1987, in stating that "the most important function of our foreign policy is to create the optimal conditions for the economic and social development of our country."[15] In short, the grand strategy of Gorbachev's foreign policy includes at least the following principle: to *withdraw* from the world arena when the present position causes economic burden and maintains the perception of imminent Soviet threat. If fully implemented, this strategy would be felt both within the WTO structure and European politics in general.

During the Brezhnev era, the Soviets aimed at making "deals" with the United States about the future of Europe over the heads of the Europeans. The policy of detente was overwhelmingly interpreted in Moscow in terms of superpower conciliation and negotiation.[16] Yet this did not halt the Soviet military buildup; in fact, it accelerated it. As Viacheslav Dashichev points out in his article of May 1988:

As the West saw it, the Soviet leadership (during the Brezhnev era) was actively exploiting detente to build up its own military forces, seeking military parity with the United States and in general with all the opposing powers—a fact without historical precedent . . . the expansion of the Soviet sphere of interest reached critical limits in the West's eyes with the introduction of Soviet troops into Afghanistan.[17]

The difference between Brezhnev and Gorbachev is most striking in their definitions of general Soviet security needs and the Soviet role in Europe. As Paul Marantz puts it: "[Gorbachev's] is a long-term strategy to create a new identity and a new image for the Soviet Union as a country which is not threatening anybody."[18] But how will it be possible to implement this strategy in the WTO?

The Warsaw Pact has been a crucial political and military tool for the Soviet Union. However, the WTO also has performed several important political functions vis-à-vis the outside world. In this respect, some WTO leaders worked to further Soviet foreign policy ends. In military terms, the Soviet Union did not absolutely need the

WTO because the stationing of its troops had already been settled on a bilateral basis. Yet the WTO's military posture overwhelmingly served Soviet strategic interests and only narrowly took into account the national interests of its member states.[19] One can only ask whether the enforcement of WTO cohesion by coercive means truly benefited the Soviet Union, or whether the same basic goals could have been achieved with a much more flexible and democratic security arrangement.

The post-Brezhnev leadership of the Soviet Union has stressed the political, as opposed to the military, components of security. It has repeatedly been declared that the Soviet Union must take into account the anxieties and perceptions of other nations, since the Soviet Union will not be secure until other nations, foremost among them the United States, also feel secure. Furthermore, it has been stressed that the threat of war, although not entirely removed from the agenda of world politics, is no longer a part of the realities of Europe. Security can be achieved chiefly by political and cooperative means rather than expensive military arsenals. Indeed, Gorbachev has been consistent in applying perestroika to all segments of Soviet society. He has gradually strengthened the primacy of political considerations and of the new legislative body, the Supreme Soviet, whose president he was elected in May 1989—in Soviet civil–military relations. After these political steps and numerous proposals in the field of conventional and nuclear disarmament, it seems obvious that a historical turning point is at hand for the Eurasian security system and its role and goals. In the Soviet Union, however, the crises are becoming an increasing threat to Gorbachev and perestroika in the early 1990s.[20]

At the outset of Gorbachev's rise to power, his aim was to strengthen bloc cohesion and the economic integration of WTO member states. He also tried to implement Soviet policies in Eastern Europe without coercive methods, especially the use or threat of force. Already the repercussions of this approach have been dramatic. It has encouraged, for instance, the articulation of nationalism without historical precedent even within the Soviet Union.[21]

As for East–West relations in general, the biggest risk lies in the possibility that internal uprisings or the demise of the Warsaw Pact structure in Eastern Europe could lead to a harsh Soviet crackdown. When visiting the site of the Armenian earthquake in December 1988, Gorbachev stated that the continuing nationalistic unrest in Armenia over the fate of Nagorno-Karabakh threatened to bring to an abrupt end all his efforts to change the country. "This is the edge of the abyss. One more step and it's the abyss."[22] This comment clearly indicated how delicate a phase the process of perestroika had reached already by the end of 1988. And this was nothing but a starting point for a series of national uprisings in the Baltic states and, for example, in Soviet Azerbaijan. The disintegration of the Soviet empire began to seem a real possibility in the winter of 1990. In particular, the Baltic states' striving for independence challenged the Soviet leadership in Moscow. As Zbigniew Brzezinski predicted in April 1990: "Lithuania, in many respects, is the litmus test of the process of change in the Soviet Union." Brzezinski also stated that if Gorbachev permits Lithuania to secede, then he is also "tolerating the process of dismantling the Soviet Union."[23] The question was no longer whether the Soviet Union would be dismantled, but what course and pace this process would take.

Gorbachev's disarmament proposals clearly suggest that the Soviet Union is also accelerating perestroika within the military. In fact, a new kind of relationship has emerged between Eastern Europe and the Soviet Union. Soviet readiness to reduce drastically its military presence in Eastern Europe and to restructure its military posture so that it is unequivocally defensive started to increase the political room for maneuver of its East European allies.[24] In the 1990s the Soviet Union may be more content with allies that pursue a policy based more on national than bloc interests. It is difficult to assume that any of the East European countries define their national security interests in terms other than confidence, mutual trust and cooperation with their superpower neighbor. If a "new relationship" between Eastern Europe and the Soviet Union can be established, it will have added implications for the overall European security order. For one thing, by encouraging economic and political freedom in Eastern Europe this relationship could lead to increased interdependence and interaction across the dividing line of Europe, although this line may be shifted to the borders of the Soviet Union. Consequently, the relationship between the USSR and the countries of Eastern Europe, as well as a new Europe, will to some extent retain its bipolar character.

The Eurasian security system has entered a stage beyond the Brezhnev Doctrine. Each state now has a right to find its own way to socialism, or better, away from socialism. This development will, if not interrupted by quirks of history, have a major impact on the geostrategic landscape of Europe in the 1990s.[25]

THE TWO PILLARS OF THE EUROATLANTIC SECURITY COMMUNITY

The founding of NATO in 1949, with the strategic aim of providing U.S. aid to the weakened European states in the event of Soviet aggression, did militarily what the Marshall Plan had done economically: it further deepened the division of Europe into two camps. Only the traditionally neutral countries of Sweden and Switzerland, along with non-communist and soon-to-be-neutral Finland and Austria as well as socialist and soon-to-be-nonaligned Yugoslavia, remained outside the alliance for specified reasons. Finland and Austria managed to avoid ideological infiltration from the East and soon established their place in the "Western camp" by tilting the geostrategic balance at least symbolically toward the West.

The founding of NATO turned the orderly restoration of a unified Europe upside down. Kennan had stressed in 1947 that the starting point for a process of restoration should be "a political, economic and spiritual union," not a military one. To begin with a military objective would only frighten the "outlying" regions, such as Scandinavia, and would complicate any inclusion of Germany. Indeed, Kennan considered NATO a misguided perversion of the policy of containment.[26] But as the general atmosphere in Europe worsened in 1948 as a result of the Stalinization of Eastern Europe, the Europeans grew more nervous. Although the founding of NATO increased security in the short term, it created permanent problems over the long term. The partial "militarization" of containment was, to a certain extent, a logical step, but it induced people "to take their eye off the real ball," as the advocates of a less militarized version of containment claimed.[27] The question was whether there still existed, after the founding of NATO, any real option for conciliation with the Soviet Union and for the future dismantling of the division of Germany and Europe. In his famous speech in Fulton, Missouri, in March 1946, Winston Churchill had foreseen this problem. However, although he forecast the fall of the "Iron Curtain" and stressed the need to counter the Soviets militarily, Churchill also underscored the simultaneous necessity of negotiating with the Soviet Union about outstanding political problems in order to gain a peaceful solution for Europe. In Churchill's judgment, the partition of the continent was more favorable to the Soviets because it confirmed a status quo based on coercion in Eastern Europe. In the long run, Europe's

division and East–West military confrontation, although perhaps
maintaining military equilibrium, were and would remain a source
of conflict. A stable peace in Europe had to be based on military
equilibrium and strength as well as negotiations. Ultimately, it had
to be based on an organic political system.

Despite almost constant intra-alliance crises and disputes, NATO
is an extraordinary example of international cooperation. Comprised
of 16 sovereign and democratic states, NATO links a nuclear
superpower with a global outlook and worldwide commitments
located on one side of the Atlantic to a host of medium-sized and
small states with regional concerns and perspectives planted on the
other shore. It was thought that NATO would be based on "the
illusion that the Alliance would lead to a true partnership of equals
with virtually identical interest." However, as Egon Bahr has
remarked, the history of the Euroatlantic alliance has shown that
"even among equals, some are more equal than others."[28] NATO
has survived its crises because they were caused less by fundamental
disagreements over central alliance issues than by differences over
marginal problems. NATO's three chief tenets have never been
seriously in doubt: a common purpose, a common strategy and a
common defense.[29] The legitimacy of the Euroatlantic system is
stable—and thus status quo oriented—and thus it seems certain that
"the Atlantic Alliance won't die of its feud," as Anton DePorte
noted in 1982.[30] Although this forecast has by and large remained
valid, the Euroatlantic, or Atlantic, security community has gradually become a kind of Euro-American security system of cooperation
between two partners—the United States and Western Europe—
instead of among 16 participants. This process has been evolving—
as described above—since the early 1960s, although its roots
certainly date back to the late 1940s.

From the strategic perspective, NATO's principal objective was to
deter any Soviet attack; the threat posed by Soviet military power in
Eastern Europe was to be balanced, psychologically as well as
militarily, by formally linking U.S. nuclear power to the protection
of Western Europe—that is, by throwing a nuclear cloak over
Europe. This was the first attempt to use U.S. nuclear power in an
explicitly political way, and the U.S. nuclear guarantee has remained
the keystone of the alliance. Thereafter, crises within NATO were
primarily related to nuclear risk-sharing.[31] Since the signing of the
INF (Intermediate-Range Nuclear Forces) agreement in 1987, the
debate on risk-sharing has ranged far and wide, and Eurostrategic

interests and U.S. global interests have been on a collision course more often than at any other time in the history of NATO.

Since the mid-1960s, the relative power of the United States in the Euroatlantic community has gradually diminished, while Western Europe has made considerable progress in economic integration. However, since 1970 a cumulative process of foreign policy coordination has also taken place and the institutions of European Political Cooperation (EPC) have emerged. The EPC was originally designed in part to try to develop a corporate foreign policy distinct from that of the United States. In its early days, the EPC generally focused on issues well beyond the immediate concerns of the member states, in addition to its coordinating role for CSCE review conferences. In particular, EPC often commented on Arab–Israeli peacekeeping, and, by providing advice without facing responsibility, it was not popular with the United States. A really new phase of the EPC took place at the end of the 1980s.[32]

Above all, the process of European Political Cooperation has demonstrated an increasing degree of dynamism. Nevertheless, the United States has maintained its key role in the defense of Western Europe. The core of the problem is the nuclear issue, which has, in fact, deepened the division between the allies to the extent that, as in the mid-1960s, the basic credibility of the alliance has been called into question. As a result, the Atlantic alliance has, at least superficially, disintegrated into a "two-pillar system," in which a militarily more independent and assertive Western Europe faces a United States prone to giving priority to its global superpower interests. In addition, the role of NATO is at stake: should it be purely a military organization or should it adhere to the dual definition elaborated in the Harmel Report? One West European observer forecasts that in the short term—and as a part of the transformation of NATO—we may see reduced political ambitions for NATO and a return to the initial premises of the Atlantic alliance, that is, an emphasis on a primarily political alliance.[33] In the late 1980s the two-pillar structure of the Euroatlantic security community became still more obvious. Disputes erupted between the United States and Western Europe over the Soviet pipeline in 1981, President Reagan's Strategic Defense Initiative in 1983, and finally the Reykjavik mini-summit in 1986. These disagreements acted as catalysts in the Europeanization of detente, as well as in the creation of a "European security union" that would empower Europe to participate in all negotiations directly concerning its own security, including negotiations on nuclear disarmament. Such concerns have been especially strong in the FRG. The process of reunification of Germany, which really began to take shape after the March 18, 1990, elections in the GDR, has, of course, drastically changed the situation in NATO.[34]

The division of the Euroatlantic security community into two pillars was tried again in the late 1980s, but its political implications have yet to be seen. If it reaches a stage in which it functions more fully, will it tilt the West toward the East or vice versa? First and foremost, Europe needs a political framework for the ongoing and largely unpredictable processes of change.

In the early 1980s, a "new chill" between the superpowers strengthened the process of Europeanizing detente. By the end of the 1980s, a revitalized dialogue between the superpowers pushed the Europeanist approach to Europe's defense further ahead. Over the long term, while the Soviet Union would welcome a diminished U.S. role in Western Europe, it would not wish to see the emergence of a more powerful West European defense capability, especially if it were to involve a more prominent role for a reunified Germany, including what the Soviet Union would call "a finger on the nuclear trigger." Nevertheless, to be successful, the incipient West European security option must include both conventional and nuclear weapons, so long as the nuclear component is subsumed into the Western defense posture in general. All conceivable security options for Europe should, as Lothar Ruehl has argued, be pursued under the NATO umbrella, even strengthening NATO synergy through French reconciliation with NATO's strategy.[35] But will the end result, then, be a Europeanization of the East–West military conflict—a bipolarity between Moscow and Brussels—or a new security order based, not on a bipolar military conflict, but on non-military and cooperative components?

In any event, the role of NATO is in transition. This process primarily reflects the developments in Moscow and in Central Europe, but it can also be regarded as resulting from the European Community (EC)'s emergence as a great power of sorts. The ongoing processes of disarmament and rapprochement between East and West provide new opportunities to readjust NATO to a function that does not hinder the dismantling of the division of Europe, but in fact even advances it. The challenge is to find a function for NATO beyond bipolarity and the Cold War.[36]

EUROPEANIZATION AND THE EMERGENCE OF A CONTINENTAL EUROPE

It is well recognized in Europe that the new and probably consistent rapprochement of the superpowers does not resolve Europe's security dilemma per se. Nor can the superpowers directly influence the course of Europe's political future as before, as the revolutions of 1989 and reunification of Germany have shown. On the whole, the United States and the Soviet Union seek mutual cooperation in an effort to adjust themselves better to the newly emerging multipolar world.[37]

The first period of East–West rapprochement took shape on two distinct levels: the traditional bipolar level of the superpowers and the military alliances; and the intra-European, or "regime," level of Eastern and Western Europe. In terms of timing, these two levels of rapprochement have evolved autonomously or in an ad hoc manner. For years it was argued that East–West confrontation was based on ideological and political cleavages. As a consequence, it was commonly agreed that differences between socioeconomic systems could not be reconciled: there was a totalitarian system on the one side and a pluralistic one on the other, or, as orthodox Soviet and East European rhetoric would have it, Western capitalism could not be reconciled with socialism. Now the ideological competition seems to be more or less over, as pragmatism supersedes ideological jargon in Europe. This development results from a long-term process encompassing both intra-alliance factors and factors related to the changing roles of the superpowers in the world community. Yet Europe is still made up of different socioeconomic systems. Primarily because of the "stalemate" over the use of military might—especially nuclear weapons—competition can be converted into favorable political processes that are indirect and necessarily involve large amounts of highly subjective components.[38] Thus the Europeanization of Europe in terms of security and political development could also connote Europe's tilt toward a continental orientation. This process was highlighted by the signing of the INF Treaty, which, as one French observer put it,

> marks an American disengagement in Europe, and all at once it is the entire Western European setup that is going to shift from an Atlantic or Atlanticist orientation to a continental orientation.

Ostpolitik is becoming European and Europe is resuming its continental dimension.[39]

If the U.S. anchoring of Western Europe is severed, there is nothing that will offset Europe's continental pull. This process of "decoupling" is taking place while Europe is still divided and "helpless" vis-à-vis Soviet military might. Even if partly true, this threatening image of the problems related to the continental orientation of Europe depicts the East as an unchanged entity, certainly contradicting the realities of the late 1980s and early 1990s. However, it illustrates what the "potential" threats would be if the East were to return to Stalinism.[40]

Historically, Europe can be seen to be resuming its continental orientation, for the most part with little regard for its Atlantic security commitments or "unilateral" actions taken by the United States. The INF Treaty, for example, might have accelerated the process, but did not in itself trigger anything new. In the long run, Western Europe has had to face its political problems and its unfinished political agenda in the East with self-reliance and without the automatic support of the United States. Yet political self-reliance requires considerably greater military self-reliance than Western Europe can presently muster. Ultimately, it is up to the Europeans themselves, as Kennan once counseled, "to discover the paths of escape"[41] from the continent's division into hostile blocs. The superpowers cannot do this for them, nor do they have a compelling need to do so.

The post-INF environment and the incipient detente it has nurtured also intensified discussions about military integration in Western Europe. The Soviet Union's ostensible interest in minimum deterrence, along with Gorbachev's relaxation of control over Eastern Europe, may improve the systemic disintegration of the Warsaw Pact, thus facilitating the continental orientation of Western Europe and, as a consequence, that of Eastern Europe toward the West. The remaining question is how change can be managed and stability maintained if certain features of the transformation are no longer under superpower control. For its part, the Soviet Union kept alive and further developed its concept of a common European home, thus signaling its intention to remain an integral part of a post-INF Europe. Here again, the question is what this would mean in the medium term. So far, the concept of the common European home has not produced any concrete result except, perhaps, certain

changes in Western public opinion and a rapprochement between the
CMEA and the EC. In psychological terms, Soviet acknowledgment
of the EC illustrates a sense of political realism and a waning of
ideological rigidity in Soviet foreign policy thinking. It seems obvious
that the Soviet Union is prepared to expand its European politics
even more. In this respect, its vision of a common European home is
aimed at providing a political framework that would, in the final
stage, create a "unified continent" with socially and politically
diverse nations. In the summer of 1989, Gorbachev spoke to the
Council of Europe about his philosophy:

> The belonging of European states to different social systems is a
> reality. Recognition of this historical fact and respect for the
> sovereign right of every nation to choose freely a social system
> constitute the major prerequisite for a normal European process
> . . . . Differences among states are not removable. They are, as I
> have already said on several occasions, even favorable, provided,
> of course, that the competition between the different types of
> society is directed at creating better material and spiritual living
> conditions for all people.[42]

Gorbachev also ruled out the use or threat of force—alliance
against alliance, within the alliance, wherever—thus burying the
Brezhnev Doctrine for good. He pleaded for a Europe in which
"the only battlefield will be markets open for trade and minds open
to ideas." In order to speed up his vision, the Soviet leader proposed
that the 35 nations that drafted the Helsinki Final Act meet again to
lay down another grand design for the continent's future. The
common home could be built within the Helsinki process, although
not without endowing it with a new impetus and dynamism.
Historically, the image of the common European home meets the
criteria set by French President de Gaulle, who once advocated the
establishment of a "European Europe." Yet while de Gaulle wanted
to oust the superpowers from Europe, Gorbachev now takes the
unassailable position that the concept of a unified Europe must be
defined in terms of the CSCE goals.[43]
    It is clear that the restoration of Europe will require a kind of
reassociation of its Western and Eastern halves. The process of
achieving that goal is a complex one. Although no immediate
chance is in sight for dismantling the military alliances as the
foundation of the European security order,[44] psychological and

socioeconomic processes tending toward a more organic European system are making unequivocal progress. There have been periods—for instance, in the early 1980s—when the phenomenon of an autonomous European detente and, within it, an autonomous inter-German detente, gained ground in international politics. As an ideal, the reassociation of Europe should be attained through a gradual process of mutual involvement implemented from a stable basis in symmetrical power. Such a reassociation would mean, among other things, that Eastern Europe could be both economically and politically more involved in Central and Western Europe. In this respect, the prospects for a common European home are to be welcomed. But it is obvious that this process cannot be achieved symmetrically, which contributes, of course, to a major political problem. Therefore the political structure of Europe—both Eastern and Western—is emerging as a central issue of the 1990s.[45] The Europeanization of East–West interaction and of solutions related to the outstanding political and, to a certain extent, military questions provides only a vague framework without any concrete substance. In the long run, however, this process cannot be overlooked as proposals for overcoming the division of Europe are formulated. In the multipolar world of the future, that stubborn division would be an increasingly heavy burden for all Europeans.

For years the main asset of Europeanization seemed to be rapprochement in general. Economic cooperation between East and West, as noted earlier, had not been encouraged for a multitude of reasons. In this respect a turning point was reached during the revolutions of late 1989. Nevertheless, Western Europe will remain the most important trading partner for the Soviet Union and even more for the smaller CMEA countries. With their specialized interests, European countries in both alliances are suited to acting as mediators in the bid for more economic cooperation.[46] Cross-regional socialization processes, which can induce such changes as the adoption of new values more congenial to pluralism and the free market, have shown surprisingly limited results despite vastly increased contacts between East and West Europeans.[47] Yet their prospects have improved since Gorbachev's policies began to take root in Eastern Europe. This led one Western observer to admit in 1988 that "if present trends continue, it is not unreasonable to look ahead to a time when the West will be not, as since Yalta, a tertiary actor in East Central Europe, but a secondary actor as important as the Soviet Union, though in different ways."[48]

Domestic developments in both halves of Europe increased "ideological Europeanization." David Gress has predicted that the FRG will constitute the "gravitational" center for this process. By definition the FRG takes its policy inspiration mainly from the tradition of Ostpolitik. Consequently, Western Europe should have political interests that are not only different from the interests of the United States in Western Europe but that can and ought to be defended, as it is often put, "against both superpowers." This thinking constitutes an "ideology of Europe," since, as Gress reasons,

> it is a belief that the political conditions under which West European democracy will survive are other than they are, and that a struggle that, in fact, directly involves Europeans can be ignored and neglected. It is, therefore, an ideology, and not a reasonable prescription for political action in the true interests of West Europeans.[49]

In this sense the "ideology of Europe" had its roots in the superpower confrontation of the early 1980s. Since then, however, the process of ideological Europeanization has developed mainly as a result of superpower rapprochement and inter-European dynamics. In the latter development, new security issues such as the threat of ecological catastrophes have increased European interdependence across old ideological boundaries. Indeed, anti-superpower attitudes have de facto disappeared from European soil. Yet the process of Europeanizing East–West interaction has not ceased—a testimony to the organic dynamism of the process as such.

The first period of the Europeanization of East–West interaction ended in the early autumn of 1989. Since then a "new" Central Europe has emerged, replacing the political concept of "Eastern Europe"; the quality of interaction between Central Europe and Western Europe is rapidly rising. It is now possible to speak about the beginning of the final phase in the emergence of a whole and continental Europe in world politics. Furthermore, now that Soviet domination is crumbling, "old and new questions are raised about the German role in East Central Europe," as Jacques Rupnik puts it.[50] Undoubtedly, the question of German influence in Central Europe will be an enigma of European politics in the 1990s.

Part III
Bipolarity in Transition

PART III
BIPOLARITY IN TRANSITION

The events of 1989 in Eastern and Central Europe as well as in the Soviet Union rocked the foundations of the postwar bipolar security system. The Stalinist regimes collapsed one by one. It is self-evident, however, that without the consent of the Soviet Union, no breakthrough in the development toward democracy in Eastern Europe would have taken place so abruptly.

Undoubtedly, the move toward democracy in Eastern Europe as well as in the Soviet Union will affect every aspect of life—political, social and economic—and have a substantial impact in Western Europe. Alongside enthusiasm there is also growing concern that the political ferment, particularly in Central Europe and the Balkans, makes for an inherently unstable mix in which old demons—belligerent nationalism and demagogic populism—could win out as easily as could liberal democracy and the ideal of a common European home stretching from the Atlantic to the Urals. The Europeans know that nationalism is both a progressive as well as a destructive force.[1]

In 1989, political change became the most important factor in the European situation. Futhermore, the emergence of complex economic, political and security interdependence was now a fact of life. Yet many of the old structures of bipolarity—socioeconomic differences between "East" and "West," some of the most stubborn military arrangements of the Cold War era—will remain for at least a few years to come. Also a new division is looming on the horizon. The 1990s will therefore be a period of transition.

After the revolution of 1989, the European situation is also more paradoxical then ever before. The forces of integration as well as disintegration are molding the geostrategic landscape of the continent. Undoubtedly, Europe's top agenda item in the early 1990s will be accommodating and managing the revolutionary situation in Eastern Europe, and especially in the Soviet Union.

In the early 1990s one of the major problems in Europe is the lack of any comprehensive approach to and framework for dealing with the revolutionary developments.[2] Events often seem to take their own course. In the short term, a conceptual framework has to be designed. Also, the European change should be better defined within a global system of transformation. President George Bush for his part acknowledged this dilemma in December 1989: "The task before us is to provide the architecture for continued peaceful change."[3]

This part discusses the changing geostrategic landscape of Europe and the conceptual premises needed to cope with the changing security situation. Furthermore, a new European architecture is elaborated in terms of whether it could provide a new and alternative security order: an institutionalized structure for the third postwar peace arrangement for Europe.

5 The Changing Geostrategic Landscape of Europe

If measured by the broadest military criteria, the postwar bipolar order has not dramatically altered, and the dismantling of the two military alliances does not seem imminent in the early 1990s. Yet even a significant decrease in the level of military confrontation cannot be ruled out as a consequence of ongoing efforts in the medium term. Conventional arms reductions and troop withdrawals in particular may have a significant influence on both the strategic landscape and European stability. In any case, without arms reductions and troop withdrawals the European security situation cannot be markedly improved; such immobility would produce a permanent source of tension.[1]

The notion of a "geostrategic landscape" used in this book fits only within the framework of the postwar military–political division of Europe; cultural and economic bipolarization are considered a consequence of the division. However, in the discussion of the emergence of a multipolar world, reference is made to new spheres of influence on a continental scale being established around the world. Within the context of this study, a related question might be whether changes in the geostrategic landscape of Europe will tilt Western Europe toward the East or vice versa, or whether we need a new concept altogether to describe the possible geostrategic repercussions of change.

As a part of the systemic as well as political processes of change described in the previous chapters, a geostrategic setting is emerging in Europe in which new power centers are replacing the bipolar structure. This development makes it imperative for states outside the military alliances– such as the European neutral states—to adapt, which in turn may have an impact on the geostrategic landscape.

THE EMERGENCE OF A NEO-NEUTRAL CENTRAL EUROPE

In retrospect, perhaps the most important turning point in the postwar East–West configuration took place between August 1989 and January 1990. All the Central European states managed to escape the Soviet-led ideological camp. It was much more difficult for them to escape poverty and the Eurasian security system. The return to Europe of the Central European states will in any case require years or even decades.

The quest for democracy—demonstated by such events as the ascension of a Solidarity prime minister in Poland, East Germans "voting with their feet" and leaving in droves for West Germany, and the violent overthrow of the Ceausescu dictatorship in Romania—were necessary preconditions for Europe to get rid of the "Yalta legacy" and to start building a new Europe, one in which "East" and "West" would have less, if any, meaning.

It was no surprise that the political earthquake in Eastern Europe had the most dramatic impact on the German question. However, the tempo of events surprised not only the Germans but the rest of the world as well. The unification of Germany now had a historical momentum (this question will be dealt with primarily in the next section).

The revolution of 1989 restored a geographic Central Europe. As a result, the Soviet Union became Europe's real geographic and, in particular, geopolitical East. However, the reemergence of Central Europe poses, as Zbigniew Brzezinski reasons, "a special problem, dangerous to stability of Europe as a whole." He expresses a number of arguments:

This postcommunist region is threatened by chaos and instability even as it yearns for a Western European style of life and for Western-type institutional arrangements. It is fragmented and weak. The economies of Central Europe are in a shambles. Their political systems have to be built from scratch. Their political cultures are imbued with intense nationalism that has been intensified by the communist experiences. The threat of national and territorial conflicts overhangs the internal difficulties that every Central European regime will have to overcome on the way to the stable democracy which all profess to seek.[2]

Undoubtedly, upheavals in Central Europe and in the Balkans will continue. As a result of the 1989 revolution, the differences of the states concerned became evident. It is not possible to find one simple solution or model that could resolve all political, economic and social problems arising in Eastern and Central Europe after the collapse of authoritarianism. It is generally recognized that it would take at least a generation, if not longer, to effect these changes in Eastern and Central Europe. One could express a justified fear that beyond the collapse of authoritarianism, a more general deterioration of a variety of social links in all areas of life could develop. This could create the danger of chaos or a return to some sort of hardline, authoritarian rule. This has taken place, in fact, in Romania in 1990.[3]

In the short term, the revolution of 1989 "liberated" the East Central European states. One could agree with Stephen S. Rosenfeld, that "the time of smaller or defeated nations does seem to be coming again." He may be equally right in adding, however, that "their future depends not only on their courage and steadfastness, but on their modesty and realism as well."[4] In the future they have to establish a new kind of security arrangement among themselves and also vis-à-vis the "East" and the "West."

In the future, Central Europe's ability to identify itself as a part of the whole of Europe rather than as a part of a "political" region will be strongly linked to the overall process of dismantling the division of the continent. George F. Kennan's misgivings about the long-term implications of decisions reached in the late 1940s and early 1950s have actually gained ground, as he himself put it in 1989, "with the passage of the years":

> And now it is becoming increasingly evident that certain Warsaw Pact countries, encouraged by the more liberal policies of Mikhail Gorbachev, are feeling the need for a relationship with Western Europe that is inconsistent with the concepts underlying the initial decision to divide Germany and Europe.[5]

In the postwar era, the coerciveness of the WTO structure has been demonstrated by a series of military crackdowns and interventions by Soviet or Soviet-led troops in several East European states. Since the signing of the Helsinki Final Act in 1975, however, military means have not been used in a direct way to resolve problems between Eastern Europe and the Soviet Union. Yet the presence of Soviet troops in Eastern Europe remains a symbol of unresolved political problems there, though the function of these troops must be seen also within a strategic context.[6] Indeed, it should be taken more or less for granted that Gorbachev's primary interest has been strengthening the WTO structure. "Perestroika should not change the status of Eastern Europe from a Soviet sphere of domination to one of mere influence," as one Western observer has said.[7]

The political erosion of the WTO had been a fact for years, as described in Chapter 4. Mikhail Gorbachev had not managed to strengthen the political cohesion of the Eurasian security system either. On the contrary, perestroika led to demilitarization tendencies in Central Europe. This development has made it necessary for the Central European states to create a new form of relationship with the Soviet Union. As Peter Hardi of Hungary states: "The efforts to strengthen the political structure of the WTO would have further politicized it and increased Soviet dominance."[8]

It seems that the revolution of 1989 did not affect primarily Soviet military goals, because Soviet military thinking had already been moving away from its traditional emphasis on the capability for attack. Nevertheless, developments in East Central Europe accelerated the arms control process. Earlier arms control thinking was far ahead of the political process in creating goals for reductions in weapons and troops. After 1989, events rapidly moved political realities beyond the ongoing negotiations. But because the transition period is likely to be difficult and potentially destabilizing, the removal of troops will have to be more gradual.[9]

The search for a new relationship between Eastern Europe and the Soviet Union has incorporated one approach to resolving, at least partially, the division of Europe. In fact, from the Soviet point of view, the rationale for this search derives from the opportunities it presents to promote the realization of the common European home. Sergei Karaganov of the Institute of Europe of the USSR Academy of Sciences defines the concept of the common European home as follows:

> The conceptual key to this new security system in my view should be demilitarization and humanization of inter-European politics. That needs parallel and interdependent movement in all spheres of interaction between peoples and nations of our continent. In the political sphere it means redirecting the CSCE from being an instrument of status quo, into a means of changing and overcoming it.[10]

Karaganov makes it clear that if the military division has not been radically softened by 1992—the year the single European market is slated to go into effect—it will be much more difficult to accomplish this later on. Although Karaganov's views are not authoritative, he does point out some new attitudes in Soviet thinking vis-à-vis Western—and also Eastern—Europe.[11]

By definition, the common European home provides a political framework for overcoming the status quo that would ensue as a result of the demilitarization and humanization of inter-European politics. Without a doubt, at least the pillars of the European house should be erected by 1992. The evolution of a new relationship between Eastern Europe and the Soviet Union should thus be considered part of a process of demilitarizing and humanizing inter-European politics, too.[12]

Since the 1950s, the Soviet Union's European policy has been widely regarded in the West as expansionist: its short-term aim is to legitimize the status quo, particularly the existence of two German states; and its long-term aim is to promote the eventual neutralization of Western Europe. As Brzezinski stressed in 1968:

> Although it may be exaggeration to say that the Soviet goal is to make Western Europe into a Finland, the Soviet leaders could not be unaware of the increased political leverage that they would gain over a Western Europe less intimately tied to the United States in matters of security.[13]

Brzezinski goes on to state that the Soviets disregarded the fact that "the unsolved legacies of World War II cannot be resolved by a fiat that transforms them miraculously into a generally accepted and enduring settlement."[14]

During the postwar era the overriding Soviet concerns in Eastern Europe have been forward defense and maintenance of the region as a "buffer" between the Soviet Union and Western Europe. Thus the Soviet sine qua non in Eastern Europe is *stability*. The question is whether the Soviet Union would actually safeguard stability in Eastern Europe more effectively by forging a more realistic relationship with its East European allies. The declared aim of a common European home provides the Soviet Union with a political and diplomatic framework for adjusting to change while also securing its most vital interests in Eastern Europe. One Western observer has stated that the needed adjustment process would amount to a gradual Finlandization of Eastern Europe: "If such a solution could create stability where instability was increasing and chaos appeared likely, it would be a move worthy of a political culture which has tried to stress long-term concerns."[15] In the fall of 1988, Kissinger posed this question in *Newsweek*: "In the long run, aren't arrangements in Finland more useful to Soviet security than those in Eastern Europe?" He went on to state:

Is it possible to devise arrangements that would give the Soviets security guarantees (widely defined) while permitting the peoples of Eastern Europe to choose their own political future? Under such a system, it would be possible to conceive a drastic reduction of all outside forces in Europe—including those of the U.S.—that might revolutionize present concepts of security.[16]

In the 1960s and 1970s—but not so much in the 1980s—the concept of Finlandization was used in the West as a threat image. It was feared that the decline of the bipolar system would lead to Western Europe's disengagement from the United States, to the collapse of NATO and to an increase of Soviet influence in the "buffer zone" along the eastern border of the West European community. The term Finlandization was a stereotype, a simplification, undeniably very convenient for evoking certain specters, but it did not reliably reflect reality. In fact, Finland's postwar policy vis-à-vis the Soviet Union should be understood primarily in terms of its realism. A peaceful relationship between neutral Finland and its superpower neighbor, the Soviet Union, was achieved by putting great emphasis on certain historical lessons and geographical factors (e.g., the fact that Finland shares a border with the Soviet Union of more than 1,000 kilometers). Finnish statesmen are fond of quoting the English historian Thomas Macaulay: "The genesis of wisdom lies in the recognition of facts." This insight resulted in a small nation's realism: in a nutshell, if the Soviet Union perceives that there is no threat to its security from Finland or through Finnish territory, there is no reason that the two countries cannot live side by side in peace.[17]

The debate on a new relationship between Eastern Europe and the Soviet Union has occasionally produced the suggestion that Finland serve as a model for Eastern Europe. In and of itself this model does not work. Finland's case is unique and cannot be applied to other states. However, the image of Finland may generate thinking in the right direction. Stability in Eastern Europe can be most effectively guaranteed by taking into account the vital interests of the Soviet Union; a new Realpolitik in Eastern Europe would permit political change according to national needs, aspirations and traditions, along with the freedom to pursue close relations with Western Europe. Furthermore, an organized "community" of nations in Central Europe would tie these states closer together and make them less vulnerable in their extensive dealings with the rest of Europe.[18]

Although the concept of a Finnish model was generated in the West, it has been the subject of serious thought in Eastern Europe, albeit in slightly different form. As Timothy Garton Ash asks: "Does [the application of Finland's model in Eastern Europe] mean that the East Europeans should first give the Russians a bloody nose in a winter war?"[19] Ash reasons that if the term signifies a "new Yalta" or a basic renegotiation of the status quo in Europe, nothing has hinted at that possibility so far.

A new relationship between Central Europe and the Soviet Union is not, of course, emerging in a vacuum, but largely as a result of the development of a more organic setting. If this setting is realized, Central Europe will probably "tilt" toward the West. However, this kind of tilting within the European geostrategic landscape should not increase military confrontation; rather, it could strengthen stability by resulting in a more organic setting.[20]

It was difficult to believe that, as Charles Gati puts it, "Gorbachev would permit Eastern Europe to combine membership in Soviet-led military and economic alliances with internal and even considerable external independence."[21] However, this is what is currently taking place. Indeed, the Soviet Union has retreated from the quest for power and control in the world and has begun a new offensive to obtain a necessary amount of influence. However, in order to gain influence in Central Europe, a new *raison d'être* is needed for the Eurasian security system.

From the Soviet point of view, the bipolar security structure may pose an unnecessary obstacle to the further development of Soviet–German relations in particular, and as a consequence, rapprochement between Eastern and Western Europe may constitute a precondition for their improvement. One Western observer assumes that the whole idea of a common European home is merely a metaphor for *Soviet–German entente*, with the Americans excluded.[22] It has been questioned whether Central Europe lives under a threat of a new Rapallo.[23] Although the division of Europe has so far served Soviet interests well and any effort to change fundamentally the postwar political order could unleash forces such as German nationalism that Moscow might find difficult to control, the USSR's need to become a more integral part of the world economy is at stake. In such circumstances surprising developments are also possible. Undoubtedly the Soviet Union prefers gradualism, but the overall changes in both the Soviet Union and Central Europe have merged in a historic watershed. In any case, the Soviet–German factor will be crucial to any new relationship between the Soviet Union and Eastern Europe. Indeed, the evolving role of the FRG—a unified Germany—within the general framework of change in Central Europe is a key question of the 1990s.

In light of the revolutions of 1989 and the constructive launching of the process of democratization, the countries of Eastern and Central Europe will most probably constitute a fairly identifiable geostrategic entity. This entity's political status could be defined most accurately in terms of neutrality *à la finlandaise*. As Curt Gasteyger predicts, "considering the alternatives, the Soviet Union itself may eventually come to the conclusion that such an option is by far not the worst."[24] Yet neutral status cannot be easily applied to a unified Germany in the near future because of its special status (see the following section). However, in the case of East Central Europe, the temptation of neutrality is increasing, and natural.

FROM A "NEW" GERMAN QUESTION TO THE RISE OF A UNITED GERMANY

The fall of the Berlin Wall on November 9, 1989, became the symbol of the beginning of the final phase of erosion of bifurcation in Europe. For many, both in the West as well in the East, the emergence of a sudden momentum for German unification was a shock. Yet, in light of the developments between the two German states, particularly since the early 1980s, the collapse of the "artificial" walls between these states was a logical consequence.

In retrospect, it can be stated that at least two preconditions emerged to facilitate the unification: 1) the policy of the Soviet Union to build a common European home; 2) the deepening of the sense of German unity between the two German states. Of course, one can add a number of other factors, but without these two preconditions, no real possibility for unification would have occurred in 1989.

What seems to be a puzzle for many observers is the ease of the unification process that was actually triggered in December 1989. In retrospect, again, one could imagine that there would have been a "secret" plan between the Soviets and the West Germans to proceed toward unification on mutually acceptable terms. Since the end of 1986 the West German government—or at least Foreign Minister Hans-Dietrich Genscher and President Richard von Weizsäcker— have started speaking favorably about perestroika, and even have made public statements with respect to the conditions for ending the division of Europe. Genscher was distrusted by other NATO leaders and even by his Christian–Democratic allies in the government for his "softness" vis-à-vis the Soviet Union. Craig R. Whitney states that Genscher apparently formed his view that Gorbachev might deliver the key to German unity during his first encounter with the Soviet leader in the summer of 1986, a little more than a year after Gorbachev came to power. In early 1987, in a speech in Davos, Switzerland, Genscher sounded prophetic:

> If there should be a chance today that, after 40 years of East–West confrontation, there could be a turning point in East–West relations, it would be a mistake of historical dimension for the West to let this chance slip just because it cannot escape from a way of thinking which invariably expects the worst from the Soviet Union.[25]

It took about three years to achieve the first parts of the goal dreamed about in Davos: a comprehensive package of arms reductions, an all-European security structure building on the mechanisms set up in 1975 by the CSCE process, large-scale financial help for the Soviet Union to modernize its economy and a gradual end to the divisions of the continent. Undoubtedly, this development could not have been possible without the consent—or a plan—of the Soviet Union.

Since the 1960s the Soviet Union had been unwilling to contemplate reunification under conditions that would remove the GDR from its sphere of control. However, the concept of the common European home complicated this matter for the Soviets. The United States, for its part, has never judged that its interests would be served by reunification under terms that would neutralize a reunited Germany. In recent years, there were significant changes in the relationship between the German states, major shifts in public opinion and elite attitudes within the states, and adjustments in the relationship of each to their respective superpower allies. These changes were of consequence for East–West relations in general as well as for inner-German ties. In the 1980s "a new German question" emerged, which consisted of two interrelated processes: 1) a special relationship between the two German states; and 2) the special role of the FRG in the political resurgence of Europe.[26]

The "new German question" largely stemmed from three factors, which have both internal and external explanations. First, there was Ostpolitik, which was initiated by the FRG in the late 1960s and was inspired by the lessening of tensions between the superpowers. In concrete terms, Ostpolitik consisted of the FRG's treaties with the Soviet Union and Poland on the renunciation of force of 1970, the 1971 Quadripartite Agreement on the status of Berlin and the FRG–GDR Basic Treaty of 1972. In political terms, Ostpolitik was to a large extent a compromise between the Soviet goal of achieving general approval of the postwar territorial status quo and, by extension, the division of Germany, on the one hand, and the realistic modified West German approach to ending a frustrating stalemate in inner-German relations, on the other.[27]

Second, the process of Europeanizing detente has had a strong German impetus. In particular, the breakdown of superpower negotiations on intermediate-range nuclear forces in 1983 created an incentive for promoting inner-German relations in order to preserve detente and East–West cooperation during times of superpower tension. Since the signing of the INF Treaty in 1987, both German states have recognized more clearly that it is in their common security interest to avoid any "Germanization" of the nuclear option in Europe.[28]

Third, increased economic, cultural and social interaction strengthened pan-German thinking, as well as the German identity in general (i.e., the notion of two states within one nation). In the late 1980s, it became more difficult to convince Germans that they should remain divided for the good of Europe. On the contrary, the "new German question" and the issue of European unity were more consciously linked, which signals a change in traditional German thinking. As FRG President Richard von Weizsäcker said in 1987:

> The subject of unity, as it presents itself to us today, is primarily a pan-European matter. Unity of Europeans means neither administrative unity nor equivalence of political systems, but rather a shared path based on human progress in history. The German question is, in this sense, a European responsibility. But to work

towards that goal in Europe, by peaceful means, is above all a matter for the Germans.[29]

The interest of the two German states in continuing the build-down of East–West military confrontation was stronger and more persistent than that of any other participant in the confrontation. As the demilitarization of East–West relations continued, the political repercussions for both German states and a reunited Germany of the dismantling of Europe's military division became even more obvious. The deepening dialogue on military issues also included the question of Germany's military status and whether it is the most important precondition for European stability.[30]

For years, East and West German public opinion polls had revealed increasing support for the ideal of a reunified Germany. Polls taken in 1987 already showed that about 80% of the respondents wanted German reunification, but only 8% considered it possible in the 1990s. But, in what seems to have been an even more indicative trend, more than the customary one-third of the West German public conceived of neutrality guaranteed by the United States and by visible relations within the framework of future East–West arms control agreements. There is no doubt that the German question will be addressed explicitly in terms of the European question, which will be, by most expectations, high on the agenda of international politics during the early 1990s. In any future scenario it is dynamic enough to change or tilt the geostrategic landscape of Europe, though in which direction remains to be seen.

Thus the German question remains—even after reunification—open in terms of its strategic and political implications for the rest of Europe. Between November 1989 and January 1990 German power finally became an increasingly identifiable center of gravity in European and world politics. In August 1989, East Germans began streaming to the West (initially through Hungary), which rapidly weakened the credibility of the communist regime of the GDR. A "revolution" broke out and quickly led to the collapse of the Berlin Wall on November 9, 1989. Consequently, it was no longer possible to contain the process of reunification of the two German states by diplomatic means. The main issue of reunification was no longer whether it would take place, but when and how.[31]

The superpowers and the other European powers moved rather quickly to adapt to this development. The superpowers appear to have rejected the traditional zero-sum game, and instead pursued a policy of positive follow-up emphasizing the need to consider the question of reunification within the framework of the European question. On January 31, 1990, Soviet President Gorbachev expressed Soviet acceptance of the step-by-step union of East and West Germany. At this stage the Soviets and the East German Communists emphasized the need to establish a politically neutral Germany, while the rest of the world preferred Germany as part of a larger political structure. As Gregor Gysi, the leader of the East German Communists in the post-Honecker era, stated in an interview on January 30, 1990: "This process cannot be stopped anymore. But it is irresponsible to do things in such a way now as if it were possible tomorrow . . . . I am against a German Europe but in favor of a European Germany."

In December 1989, West German Chancellor Helmut Kohl introduced a concrete ten-point plan for reunification, but he left the timetable open. He did say, however, that the negotiations on reunification could not start before free elections were held in the GDR on March 18, 1990. On February 3, 1990, Chancellor Kohl stated in Davos that Germany would first be reunified economically—a common currency would be established. Kohl's Davos speech also confirmed the order of West German priorities in European politics: first the reunification of Germany and second the political and economic integration of Western Europe. Undoubtedly the new situation with respect to the German question has created a major headache for the advocates of West European integration. The rise of German power in Europe will certainly change the structure and ambitions of the European Community.[32]

During the eight months following the fall of the Berlin Wall the steps toward the final unification of Germany were taken without major setbacks: the first free elections were held in the GDR on March 18, 1990, resulting in the overwhelming victory of parties favoring rapid unification. The treaty establishing a monetary, economic and social union between the two German states was signed on May 18, 1990, entering into force on July 1, 1990.[33]

The domestic as well as external parameters of German unification were worked out in the heady atmosphere generated by the end of the Cold War. The negotiations on the conditions of the unification actually took place at the Ottawa conference on "Open Skies" in February 1990. An agreement was reached between the two German states and the Four Powers on the procedural matters concerning the "two plus four" negotiations. As a result of this agreement—and the

GDR elections—the situation in arms control negotiations changed dramatically and led, as Joachim Krause states, "to a totally new set of functions for arms control and arms reductions." Krause draws the following conclusion:

> Negotiations on arms control and arms reductions now have to fit into the evolving international order, and they should be considered an important—but not exclusive—tool for forging a European Security System (ESS), which would supersede the old bipolar security order.[34]

The security parameters of the unification of Germany touched upon the premises of a post-bipolar security order. In the months after the revolution of 1989, the political forces in Central Europe were prodding politicians in both East and West to proceed much faster. As a result, "the dynamics of German reunification are determining the speed of further action."[35]

Now it was evident that the parameters of a new post-bipolar security system served as an integral linkage with the security parameters of a unifying Germany. The debate about the solution of this puzzle had been to a large degree ended by Chancellor Helmut Kohl and President Mikhail Gorbachev in the Caucasus on July 16, 1990. Briefly, the Soviet Union accepted that a united Germany is free to join NATO, that Soviet troops in East Germany (350,000) will be withdrawn in three to four years, that the FRG will be an economic ally of the Soviet Union, and that the united Germany's combined troop strength will be cut from the present level of 600,000 to 370,000.[36]

After the Caucasus agreement there were no longer any external obstacles to the unification of Germany. However, the debate about the political and geostrategic repercussions of that deal began immediately in both the West and the East. It was obvious in any case that the Kohl–Gorbachev deal had finally brought the West closer to achieving the failed promises of Yalta in February 1945 for freedom, democracy and self-determination for all of Eastern Europe. Nevertheless, it was seriously asked whether both leaders had gone "too far."[37]

It can be said that both the Soviet Union and the unifying Germanies won at least something vital in this diplomatic "power game." For the two Germanies, the Caucasus agreement brought unification; for the Soviet Union, it brought urgently needed economic assistance; moreover, it brought the option of a permanent politico-economic relationship between a declining superpower and a new economic–political "superpower." Undoubtedly, the Caucasus agreement laid the groundwork for a significant change in the European geostrategic landscape. One can agree with the Western observer who stated that, as a result of the Kohl–Gorbachev pact, "it is blindingly clear that the geopolitics of the new Europe will be determined, for good or for ill, by the character of the new Germany."[38]

A united Germany's combined military and economic-political power does not necessarily make Germany a full-fledged superpower in the traditional postwar sense. Even a reunited Germany will lack the continental size, the nine-figure population, the deep-water navy and the nuclear arsenal needed to match the United States and the Soviet Union. In any case, the traditional superpowers are in relative decline—in particular the Soviet Union—and military might counts for less while economic and technological power count for more. The international system transformation is, then, conditional on the rising power status of a united Germany.

At least a reunited Germany is emerging as a superpower on the European stage. As a consequence, the geostrategic landscape of Europe will certainly tilt toward Eastern and Central Europe and a new geopolitical reality will emerge in the geographic heart of the continent. Undoubtedly, the European economic integration will be influenced by this development. In the 1980s, France was the politico-economic engine of the European Community. In the 1990s, the initiative is being taken by the Germans.

In retrospect, it can be argued that Gorbachev never had any real option but to agree with the German unification on "German terms." In a delicate diplomatic and domestic power game, Gorbachev first took a number of steps backward in order to take a major leap forward. In any case, Gorbachev is now more free to influence the pan-European arrangements and even the further dilution of NATO. The new Bonn–Moscow link gives him a better lever to do so. However, the Soviet Union itself is in the process of disintegration. In the future, this development may further influence the shape of the geostrategic landscape of Europe.

A reunified Germany must, however, find a new role for itself in both European and world politics. This can come about only if Germany is a member of the Western economic and military–political structures. Therefore, in order to be successful in these efforts for a unified Germany, the new European security and economic architecture will remain the key question. In this respect one can easily agree with Rita Süssmuth, President of the West German Bundestag, that "the key to a peaceful and stable European framework lies in the process of the Conference on Security and Cooperation in Europe."[39] For a unified Germany, the option related to the strengthening of the CSCE does not include the weakening of its Western alliance structures. Yet one could ask whether there still is room for an alliance that has its roots in the Cold War heyday. A political puzzle is emerging that cannot be resolved without a strong German political contribution in the 1990s.

THE EUROPEAN COMMUNITY AS A GREAT POWER FRAMEWORK

The 40-year history of West European unification has been marked by numerous attempts at political integration. Today, however, the European Community (EC) is the heartbeat of Europe. All other states must adjust to this development, and undoubtedly the number of EC member states will increase. Even in the new democracies of Eastern and Central Europe there is a debate over the possible "affiliation" of any or all of these countries with the EC. Of course, West European states not now included in the EC are also viewed as potential members in the 1990s. Above all, the EC is still seeking a political and geopolitical role: it should not become a new Germany, nor should it remain a faceless "Western Europe."[40]

Thus the main issue is the process of transition at the end of this century. The situation is, as Paul Kennedy observes, in some ways similar to that which, on a smaller scale, faced the members of the German Federation in the mid-19th century:

A customs union existed which had proved to be so successful in stimulating trade and industry that it rapidly attracted new members, and it was clear that if that enlarged economic community was able to turn itself into a Power state it would be a major new actor in the international system—to which the established Great Powers would have to adjust accordingly. But so long as that transformation did not occur, so long as there were divisions among the members of the customs union about further economic integration and, still more, about political and military integration, [then it would] stay divided, unable to realize its potential, and incapable of dealing as an equal with the other Great Powers. For all the differences of time and circumstances, the "German question" of the last century was a microcosm of the "European problem" of the present.[41]

History does not usually repeat itself. Other global power centers are already adjusting their policies and interests in light of the prospect of a rising West European center. It is evident that the European states outside the two military alliances in particular must find a new formula for their policies that comes to terms with a Western Europe made up of the 12 member states of the EC.[42]

Although the history of the EC is replete with stories of competition between selfish nations, it also evinces the gradual establishment of a more coordinated and unified political and economic entity. Since the early 1970s the EC has gradually taken on a more coherent shape within the changing international system and especially within the European geostrategic framework. *The EC will provide, in one way or another, a partial framework for the transformation of the Euroatlantic security community into two pillars.* However, the events of 1989 have also brought new impetus to the transatlantic structure. In short, the EC will not replace NATO, but its tasks will change. U.S. Secretary of State James Baker stated in Berlin on December 12, 1989: "NATO will become the forum where Western nations cooperate to negotiate, implement, verify and extend agreements between East and West."[43] In other words, the United States will remain a European power and NATO's primary task is to provide a framework for a European security community in the new Europe.

A more independent and politically autonomous Western Europe is emerging, and it increasingly presents itself as a major gravitational field that could, for example, enable Eastern Europe to serve as a counterbalance and thus substitute for previous levels of Soviet influence in such a way that there would not be any direct repercussions on the balance between the two superpowers. This arrangement would allow more room for political maneuvering in Eastern Europe, at least over the longer term. Yet, as mentioned earlier, the EC itself is undergoing a process of rapid transition. In this regard, the most important turning point in its history since the signing of the Rome treaties in 1957 has been the official signing of the Single European Act in 1986. This agreement set some new and ambitious targets, including the completion by 1992 of an all-encompassing West European internal market of 320 million people and "citizens'" Europe. The Single European Act was aimed at activating a common European foreign policy that would take into account the political and economic aspects of security. At the end of the 1980s it was clear that there was no realistic alternative to the process of European integration, the final goal of which is a European union. This gathering of nations is evolving toward a kind of federation of states with great power potential.[44]

The EC should be more or less "obliged" to take stronger hold of its own defense responsibilities. There seems to exist an "iron law" according to which economic integration, once it is stuck in neutral, can be reactivated only by improving cooperation on political and security questions. As a result of factors that are both external (concerning the redefinition of the U.S. role in the defense of Europe) and internal (relating to this "iron law" of integration), the prospects for a more independent European security option within the framework of the EC could be strengthened over the longer term. But already the formation of a European security community is rapidly making progress, although the countries in question are in many ways still split over the terms of both the concept and its organization.[45] The revolutions in Eastern Europe, however, have also changed the prospects of the EC; they have "weakened" its security identity and "strengthened" its economic function. This means that in security issues the EC must still hew primarily to NATO and the CSCE, as was largely confirmed by the heads of state and government participating in the meeting of the North Atlantic Council in London on July 6, 1990. Their "London Declaration" stated that "the move within the European Community towards political union, including the development of a European identity in the domain of security, will also contribute to Atlantic solidarity and to the establishment of a just and lasting order of peace throughout the whole of Europe."[46]

Within a month, the European identity in security affairs was tested when Iraq invaded Kuwait on August 2, 1990. It took weeks before the member states of the EC were able to begin to support with concrete military means the U.S. and Arab opposition to Iraq. The dilatory response to the Gulf crisis may, however, have strengthened arguments for a defense role for the European Community. This role could be worked out most practically through the Western European Union (WEU) in operations outside Europe. It can be assumed, however, that it will take years before any kind of really functioning defense role of the EC can be developed. First the EC has to find out whether it can create the European Monetary Union and the European Political Union.[47]

A sticking point in any plan for a European Defense Community is the role of nuclear weapons. The Soviets are not the only ones opposed to a Germany that possesses nuclear weapons: the French and the majority of Germans themselves are unlikely to let the German military-political leadership have its finger on the nuclear trigger. However, discussions of Franco-German military cooperation have already touched at least preliminarily upon the possibility of extending French nuclear forces to cover the FRG. This theme has been especially prevalent since the signing of the INF Treaty, which increased fears in Germany about the "Germanization" of a possible nuclear exchange on the European continent.[48] As for the idea of a European defense community composed of independent defense forces of the EC and perhaps loosely linked with the United States in a kind of post-NATO structure, a more innovative proposal has been put forth by François Heisbourg, Director of the International Institute of Strategic Studies. He argues that France should abandon its muddled ambitions to be a "mini-superpower" and should instead hitch its armed forces firmly to those of its neighbors. In short, France should devote fewer efforts to shoring up its own nuclear forces and do a lot more for Western Europe's conventional defenses in the FRG. Heisbourg has at least begun to elaborate a concept that by and large would meet the challenges posed by the possible withdrawal of U.S. forces from Europe.[49]

Primarily for political reasons, European defense is not going to be denuclearized, at least in the immediate future. Otherwise fears of a West European geostrategic tilt towards the East would erupt. As one U.S. observer puts it: "So the alternative to nuclear weapons in Europe, which provided cheap deterrence, will be European insecurity, and Finlandization."[50] This kind of threat image may still exist, although rapidly increasing prospects for conventional disarmament in Europe and especially the withdrawal of Soviet offensive forces from Eastern Europe are certainly eroding its reliability.

In the end, the basic question is whether the West European nations—that is, the EC, with its own political and security capacity and identity—are capable of counterbalancing the Soviets in Europe and are in fact willing to do so. It has been argued that the United States should continue to participate in Europe's defense while NATO is Europeanized on the basis of French and German conventional forces and French and British nuclear forces. The Franco-German coalition within the EC, whose purpose is "balancing the Americans in the economic sphere" would then "acquire the new purpose of balancing the Soviets in the military sphere." The Franco-German "minuet," halfhearted as long as U.S. protection is certain, will become more intense once the protectorate disappears. Yet the rapid change in Europe seems to be strengthening the transatlantic relationship. Moreover, European nuclear deterrence should facilitate rather than complicate superpower arms control because it is precisely "the need for extended deterrence" that has driven the arms race.[51]

The nuclear dilemma is but one obstacle to achieving a common defense posture within the EC framework. As a matter of fact, there are still plenty of political obstacles related to the foreign and defense policy priorities of the EC. The traditional stance on neutrality of the Republic of Ireland, the only EC state outside NATO, prevents the EC from formally discussing defense issues. Also, "radical" EC states such as Greece and Denmark are often reluctant to go along with the mainstream EC nations. How, then, can special German security concerns be incorporated into EC policy?

Given some impetus by the fall of the Berlin Wall, the EC is increasingly becoming a gathering of 12 countries tending toward closer economic and political unity in most areas, though never arriving at a "single European nation." The EC has already established its position as an economic power center, although it has been losing ground in some key areas of international competition. As a political and security power, the EC has yet to shape itself into a great power entity.[52] Here a rapid erosion of bipolarity may yet play a critical role in the early 1990s. The idea of "concentric circles" in Europe of Jacques Delors, President of the Commission of the EC, was to safeguard the maximum implementation of the single market in 1992. In fact, Delors wanted to prevent the EC from being dominated by any single member state. In order to achieve this goal, the number of EC members should be limited to twelve; countries outside the EC should be allowed to adopt a "third way," like the European Free Trade Association (EFTA) countries, by reaching an agreement on the European Economic Space (see next section); and the division of Europe (and Germany) would remain. One can say that from the French point of view, the revolutions in Eastern Europe took place a bit too early. On the other hand, French diplomacy has quickly moved ahead on the basis of changing realities. In his 1990 New Year's message, French President François Mitterrand announced a concept of a confederal Europe, which would consist of the 12 EC members and other categories (circles) of Europe working in close cooperation with each other. In short, this is a last-ditch effort to save the EC made up of equals before the emergence of a reunified Germany.

Undoubtedly, the upheaval in the East pushed the European Community to the center of the geopolitical arena. This development has been assessed by one prominent research center as follows: "The Community's political, economic, and psychological resources must be regarded as strategic assets of the highest order during the period beyond East–West military confrontation that lies ahead." However, at least four decisive tests are at hand. First, the Community must absorb the political and economic weight of a united Germany. Second, the transition in Eastern Europe must be tackled. The burden of reviving and sustaining this diverse and increasingly fragmented region has shifted from Soviet to Western hands. Third, the EC must develop a comprehensive and effective strategy toward a politically turbulent Soviet Union, which is heading toward economic catastrophe and is losing its political cohesion, but is still able to maintain immense military power. Fourth, the Community must finally decide how active it wants to be in the development of new or revised security structures for Europe.[53]

In the short term, it should be decided whether the EC should be "deepened" or "widened." The EC has been divided in this respect. After the emergence of a united Germany on October 3, 1990, strong support was expressed by the leaders of the EC to the "deepening" versus the "widening." Yet the only way out of this dilemma must be, as Pierre Hassner reasons, to combine the two. Hassner is of the opinion that the EC should be widened to cover the whole of Europe, even the Soviet Union, in the longer term. This is possible by a double process of a political strengthening of the Community and a reorientation of its activities towards the East. One can agree with Hassner that "the success or failure of this combination holds the key to the decline or revival both of the Community and of Europe as a whole."[54] It has also been stressed, however, that the EC should retain its "narrowness" in order to cope with revolutionary changes in the wider Europe. Thomas Pedersen argues that "the EC's Pan-European identity will in the short term be more a question of new functions than of new memberships." It is obvious that the problem related to the widening or deepening of the EC will not be resolved before the year 1993. One could expect, however, that in the case of the EC accelerating the "broadening" process, this would also lead to "deepening." In the history of the EC this has been a general pattern.[55]

It is impossible to predict whether the division of Europe could be softened, or even eliminated, if the EC replaced NATO as a counterbalance to the Soviet-led alliance. There does seem to be a self-evident interrelationship between the integration of Western Europe and the restoration of East Central Europe. Perhaps this interrelationship is more important than previously recognized insofar as the final outcome of the European landscape is concerned. In any case, the EC will be a great power framework of 12 or more nations, and it will cultivate—at least temporarily—a more historical and organic landscape.[56] This development could lead to a more stable and just security order. But one of its preconditions would be that the emerging "new framework" pose no security threat to other European political entities.[57]

THE EURONEUTRALS' ADAPTIVE STRATEGIES

At the height of the Cold War, the Euroneutrals (Austria, Finland, Sweden and Switzerland) largely remained "invisible." John Foster Dulles described neutrality as an "immoral" stance in the global psychological war that was then being waged between East and West. The Soviet Union also had a hostile view toward neutrality, particularly because it did not fit in with Soviet interests in the 1940s and the 1950s. Since the late 1950s, however, and especially since the early 1960s, the Euroneutrals have succeeded in establishing for themselves a special systemic role within the structure of increasing East–West interaction. Their policy of neutrality has also been well suited to the interdependence that has characterized the most recent phases of international politics.[58]

One of the paradoxes of the strict division of Europe is that it has de facto strengthened the security of the Euroneutrals. Although superficially the exclusion of the Euroneutrals from the bipolar security order seemed to have weakened their security, postwar history has shown that they have in fact increased their room for maneuver, are more accepted than ever before and have not had their security endangered—at least not more than international security in general has been. The great powers trust the neutrals and have many more difficulties with their own allies, especially those with neutralist tendencies. Another paradox is, as mentioned, that the Euroneutrals have been considered the most eager promoters of the status quo in Europe and, accordingly, advocate gradualism in efforts to undo the division of Europe. It should be stressed, however, that even if the neutrals are strong supporters of the stability created by the bipolar security order, this does not mean that they would prefer bipolarity to a lowering of the partition in Europe.[59] Although the Euroneutrals often present themselves as a permanent and integral part of the present order, at the same time they advocate a gradual transition to a more stable European peace order. In particular, the Euroneutrals seek a more stable security order through cooperation at the all-European level. To quote President Mauno Koivisto of Finland: "Although our continent remains divided ideologically and militarily, security can best be built on growing mutual dependence and cooperation. Europe would benefit if its bifurcation could be softened."[60]

As mentioned above, the Euroneutrals established a systemic role for themselves during the era of detente and in particular within the CSCE process (where they are part of the NNA group). They had no aspiration, however, to form a bloc or establish a firm position as a collective formation of neutrals, although certain ambitions to take steps in this direction persist within the NNA group. However, the fact that the Helsinki Final Act recognized neutrality can be taken as a major gain for the neutrals and an impetus for further aspirations.[61]

By definition, "bloc thinking," even in neutralist terms, is very much against the interests of the neutral countries, which also want to retain their individual freedom and room for maneuver. This is the main reason that the Euroneutrals sometimes distance themselves from "neutralist thinking" and do not side with various "neutralist elements" in the military alliances.[62]

In sum, the Euroneutrals want to present themselves as stabilizing elements in the European security order. For them the type of order is not the decisive question, and as they have become more active advocates of peaceful change and a softening of the division of Europe since the early 1980s, they have to a certain extent promoted the Europeanization of detente as well. But will the Euroneutrals lose their credibility if the process of overcoming the division of Europe progresses in the 1990s? Is neutrality really only a function of East–West confrontation, as one Western observer has argued?[63] Neutrality for any of the neutrals is not a goal but a means. And stability is only partly a function of structure; it is also a result of the conscious behavior of nations. As a consequence, sticking to the status quo does not of itself strengthen stability.[64] Security must be achieved equally through cooperative means and within the framework of what will be rather than what is. Given the changes of 1989, the Euroneutrals have to redefine their neutrality, maybe even jettisoning it.

The Euroneutrals also have to adjust to the changing political and economic environment of Europe. The European political structure should be based on socioeconomic realities rather than coercive power interests, and the ongoing processes of transformation also need a political framework. The Euroneutrals cannot stay on the sidelines in this process. They will not be the losers if the emerging security order is based on broadly rather than narrowly defined security interests and on a more organic structure. The greatest danger for the Euroneutrals derives from the threatened isolation of key security and economic processes in Europe, which would have a major impact on the emerging security order. For one thing, the CSCE structure has not provided a forum for neutrals to be involved in negotiations on arms reductions on an equal footing with members of the military alliances. On the other hand, none of the neutrals poses a military threat to anyone at their present level of military preparedness. The Euroneutrals must also adjust to the challenges of the single market in 1992, which poses particular threats with which each neutral state must come to terms. If the EC should become a major military factor, the inclusion of the Euroneutrals in it without a radical lowering of Europe's present military division would automatically heighten the level of confrontation on the continent.[65] At present, it is still difficult to articulate the possibility of a kind of "neutral entity" existing within the political–military framework of the EC. Yet an alternative solution seems to have become more obvious since the events of the fall of 1989. Since the division is rapidly losing its importance as a guiding principle for neutrality, it no longer guides the policies of the Euroneutrals vis-à-vis the EC to the same degree; the EC is less and less an organization of a divided Europe.

The debate over EC membership for the European neutrals will gather steam in the coming years.[66] While each neutral country must solve its own problems vis-à-vis the EC on the basis of its individual premises, no neutral country is going to choose a strategy of isolation. The prevailing neutral strategy of adaptation has been based thus far on the so-called "EFTA card," which could be described as a cooperative integration strategy. The main aim of the "EFTA card" is to buttress EFTA and arrive at a common EFTA view on as many issues as possible. If the "EFTA card" is lost, finding other alternatives for EC participation may be difficult.[67]

If the Euroneutrals believe that only full membership in the EC can, in the final analysis, safeguard their economic prosperity, they will try to maintain their role as stabilizing and peacemaking elements in the evolving European security system. Economic success is, of course, one of the key conditions for ensuring a credible neutral status. If such a condition cannot be guaranteed by staying outside the EC, then the necessary conclusions must be drawn. It would be much easier for the neutrals, however, if Europe were to move toward a radical lowering of all remaining ideological and military barriers—in short, if Western Europe were to become a "security partner." Undoubtedly the neutrals' membership in the EC would be more obvious if the old political-military division of Europe no longer constituted the European security order, if the neutral states could decide upon their membership purely on economic terms. Otherwise the final result may bring confrontation rather than security. Solutions offered by the neutrals—regardless of whether any or all of them join the EC—will modify somewhat Europe's changing geostrategic landscape, and in this sense their solutions are interrelated. The neutrals' basic goal in changing circumstances is to preserve their traditional function as system stabilizers.[68] Whether they are able to become a more dynamic part of the system in this sense remains to be seen.

In any case, the Euroneutrals could also establish for themselves a more active role—as system stabilizers in the redrawing of the economic map of Europe. For example, the organic dynamism is already creating closer ties, in particular between the Nordic states and the Baltic states and Poland, as well as between Austria and its East Central European neighbors. Consequently, one could ask whether the EFTA countries should actively promote such an economic map, which would contain a European Economic Space (EES) expanded by the addition of the new democracies of Eastern and Central Europe.[69] Such an enlarged EES would be beneficial to all participants in the political and economic integration of Europe.

As a result of the revolutions of 1989, a market economy, privatization, pluralistic forms of ownership, market prices, convertibility and liberalized trade were declared the objectives of all economic activities on which the work of relevant organizations would be based. This development has dramatically changed the process of integration in Western Europe (as described in the previous chapter). Now it is possible that mounting pressure from new Eastern European countries may leave the EFTA countries in secondary position, "transforming EFTA from a waiting room to a cul-de-sac," as Thomas Pedersen reasons. Indeed, increasing East European pressure to join the EC would weaken the bargaining position of the Euroneutrals—both economically and politically.[70] Not surprisingly, the debate about the application for a full membership of the EC gained new and politically important impetus for the Euroneutrals in 1990. Besides the new situation in the East, it also became clear that the EES agreement did not offer EFTA countries a real share in decision-making power. Even the ministers of the governments of Finland, Sweden and Switzerland began to speak about the "EC option" in 1990. The most convincing argument for membership in the EC is that only within it can European states really influence the most important decisions that will affect the region for the foreseeable future; the argument is particularly telling since the emergence of a united Germany.[71]

The main question is how harmonious economic development in Europe can be secured. Economic strength, increasingly the determinant of the security structure, has brought the European Community and (in connection with the Soviet Union) a unified Germany to the forefront as guarantors of stability in Europe. The intensity of the economic relations between the United States and Central Europe cannot be compared to those of the Community.

The Euroneutrals are searching for a parallel approach through EFTA with the EC in their relations with Central European countries. The great emphasis on socioeconomic stabilization in Central Europe as well as in the Soviet Union is, then, becoming a priority also in "neutral" security thinking in the 1990s. The question is whether a new economic architecture is needed in Europe, at least from the neutral point of view, or whether the Euroneutrals have to join the EC for "security" reasons too. The answer will primarily depend on the nature of the further development of the EC, not as a great power, but as a great power framework.

6 The Outlook for European Security in the 1990s

In previous chapters this book has examined the political factors that have played a key role in maintaining or changing Europe's bipolar security order. In the next two chapters I will risk making predictions about the future. The Canadian media theorist Marshall McLuhan once said that anyone who truly perceives the present can also see the future, since "all possible futures are contained in the present."[1] Unfortunately, the future of Europe must appear to any observer as inordinately complex, a combination of processes that could produce contradictory outcomes. Nevertheless, some of these processes are developing into a coherent pattern of change, and the time may be ripe for fairly accurate predictions.

To begin with, the concept of security is in transition. For example, the concept of security as a zero-sum game in the superpower context is losing ground. As Robert Jervis states, "just as the two sides' fates would be linked together in a nuclear war, their general levels of security are also linked: if one is highly insecure, so will the other be." Jervis also notes that Gorbachev has insisted that there can be "no security for the USSR without security for the United States."[2] If the superpowers respect this principle, the Europeans in particular will benefit quite a bit. But what exactly is security thinking beyond the zero-sum game? Obviously, it should contain old ideas as well as innovations. Indeed, new security thinking should even try to transfer the stability of the status quo to the newly emerging security order. In addition, it should seek to increase security by non-military means and it should find common causes for security. Many new security problems can be solved only through cooperation. The basic question is, then, whether changing security needs and threat images can constitute a reliable basis for setting up a more stable and just security order. This study concludes that by definition the new security thinking now taking shape in Europe is more "neutral" in its essence as advocated by the European neutral states. Neutral security thinking is based on a broad interpretation of security, and it emphasizes political and pragmatic means for solving disputes between states. Consequently, the two superpowers have to adjust themselves to a kind of "neutral postulate" in order to maintain their central role in Europe.

Second, although the structural framework of European security will become more complex in the short term, over the longer term the process of organically restoring a unified Europe will eradicate a significant part of this complexity. If Europe avoids developing a new Euro-Soviet bipolarity, its new security framework will likely consist of "political entities" that are partly identifiable by national factors, but even more so by various kinds of cooperative and transnational arrangements.

THE EMERGENCE OF COMMON SECURITY

The transition in European security thinking is being manifested primarily in two ways. First, the definition of security is widening to reflect the changing security needs and threats in general. This is due partly to the evolution of popular consciousness and partly to the changes in the international system. Second, as a result of the strengthening of organic processes, national interests are gaining a more dominant position in national security strategies. In Europe this means that national interests must increasingly be taken into account in the security strategies of the two blocs. Specifically "European" and national or regional security interests may supersede alliance interests. For the moment, the challenge will be one of finding a new balance of national, European and alliance interests in both East and West.

It is widely agreed that a precondition for stable peace in any international system is that it should be based on shared values and common approaches to basic problems. In practical terms this assumption can be tested by comparing the threat images and security values of the states involved. Measured thus, Europe is now less divided than at any other time since the late 1940s. The old enemy images are fading away, making room for a more friendly climate of interaction among peoples. To quote the chief of the Soviet General Staff, General Mikhail Moiseev, who spoke at a CSCE seminar on military doctrines held in Vienna in January 1990:

Personally, I am convinced that today the U.S. and NATO do not nurture aggressive plans towards the Soviet Union and its allies. Tensions in the world have diminished thanks to positive changes, but the military threat has not disappeared.

The West has understandably rejected the notion that the West poses a military threat to the Warsaw Pact members. But many things look different from the other side. As Michael MccGwire points out in his book, *Military Objectives in Soviet Foreign Policy*, the West has been unable to understand how it could possibly be perceived as a military threat to the Soviet Union.[3]

Furthermore, welfare and social values are superseding ideological values in both the East and the West, thus improving possibilities for finding security solutions based on shared interests. This is due in part to the emergence of common threats, such as ecological catastrophes, which obviously can be overcome only through joint efforts.[4]

The European system of nation-states, however, will not disappear in the foreseeable future. Undoubtedly, security will continue to be defined primarily in military terms. Yet national armies are undergoing a doctrinal transition as they increasingly adopt defensive postulates to legitimize the maintenance of a state of military preparedness. Even if this process continues to advance without major delays, it will still take many years to play out fully. The most difficult political problems related to this development are found in Central Europe.[5] In the final analysis, the question is whether the old definition of national power still has any validity. Many decision-makers still believe that the more power a state has, the greater its security. But today a great deal depends on how these terms are defined. Undoubtedly, most leaders still give great credence to military definitions, and yet power has come to be defined more and more in economic and political terms. In today's Europe a search is under way for a new balance between socioeconomic and military terms in formulating the most constructive national security strategies. A shift is rapidly taking place toward new and more "European" security thinking, which, by definition, will be based on a more regional definition of national interests, as well as on greater recognition of changes in the "hierarchy" of threat images.

What, then, could concretely result from the emergence of "European" security thinking defined in terms of common security interests? It should be taken for granted that changes in security thinking will have repercussions on national security postulates and, later on, on the security order as well. But all scenarios aimed at formulating a new, more effective security order designed to cope with changing security needs and guarantee maximum security will of necessity fall short of their goal. It is widely agreed that security can be defined and pursued only in relative terms. This means that states have to reconcile their competing interests and seek in a cooperative manner such relative shares of security as are mutually acceptable. The alternative to mutual adjustment of security interests is absolute insecurity for one or both powers involved in a bilateral conflict. Thus the term "common European security thinking," interpreted as the ongoing development of ideas along these lines, hints at *an alternative security system, in which the reduction of military power and the equitable resolution of conflict have replaced the accumulation of arms and the use of force.* It has been stressed that if security is defined as a "common effort and cause," all policies pursued according to it should reduce the role of military factors in international affairs—nuclear weapons, in particular—and direct more attention to political management and conflict resolution.[6]

A doctrine of security defined in these terms is generally compatible with the present European security situation in which outstanding problems are primarily political in nature and thus need to be solved by political means.

Consequently, a common security structure can be implemented within the framework of the state system and does not absolutely demand the transformation of its basic organizing principles. As Raimo Väyrynen puts it: "It may be argued that the system of international security embedded in the hierarchical international relations, whether an empire or a world government, does not necessarily meet the criteria of common security." However, regarding the need to work out institutionalized structures of cooperation such as the CSCE process, Väyrynen argues that "the pursuit of common security would produce, though, more results if the underlying political strategy would conceive this system as a rule-based international society rather than an interest-based anarchy."[7]

Common security, if applied in Europe, could be regarded as an inter-actor strategy in that its aim is to ameliorate the security dilemma among states by transforming relations between adversaries into a more peaceful, equitable and stable pattern. If positive actions by one state are rewarded in a roughly comparable manner by other states, it can become a learning process in which national decision-makers start trusting each other as new patterns of communication and confidence evolve. By the late 1980s there were a greater number of interactions in Europe that contained a high degree of reciprocity, German-German relations and the deepened superpower dialogue being just two examples among them. Although the basic structure of European interaction has reached only an early stage of reciprocity, the learning process, which is of course difficult to comprehend, may have progressed significantly. The 1986 Chernobyl nuclear accident, for example, did not increase hostility toward the Soviet Union, but in fact strengthened common concern and awareness of shared security interests, thus functioning as a unifying factor in the common European home.[8] In the area of ecological security the "common European home" is no longer a metaphor but a reality.

The common European home is being erected largely against the backdrop of a European state system. It is logical to expect that in the long term this will entail dismantling the political division of Europe. Its structure will emerge as a gradual and organic process. By definition, the sociopolitical factor in Eastern Europe and the Soviet Union took on an important role in overall policy thinking and strategies, a fact that Gorbachev already made clear at the January 1987 plenum of the Communist Party's Central Committee. He stressed that sociopolitical change was a prerequisite for successful economic reform. His remarks expressed the realization that in the environment of the 1980s the "human factor" had become decisive.[9] Such an attitude will work to strengthen organic developments in the Soviet security system. Competition and even rivalry among the participating entities cannot be fully discounted. Competition, in fact, should even be encouraged in order to strengthen certain preconditions of a stable peace, such as economic prosperity. In the final analysis, the maintenance of stability, a precondition of a stable peace, is a matter of "caution, maturity and responsibility on both sides," as John Lewis Gaddis puts it. He goes on to state that stability requires the ability to distinguish posturing from provocation. Indeed, it requires:

> recognition of the fact that competition is a normal rather than an abnormal state of affairs in relations between nations, much as it is in relations between major corporations, but that this need not preclude the identification of certain common—or corporate, or universal—interests as well. It requires, above all, a sense of the

relative rather than the absolute nature of security: that one's own security depends not only upon the measures one takes in one's own defense, but also upon the extent to which these create a sense of insecurity in the mind of one's adversary.[10]

Security cannot be increased through unilateral efforts. A modern sense of realism in international relations must be based on the assumption that there is an interdependence—or at least an integral linkage—between the prosperity and security of all participants. Yet the development of interdependence and a sense of common cause should not produce conditions conducive to the growth of new coercive structures. Cooperative solutions are often compromises and involve adjustments among various kinds of interests. If Europe is heading unequivocally toward greater integration but not organic restoration or, for that matter, national revitalization, then new sources of conflict may arise in the longer term. Indeed, the only possible authority for all European nations and political entities is a sense of increasingly common responsibility and positive interdependence, which would partly replace nationalism with Europeanism as the ideological driving force of development. Perhaps the maximum result would be derived from a mixture of nationalism and Europeanism.

Today, the differences among prevailing sociopolitical systems still rule out any temptation to build an entirely uniform European civilization that transcends each state's specific sociopolitical nature. There is no need to prove that each nation and each system or "political entity" creates its own climate for civilization, its own political and cultural notions, and its own unique interpretation of moral principles and ways to apply them. Although common foundations and parallel goals can and should be sought, it would be harmful, as Michael Dobroczynski states, "to try to unify them. The unity of European civilization presupposes mutual respect for the sovereignty of cultures and aspiration of the peoples."[11] In sum, the new European security thinking appears to include at a minimum the following features:

- Security is increasingly based on a "neutral," that is, broad, interpretation that puts more emphasis on political over military means of solving outstanding problems.
- A "value revolution" is taking place at the grassroots level throughout Europe, most particularly in the Soviet Union and Eastern Europe. This development is strengthening the common

basis for security and contributing to the waning of old enemy images and the emergence of new unifying threat images everywhere in Europe. Indeed, the common European home is to some extent already a reality in the minds of Europeans.

- As a result of the tendency toward the restoration of Europe as an organic whole, the member states of the military alliances are increasingly distinguishing national from bloc interests. This means that these states seek national room for maneuver particularly in political and economic issues.

Although a major change has already taken place in security thinking at the grassroots level, national military–political threat perceptions, defined in terms of military doctrines and related postulates, are changing very slowly. National security policies are based on historical experience and geopolitical realities. Temporary twists in opinion polls seldom have an impact on decision-making in security questions. Yet the growing idea that the Soviet Union is a "security partner" in Europe (and no longer the adversary against whom defenses are maintained) has given the Soviets, as David Gress points out, "a leverage on Western policies they did not have in the 1960s."[12] This development is currently most striking in a united Germany, where the changing threat perceptions in the domestic structure have already found expression in German security thinking at the government level.

In order to comprehend the durability of threat perceptions, one only has to glance at the history of East–West rapprochement. Unfortunately, detente did not bring many concrete results in this respect. For instance, the process of disarmament was relatively ineffectual in penetrating the root causes of confrontational perceptions on all sides. The maintenance since the mid-1960s of NATO's strategy of "flexible response" toward the WTO has also meant that, for the Soviet Union, neither of its traditional threat perceptions (the fear of nuclear weapons and the fear of encirclement) has disappeared. In this context, the Gorbachev–Reagan Reykjavik summit in the fall of 1986 may have been a watershed, for the prospect of eliminating nuclear weapons became real and certainly had an impact on Soviet thinking vis-à-vis the United States and NATO in general.[13]

Yet traditional threat perceptions will linger because of institutionalized bureaucratic and economic vested interests. In addition, old enemy images tend to be easily reinforced by unfavorable events. As

Kenneth Boulding observed many years ago, while it may take a
long time to create and nurture favorable images of others,
unfavorable ones develop rapidly.[14] Ole Holsti claims that the
history of Soviet–American relations during the past four decades
could provide plenty of empirical support for Boulding's "dolorous
observation about the human condition."[15] Since the early 1970s, the
stubborn structure of East–West threat perceptions has constituted a
special problem for talks on conventional disarmament. Undoubtedly one of the main barriers to conventional arms control in the
past has been the lack of political will to reach agreement. One could
also agree with a Hungarian observer who stated that the emphasis
should instead be on the fact that "the whole evolving problem of
the military balance is largely built on diverging perceptional
foundations, which are certainly further complicated by emerging
new technologies."[16] Today it seems obvious that major reappraisals
of each other's images are taking place in both the United States and
the Soviet Union. If this process continues without major breaks, it
will find expression in the progress of the CFE (Conventional Forces
in Europe) talks in Vienna in the early 1990s. It is also giving a
major boost to cooperative security options in Europe. To be
successful, it requires, as John Steinbruner notes, "not only that
Soviet conventional forces be put into a defensive posture, as the new
Soviet operational doctrine requires, but also that NATO subordi-
nates its reliance on tactical nuclear weapons to plans for a strictly
conventional defense of forward positions." These changes would be
of particular importance in crisis situations. Steinbruner points out
that "no other circumstance worldwide could strain the two military
establishments as seriously as a mutual alert in Central Europe. If
that situation were stabilized, all other potential crisis engagements
would be notably eased."[17] This means that the role of the military
alliances will also be gradually changing. As Soviet Deputy Foreign
Minister Viktor Karpov stated in June 1989, "both alliances should
be transformed into new organizations with cooperative relations."
But even before this goal has been achieved, the alliances can
consider, as Karpov proposes, "the possibility of new relations not
based on the assumption of military threat."[18] Karpov has touched
upon the core of the problem. If the military threat is finally
eliminated from Europe, the military division can be eliminated,
too. This goal cannot be achieved very quickly, for the outstanding
political problems must be solved first. Nevertheless, it seems evident

that for the first time since the establishment of the military division of Europe, the traditional military threats have definitively begun to fade away.

If, then, disarmament were really to take off in the conventional as well as nuclear fields, military security would be based primarily on a notion of cooperation defined largely in "neutral terms." At present, the neutral and nonaligned nations of Europe have based their military postulates on a doctrine of "strategic defense."[19]

In the 1990s European security should be defined to a greater degree in cooperative terms. To state it categorically, Europe is heading toward a post-military "green" era in its security concerns. Although this is also a global phenomenon, revised security definitions are needed as urgently in Europe as they are anywhere else in the world. The states suffering the most environmental pollution in the world are found between the Atlantic and the Urals. Together with growing economic interdependence, global environmental trends are reshaping international relations, and in Europe the "greening" of domestic structures points up the urgent need for collaborative policies. As a result of revisions in security thinking, domestic and foreign policies can no longer be shaped in isolation; "now they must be merged," as Jessica T. Mathews writes.[20] It seems obvious that the essence of the ideology of "Europeanism" is significantly "green." Ecological questions are regarded throughout Europe as common concerns that unify, rather than separate, peoples.[21]

Since its early days at the end of the 1940s, the European movement, defined in terms of West European integration, was thought to aim at the realization of a lasting and just peace. It is difficult to judge, however, whether the present trends of systemic and political change continue this grand peace strategy. But the security of Europe will, in any case, be conceived increasingly as a common cause. Accordingly, new arrangements are necessary to reflect this development; security is ever more frequently sought through cooperation among still competing nations or coalitions of nations. In the 1970s this process was an outgrowth of the policy of detente, which was originally initiated by the superpowers in order to increase crisis stability and safeguard the political status quo in Europe. Today, the growth of interdependence and the emergence of common security threats are changing security thinking in Europe. In short, security is beginning to be defined in terms of European and regional, rather than bloc, interests.

STABILITY DURING THE DISINTEGRATION OF BIPOLARITY

Europe has a tragic history; even the most promising peace arrangements have proven temporary. From a historical perspective, all European peace arrangements have been based either on a consensus among major powers about the importance of avoiding a military exchange—the concert of Europe—or on the establishment of a balance of power to restrict the use of military force. Over the last two decades the European security order has gradually moved from a balance of power toward a European concert. In the 1980s, Europe managed to isolate itself significantly from the temporary chills between the superpowers, and it has discovered at least a few unifying security interests that form a basis for further efforts to overcome the continent's temporary division. In addition, we now live in an interdependent world, in which security must be mutual and relations must be grounded in a balance of interests reached through compromise. This is in fact a new and crucial factor that must be taken more consciously into account in the overall European security order in the 1990s.

Yet the question remains whether humanity will ever be able to escape its basic security dilemma: that in order to strengthen its own security, a given state usually increases the sense of insecurity of other states. In Europe the most durable and stable security order has always been a compromise between the worst and possibly better alternatives. Henry Kissinger dealt with this problem in his book, *A World Restored*:

> Any international settlement represents a stage in a process by which a nation reconciles its vision of itself with the vision of it by other powers . . . . Could a power achieve all its wishes, it would strive for absolute security, a world order free from the consciousness of foreign danger and where all problems have the manageability of domestic issues. But since absolute security for one power means absolute insecurity for all others, it is never obtainable as a part of "legitimate" settlement, and can be achieved only through conquest.[22]

In Kissinger's view, this explains why an international settlement that is accepted and not imposed will always appear *somewhat* unjust to any one of its components.

Paradoxically, the generality of this dissatisfaction is a condition of stability, because were any one power *totally* satisfied, all others would have to be *totally* dissatisfied and a revolutionary situation would ensue. The foundation of a stable order is the *relative* security—and therefore the *relative* insecurity—of its members. [emphasis in original].[23]

Thus the preconditions for a stable order are twofold. First, the order must be accepted by all major powers; and second, its security resides in the balance of forces and its manifestation, equilibrium.

Although Kissinger's analysis deals with a multipolar European security order, specifically the arrangements reached at the Congress of Vienna in 1815, it has a certain validity for today's Europe, which is experiencing a transitional stage between the bipolar order and a more complex order that may again become multipolar. Although a number of unifying, essentially "European" processes are remolding the landscape to overcome differences, in the foreseeable future a new unity or peace order can only be achieved as a result of a process of compromise among the states involved. In addition, fundamental cultural, political and economic differences still outweigh the unifying process. Thus the maintenance of order and stability will remain of utmost importance for Europe in the future.

The postwar bipolar order, in spite of its many anomalies, has well served the interests of the major powers. To a certain degree it has safeguarded an optimal equilibrium.[24] One major difference between the postwar bipolar order and the multipolar order after 1815 lies with their basic building blocks. The multipolar order reflected, though not satisfactorily for all its participants, Europe's organic structure. All participants were *European nation-states* and no significant form of repression was applied to any of the members. In the modern world such a distinction between European and global powers has to a large extent lost its relevance, because the superpowers are and will remain European powers on the basis of their strong political, economic and even military commitments. However, the bipolar structure suffers, perhaps fatally, from its political premises. It was imposed as a "necessity" in the aftermath of World War II, at a time when order superseded justice in the East. Even then it was evident, however, that sooner or later the outstanding political problems of World War II would have to be addressed in depth. Now, at the threshold of the 1990s, the time is ripe for tackling those outstanding problems. Paradoxically, the postwar peace order must be rewritten in order to maintain stability in Europe, but not necessarily to improve justice.

The present European security order is determined by two factors: first, the bipolar concentration of military power aimed at an optimal equilibrium; and second, the absence of any transnational authority to maintain order and the existence of a largely anarchical system. One may state that the maintenance of military stability will remain the key security consideration in the future and consequently will continue to be primarily a function of superpower relations and strategic parity. By the end of the 1980s, crisis stability between the superpowers had, as John Mueller remarks, "probably gotten worse while general stability has probably improved."[25] Mueller reasons that the development of arms technology, especially the increased accuracy of multiple warhead missiles, poses the danger that one side could achieve a first-strike counterforce capability. Nevertheless, "whatever happens with crisis stability in the future, general stability is here to stay for quite some time." But as long as the political problems between the East and the West remain unresolved, one must label the present state of affairs an "unstable peace." Military preparedness or a "mutual balance of terror" will be maintained for the purpose of enforcing that unstable peace.[26]

This book has argued that security is a function of a variety of factors, some more important than others. Yet there is no longer a single most decisive factor. Furthermore, no war (despite some expectations) has been started by an arms race alone; the over-whelming majority of wars, if not all wars, have been caused by unresolved political issues. Consequently, the maintenance of peace in Europe is overwhelmingly a political concern.[27]

Regarding the absence of any transnational authority for keeping order, the situation is also changing and has obviously already changed. Though there is no institutionalized transnational or "pan-European" authority, the same effect can be achieved with the emerging sense of a common responsibility shared by the states involved in European security matters. However, plenty of new ideas have been introduced to establish new institutions to cope with the ongoing changes in the early 1990s (see next sections).

The struggle for power among European states is taking place in a new environment; it has been generally recognized that "all nations can have a stake, not just in the survival, but also in the success and prosperity of their rivals."[28] In short, a zero-sum game is no longer in anyone's interest. Although prospects for peaceful change in

Europe are more promising now than at any time in the postwar period, there is no cause for euphoric anticipation of a perpetual peace in conjunction with, for instance, the economic and technological developments of modern times. Great reform movements and economic–technological advances have usually caused turmoil and posed major challenges to the international system. The maintenance of peace in Europe will remain a demanding task for all states involved. Yet the possibilities of avoiding a catastrophe are better than ever before, and this is largely due to the "value revolution" taking place in both East and West; there is no crusading power in Europe any more; instead there is a gathering of security partners. Whether this state of affairs will constitute a more permanent situation remains, of course, to be seen and can only be answered much later. Still, it is evident that European stability will become a more important factor in a world that in many ways is heading toward turbulent times.

THE THIRD POSTWAR PEACE ARRANGEMENT FOR EUROPE

As this book is being written, a major debate on Europe's future is under way in Europe, both Eastern and Western, and, increasingly, in the United States. This debate is one of the most telling testimonies to the fact that a turning point is at hand in the postwar confrontation between East and West.

The current political map of Europe is beginning to remind one of its 19th-century counterpart and the historical configurations of the nation-states. Yet new structures in international politics are also giving impetus to this development. From the political perspective, it is time to look at the whole and not just negotiate over the parts without a clear vision of the final goal and its political ramifications. Various kinds of political plans have already been outlined for building up a new and more just as well as more stable security order beyond bipolarity. Such plans— e.g., "beyond containment," "the common European home," "revising Yalta" and Finland's model for Eastern Europe—should be regarded as sincere expressions of a growing interest in finding a common solution to the remaining political problems of World War II.

Continuity and change always characterize international politics. For years the European scene included more continuity than change.

This has led many to believe that because of its tragic experiences, Europe is doomed to be like a group of well-guarded medieval castles: peaceful places for those who obey the rules and number among the proteges of the dynasty. Yet medieval castles could not escape the pressure of change either; a long period of bloodshed and suffering followed, which finally resulted in the Peace of Westphalia in 1648, the first overall plan to restore peace to Europe.[29] Since then the basic structure of Europe's nation-state system has not fundamentally changed. Yet the peaceful order of Europe has been a metaphor, not a perpetual reality.

Europe has now experienced the longest peace of the modern era. Could any other "plan" constitute a better basis for peace in Europe? Are all plans that would restructure the division or even dismantle that order doomed to fail?

Europe's political map has been redrawn twice in this century, in the aftermath of both world wars. The third revision that East and West now face does not emphasize—if it even includes—national boundaries, though its significance could be just as great as if it did.[30] If the systemic and political processes for dismantling the division of Europe are to be controlled in a desirable way by the governments involved, the following tendencies must be sustained:

1. *NATO will most probably remain as a Western and to a certain extent "European" military alliance, but it will be transformed from an instrument of military confrontation to an instrument for ensuring that agreements reached are kept and enforced during the 1990s.* The WTO will gradually lose its members. The Eurasian security system, relying on current actors in possibly new roles, will have to maintain military stability in the area with relevant means.

2. *The freedom of the nations of Eastern Europe to pursue political and economic restructuring must be safeguarded* without interference or exploitation by East or West. Consequently, a new relationship between the Soviet Union and Eastern Europe should be gradually developed. That relationship should be built on confidence and respect for mutual security interests.

3. *Western Europe—i.e., the EC—must be further strengthened as the "adaptive" (and not discriminatory) heartbeat of the new Europe.* This process should serve the imperative that an economically successful Europe is a more secure Europe. Nations outside the EC should have access to its structures and

decision-making processes to the extent that they would benefit and not lose as the EC emerges as a "great power framework."

4. A German power center is emerging in Eastern and Central Europe that will constitute a more organic political structure and, as a consequence, a precondition for a more stable security structure in that part of Europe.

5. *An all-European security structure within the CSCE process must be reinforced.* On the one hand, the CSCE should remain a forum for all the states involved in European security matters. In short, the CSCE should reflect a more "Eurocentric" pulse in the 1990s.

The most significant goal of a third peace arrangement should be the establishment of *realistic stability in place of maintenance of the present metastability.* This book has argued that the restoration of Europe as an organic whole is the most crucial precondition for this new stability. The core of this process lies in East Central Europe, in a united Germany and in Central Europe. The best known Western propositions and plans for Europe usually address that question only.[31] Although these arguments remain valid, the restoration of an organic Europe is a more complex and demanding process, because the question is also about the (re)unification of Europe as a whole. In particular, in terms of security, a partial unification of Europe would not necessarily lead to the dismantling of the postwar division as such. As noted earlier, the possibility of a *Euro-Soviet bipolarity* also looms on the horizon.

This study has tried to examine the processes of change that are gradually finding expression in the political evolution of Europe. There is a growing need to approach European security in a more unified manner. As stressed above, it is crucial to develop a *common security concept* that would be a sort of "value organizer" for most participants in the emerging post-bipolar security system. Under such a concept, for example, disarmament could be related to larger security and foreign policy goals. Yet no real progress can be made without an open and frank recognition of fundamental—though increasingly less so—differences between the Soviet Union, some East European states and Western Europe. Any kind of common European home must include economically, politically and socially different nations, as well as new political entities. Thus a prerequisite for the successful elaboration of the concept of common security is that it should address national interests; furthermore, the concept must be based on emerging political realities. Although Europe is still oriented to nation-states, it is, in fact, beginning to be made up of new and evolving political entities that only vaguely reflect the postwar bipolar order. Major diplomatic arrangements must be handled within a political map of Europe composed of the following entities:

1. *Western Europe*, composed now of the 12 EC countries integrated into a single European Community with its own system of external relations, though perhaps not defense.
2. *The post-Stalinist Soviet Union*, possibly breaking up into independent or semi-independent units, extending geopolitically far into Asia and therefore not fully (or solely) a European country.
3. *The countries of Eastern and Central Europe*, constituting part of the Eurasian security system, but also always part of Europe. They have a growing wish to participate in certain aspects of European integration and to increase their national room for maneuver.[32]
4. *The Euroneutrals*, which are trying to maintain their role as system stabilizers, although they are to a certain extent losing their function as "neutrals" vis-à-vis the superpower conflict as a result of the erosion of bipolarity.
5. *A reunified Germany* as a political–economic power center, simultaneously an "independent" actor and an integral part of Western political–military institutions (European Germany).

The strategic stability between the superpowers will also provide a basic security framework for Europe in the future. In this respect the alliances will retain their roles as system stabilizers. Yet their roles will increasingly be ones of *system-stability guarantors*; their functions will also be more symmetrical as the WTO becomes less coercive as a structure. In particular, as Soviet troops are withdrawn from Eastern Europe and their domestic role ends—that is, as the Brezhnev Doctrine loses its last function—the political room for maneuver of the East European states will more accurately reflect the sociopolitical realities of that conflict-ridden area. The following phenomena can be expected to intensify as a result of evolving political realities:

● The importance of superpower diplomacy in European politics will not disappear.

- Political coalitions formed in Europe (e.g., the emergence of the community of the Baltic region, the Franco-German axis inside the EC, etc.) will further differentiate and could even lead to fragmentation.
- A reunified Germany will expand, potentially constituting a "new" political entity within (Western) Europe.
- Soviet–German "deals" on an array of issues, particularly improving economic ties, will increase in number.
- New dimensions for pan-European processes within the CSCE structure will emerge.

THE EMERGENCE OF THE NEW POLITICAL ARCHITECTURE

Rapid political changes presage the end of old security doctrines. Furthermore, they may presage, particularly in Europe, the obsolescence of the bipolar security institutions after the revolution of 1989. Political shifts in the European political landscape have exerted pressure for new initiatives. It would be difficult to neglect the value of the present institutions. However, new and fresh political concepts and comprehensive visions are necessary to cope with the rapidly changing conditions.

The 1990s will be, however, a decade of political and economic turbulence almost everywhere in Europe. Yet the peoples of Europe regard war among the continent's major powers as an improbable event. The security institutions of the Cold War era were based on the need to contain the threat of war between the major states of the continent; the post-Cold War era needs institutions that are able to contain political and economic turbulence. Furthermore, the new institutions should be able to create economic and political stability in the whole of Europe. In conceptual terms, a stable peace must now be based primarily on the political arrangements (international law and organizations) rather than on the military arrangements (power balances and arms control).[33] This task was eloquently formulated by Secretary of State James Baker in his famous speech in Berlin on December 12, 1989: "As Europe changes, the instruments of Western cooperation must adapt. Working together, we must design and gradually put into place a new architecture for a new era."[34]

The core of the architecture of European security comprises institutions and, of course, other political arrangements. In fact, the question is primarily about artificial configurations. To be effective and thus likely to enhance security, these configurations should reflect the organic as well as sociopolitical realities of the 1990s. Consequently, any new institution should be flexible and still efficient. The process of institutionalizing European security will comprise, for example, the changing alliances (or even their abolition), consultative commissions, periodic summit meetings, collective security treaties, short-notice challenge inspections, and weapons-free-zones. Arrangements like these could constitute a myriad of ways in which, as Richard H. Ullman states, "behavior might be codified and institutionalized to form Europe's security architecture."[35] Briefly, there are three levels of institutions in which to develop European security:

1. the pan-European institutions, like the CSCE process;
2. the regional institutions, like both military alliances; and
3. the Euro-institutions, like the Council of Europe. At present, the structures of these institutions still reflect to a large extent the bipolar divisions. This is also the case with the CSCE, because it does not constitute a security system as such.

It seems that new institutions must be created, and old ones reformulated, to meet the challenge of the disintegration of bipolarity. One could add a fourth level of institutions, economic. Undoubtedly, here the trend is unequivocal: the West European integration will step-by-step constitute an all-European economic framework (as described in Chapter 5). Indeed, the first really new institution is the European Bank for Reconstruction and Development (EBRD), which started operation in the summer of 1990. It was initiated by France and its first Director General is the former advisor to President Mitterrand, Jacques Attali. The EBRD could be described as a politico-economic instrument of the EC to "contain" the socioeconomic destabilization of Central Europe.[36] From the EC's point of view, the changes in Eastern Europe came at a bad time. The EC would have wanted to finish its economic integration process slated to go into effect in 1992 (as described in Chapter 5) and work out a similar integration of six members of the EFTA before attempting any sort of integration with Eastern Europe. The government of France, in particular, was concerned about the negative impact of changes in Eastern Europe upon West European integration. The EBRD was for France a means to maintain control over the further developments of the EC, not necessarily as much over Eastern Europe.[37]

The foundation of the EBRD, as well as the question of aiding the Soviet Union and Central Europe, reflect disputes between different schools of thought with respect to the general policy-line of the "West" vis-à-vis the "East." This dispute is to a certain extent a particular problem between Western Europe and the United States. The so-called hard-liners cling to the belief that the Soviet economy will collapse under the burden of increasing arms allocations, and hold that the Soviet Union's disintegration would serve U.S. interests.[38] At present, however, the United States should confront an apparent paradox. As John Lewis Gaddis observes: "Now that we have won the Cold War, our chief interest may lie in the survival and successful rehabilitation of the nation that was our principal adversary throughout that conflict."[39] The United States has been moving closer to the line of Western Europe, in particular the FRG, which is more favorably inclined toward aid. Yet a dispute still existed between the United States and the European Community in the summit of the so-called Group of Seven in Houston in July 1990.[40]

In brief, the question about institutionalizing European security is also a highly political issue between the Western countries as well as between the traditional "East" and "West." Although in the field of military security it is widely acknowledged that Europe should have stronger pan-European structures, the question will be whether that kind of solution is acceptable to the United States. All efforts to absorb NATO into a pan-European security organization will most probably fail. In this respect geography still matters. Yet the debate will focus, as John Mueller argues, on the idea of merging NATO and the Warsaw Pact into a new confederation. In most options of this kind, the role of the United States would diminish and, as a consequence, the transatlantic relationship would be weakened.[41] However, a rapid unification of Germany, to a large extent in "compromise terms," may foster new possibilities for a pan-European security arrangement merging both military alliances.[42] In the short term, however, the Caucasus pact between Chancellor Kohl and President Gorbachev strengthened NATO. In the longer term, there may be danger, as Henry Kissinger reasons, that "Germany's membership in NATO will be purchased by draining the Alliance of

military substance and subsuming its political role in the European
Security Conference." Kissinger is concerned that if present trends
continue, NATO will at best become a unilateral U.S. nuclear
guarantee enabling individual European nations, especially Germany, to pursue their national goals in the East on their own; at worst,
"political pressures in America could undermine that guarantee."[43]

Undoubtedly, the optimal scenario would be a slow and gradual
but purposeful development toward the expansion of all-European
structures of cooperation that would be comprised of every European nation. Yet Europe cannot return to the past. Any of the
solutions should take into account the continuing participation of
the United States and Canada in the "pan-European" structures. In
this respect, the CSCE is the most comprehensive framework for
security and cooperation in Europe. Today it is an established fact
that the CSCE norms and standards of human rights and political
freedoms, which are accepted by all European governments, had a
decisive role to play in the democratization processes in Eastern
Europe. The Vienna Final Document of 1989 was a testimony to this
progress. "As a result of the changed political situation, many taboos
of the past were swept away," as Ewa Nowotny observes. Indeed,
the events in Eastern Europe in 1989 drastically changed the political
background of the CSCE. As Ewa Nowotny argues:

> Originally conceived as an instrument to develop and further
> cooperation between the two opposing camps of East and West
> in Europe, the CSCE now can, as these differences fade, pursue
> the goal of a truly comprehensive, undivided Europe.[44]

The necessary security arrangements that are needed to equate the
ongoing political change with military security can be summarized in
five concluded or potential types of agreements: 1) a first and a
second CFE treaty on reduction of conventional forces; 2) two-plus-
four agreement on Germany (as was signed on September 12, 1990);
3) an "Open Skies" agreement providing for unrestricted aerial
observation over the entire territory of the USSR, U.S. and Canada
and of the European member states of NATO and the WTO; 4) a
treaty reducing tactical nuclear weapons; negotiations should start
after a first CFE agreement is signed; 5) an agreement on Confidence
and Security-Building Measures, like the Stockholm Document and
its continuations, will be among the most important components of
the emerging security system beyond bipolarity.

It is widely believed that the CSCE process—if further advanced—can, and probably will, be used as a forum in which the new architecture as well as the new common European home and the Confederation of European Nations will eventually be worked out. The CSCE could provide an overall framework for coping with the ongoing arms control negotiations, economic and environmental issues as well as all other questions related to the new Europe. Indeed, the CSCE has emerged as the major unifying factor in European affairs. The dynamic concept of the CSCE has prevailed; the CSCE is increasingly seen as an instrument for peaceful change.

The CSCE has established its role as a trans-European system stabilizer. To quote Hans-Dietrich Genscher, the CSCE is the "Magna Charta of European Stability." Now, however, the CSCE is increasingly needed as a system-organizer (as described in Chapter 3). International security is no longer merely a question of interstate relations; it is increasingly a question of domestic conditions and nongovernmental international relations. In Europe and related states, it is security for people and nations, not only for states. Thus the Helsinki process needs a new vision to meet this challenge properly.

The CSCE was launched in the era of a strict bipolar division of Europe. Its primary task was interpreted differently in East and West. Now these differences have to a large extent disappeared; the CSCE is needed to shape an altogether new Europe. Now is the time for the Helsinki process to advance further. In the 1990s the CSCE should fill its three baskets with new substance. The CSCE supplants the need for a European peace treaty. Furthermore, the third postwar peace arrangement—with the institutionalized CSCE as its framework—should become an open-ended process; in fact, the CSCE could constitute a trans-European peace order.

As an institutionalized framework for a European security order, the CSCE should establish new organizations as well as cooperate with the present ones. Attention has always been paid to the feasibility of institutions deriving from the process. The first hint about a possible institutionalization of the CSCE emanated from the USSR during the 1972–1973 Dipoli preliminary consultations. Soon after, Czechoslovakia formally suggested on behalf of the Warsaw Pact countries the creation of an "Advisory Committee on Security and Co-operation in Europe," which would have been entrusted with the task of undertaking "periodic exchanges of views and information" between plenipotentiary representatives of participating states as well as the task of convening (whenever appropriate) meetings of experts or working groups to prepare "practical measures" related to "the strengthening of security and the development of cooperation."

While the neutral and nonaligned countries welcomed the very idea of a standing pan-European body (which would codify their full and equal participation in European affairs), NATO members were utterly dismissive: they considered that institutionalization would provide a political bonus to Warsaw Pact countries and, more particularly, a blank check to the USSR. The notion of institutionalization was eventually dropped, replaced by the Helsinki Final Act provisions on follow-up meetings. This outcome was not only the consequence of Western opposition. It also reflected the USSR's shift vis-à-vis a process that was turning into something quite different from initial Soviet expectations—a permanent headache. After the signature of the Helsinki Final Act, the item of institutionalization vanished from the CSCE agenda, only reemerging with the dramatic political changes of 1989.[45]

The European Security Organization based on the CSCE framework could comprise the following institutional arrangements:

1. *The Parliamentary Council*, which could be elaborated on the basis of the widening of the scope of the Council of Europe.[46]
2. *The European Ministerial Commission*, a framework for the regular meetings of the foreign ministers; no equivalent system is yet in existence.
3. *The European Security Council*, which could gradually take the bulk of the tasks of the military alliances: it could become a permanent body of disarmament; the establishment of the European Peace-Keeping Forces (EPKF) could be considered as a first step in demilitarizing the European security system.[47]
4. *The Economic and Environmental Commission of Europe*, which could be developed on the basis of and devolved from the UN's Economic Commission of Europe (ECE); relatively close cooperation has existed between the CSCE and ECE.[48]
5. *The Permanent Secretariat of the CSCE*, which does not yet exist; the tasks of the secretariat could be allocated on the basis of its particular functions.

The institutionalization of the CSCE would then constitute the unifying framework for the whole of Europe as well as for the United States and Canada in most areas of security. In the course of the 1990s the CSCE could be developed as a *European Confederation* of independent states.[49] The architecture of this confederation can be elaborated in detail in the fourth follow-up meeting of the CSCE scheduled to begin in Helsinki in 1992.[50]

7   Europe in Transition

The totalitarian system in the Soviet Union and in most of its satellites is breaking down, and our nations are looking for a way to democracy and independence. This is a historically irreversible process and, as a result, Europe will begin again to seek its own identity without being compelled to be a divided armory any longer.

Vaclav Havel[1]

Only peace will emanate from German soil.

Hans-Dietrich Genscher[2]

Until the late 1980s, of all the regions of the world, Europe had experienced the least political change since, say, 1949, when the most important postwar political arrangements seemed more or less to have been consolidated. The change of the status quo appeared irreversible in the longer term, the nuclear stalemate proving sufficient both to prevent war and to prevent either side from imposing its will on the other. But the bipolar structure established after the war did contain inherent flaws, particularly within the Eastern sphere, which became apparent ultimately in the last days of the 1980s, when peaceful change was at work in Europe. A political earthquake shook Eastern Europe and a geographic East Central Europe was restored. The execution of Nicolae Ceausescu, the long-time tyrant of Romania, became a symbol of the final collapse of the Stalinist regimes in Eastern Europe.

Ultimately the people in the streets of the cities of Eastern Europe took control of events. "The initial changes were political," as Ralf Dahrendorf analyzed the revolution of 1989.[3] One of the basic assumptions of this book was that the division of Europe was based on the outstanding political problems related to World War II. The Soviet withdrawal from Eastern Europe was the key to eliminating the division. Another key factor was the unification of Germany. Yet the driving force of both these fundamental changes should be identified primarily in the longer-term historical processes. Indeed, one could draw the conclusion, as did Edward N. Luttwak, that "the force of collectively motivated ideas" is the most decisive factor,

130

more decisive than strategy or economic self-interest, among the factors of European change.[4] With the events of 1989, several historical processes gained strength: the reemergence of national sentiments, the fight for freedom and democracy, and the efforts to build a new and whole Europe. As a result, the restoration of Europe as a unified political region took a giant step forward. The problem is that it will take many more years before it is clear whether the Soviet Union will be able to establish its place within the political–economic core of Europe. It seems obvious, however, that the Soviet states, at least the western ones, want to belong to Europe. The future of Russia may remain open longer. It is large enough to constitute its own "world region." Yet in the modern world a greater Russia should be at least part of the CSCE process, and thus part of the European security system.

It is self-evident, however, that without the consent of the Soviet Union, no breakthrough in the development toward democracy in Eastern Europe would have taken place so abruptly. The two superpower leaders, Mikhail Gorbachev and George Bush, at their meeting in Malta in December 1989 closed the chapter on the postwar history of Europe opened in Yalta in 1945. In Yalta the Soviets achieved domination over Eastern Europe. At Malta the leaders agreed to put an end to the zero-sum game in European politics.

In the wake of the political events in Eastern Europe it is more evident than ever before that the postwar bipolar security order—in particular, the high degree of armament—does not adequately reflect European sociopolitical realities. Undoubtedly, Europe's top agenda item in the early 1990s will be accommodating and managing the revolutionary situation in Eastern Europe, especially in the Soviet Union.

Now, more than ever, it is difficult to predict what the 1990s will bring for Europe. Two things, however, seem certain: the new decade will produce a new internal European order, and Europe's relative standing in the world will change primarily as a function of that new order.

The overall changes under way in Europe are affecting domestic as well as international structures in both East and West. They seem likely to lead toward increased self-consciousness almost everywhere in the continent. Nationalities, ethnic minorities and, of course, nation-states are becoming increasingly assertive in voicing their concerns. There is more room for differences and nuances, the traditional richness of Europe. This process reflects the "organic" resurgence of the continent.

Meanwhile, the process of West European economic and political integration is progressing without major delays. Now the question is whether it is possible to harmonize these different processes to encourage the development of a new Europe based, not on bipolarity, but on the socioeconomic realities of the 1990s.

If there are no major delays in this development process, one may expect a new and free Europe to emerge in the early years of the 21st century. However, it would be unrealistic to expect history to progress in accordance with our most rational visions. Paradoxically, the end of the Cold War may lead to the end of the Long Peace. There can be no return to the past. The question is about a transition period to the future and its outlines are already evident. The bipolar conflict will be replaced by a number of resurgent, more localized conflicts in East Central Europe, particularly in the European regions of the USSR. Consequently, a "metapeace"will be replaced by a "conflictual peace." There is some comfort in this, however: because of change, the threat of major war seems to be waning.

Historians and political scientists have always debated whether great forces or great individuals move the world. Mikhail Gorbachev has certainly strengthened the "great man" theory. This book has underscored the "Gorbachev phenomenon" as a major factor of change in Europe. However, as I tried to stress earlier, the most important features of the ongoing change have their roots in systemic as well as political factors not necessarily dependent on the Soviet Union or superpower relations. It is obvious, however, that Gorbachev's policies of perestroika and glasnost have dramatically accelerated the pace of change. This development has also had many unexpected repercussions. Gorbachev has opened up a book with surprising and even shocking pages. In the short term, the "Gorbachev factor" will play a crucial role in the overall development of Europe. Yet even he—or his removal from power—can no longer alter the basic course of history. However, it can be assumed that if Gorbachev fails, a fatal gap between the rest of Europe and the Soviet Union could emerge, with unpredictable repercussions.

Mikhail Gorbachev, Nobel laureate, may become one of the really great statesmen of the 20th century if he can successfully complete at least one significant part of his mission: i.e., diminishing the size of the Soviet empire. One could compare him to British leaders who faced the same challenge at the end of the World War II. Their task was to bring the United Kingdom into the new era of Pax Americana, and their aim was twofold: to guarantee the status of major power for a "declining" U.K. in the postwar world order; and to make all possible efforts to influence the shaping of a new security order. In short, to try to win not only the war but the peace as well. They knew that the United Kingdom would not have been able to achieve this goal without close cooperation with its allies.

Gorbachev's vision of an interdependent and cooperative international system has already allowed the East European countries to emerge from Stalinism. This process still raises more questions than answers. Only after some years will we really be able to predict with certainty whether Eastern Europe will manage to avoid the temptation of its history: ethnic hatreds, border feuds and military juntas. Samuel P. Huntington has made a relevant comment: "Gorbachev may be able to discard communism, but he cannot discard geography and the geopolitical imperatives that have shaped Russian and Soviet behavior for centuries."[5]

Under Gorbachev's leadership the Soviet Union seems to be determined to seek for itself a new role in world politics, however. The Soviet Union may wish to remain a global power, but its current leader recognizes that it must emphasize its position as a "major European power." Gorbachev's metaphor of the "common European home" is testimony to this endeavor. Yet the Soviet Union must adjust to global developments, i.e., to the multipolarization of world politics. Moscow has to find new partners as some of the old ones disappear. The Soviet "bloc" no longer exists except as a relatively loose security structure.

As a result of the disintegration of the Soviet empire, its foreign policy is also falling apart. Indeed, "Soviet" foreign policy is more often defined outside the Kremlin, in the Baltic states, in the Russian Republic's decision-making machineries, in the Ukrainian Supreme Soviet and even in the streets of the capitals of the rebelling states. The monolithic concept of Soviet foreign policy belongs to history. Consequently, the West should pay, as Alexei Iziumov and Andrei Kortunov advise, "more attention to domestic factors that will govern Soviet international behavior."[6] Even more overtly, Professor Martin Malia proposes that the West should go over Moscow's head and deal directly with the local forces seeking to phase out communism. "The leaders of these forces are actively seeking such foreign contact."[7] It seems that emerging pluralism in Soviet foreign policy is a positive development for the Soviet Union as well as for the West and the rest of the world. It could constitute the final guarantee that the Cold War will remain in the past.

However, political stability has all but disappeared from the Soviet Union, where the difficulties of creating a democracy seem staggering. As Seweryn Bialer states, "the new tensions and conflicts do not simply mark a transitional period, but will accompany Soviet development for a long time to come."[8] It is possible that a Greater Russia, with intensely nationalistic focus, will emerge instead of a democratic Soviet Union. This development could isolate the new Russia, ultimately threatening the building in the East of a whole and free Europe.[9]

As regards European security, the unpredictability of the Soviet situation will pose a major dilemma throughout the 1990s. The Western states must pursue a strategy not of containment, but of involvement vis-à-vis the Soviet Union. In fact, the transition of European security order may really begin with the building of the institutions of crisis management, and not with the institutions of a new political architecture.

Although the Soviet Union is undergoing a major crisis, prospects for the emergence of a new and unified Europe are otherwise more promising than ever before. For the first time in the modern history of Europe, the continent's security order could be based not solely on the balance of military power, but on unifying and cooperative structures as well. Consequently, a new balance of political–economic power is likely to be established in Europe. To achieve this task, the present structures of military confrontation should be eradicated in due time. At the heart of this process lies the reunification of the two German states. Thus a European Germany ultimately should be a stabilizing factor in Central Europe. *Deutschland* should satisfy the security interests of the Soviet Union and Western Europe simultaneously. The question now is, how to tie down Gulliver? Again, the problem may be, as Otto von Bismarck put it in his last address to the *Reichstag* in 1888: "The only real threat to Germany is derived from her own power."[10]

It seems that the dismantling of the remaining structures of the division will be accomplished not by a single rational vision— although a new political architecture is needed as a guiding hand— but by a gradual and often disorderly and uncoordinated process of attrition. In this process, "collectively motivated ideas" are constituting premises for the institutionalizing of European security (as described in Chapter 6). The nation-states still remain the key players. The European international system, however, is no longer a system of nation-states, but a system of coalitions of states. Furthermore, the process is toward a transnational Europe. The problem will be whether a new geopolitical "East"—the disintegrating Soviet Union—can be adapted to a trans-European framework or whether a new Euro-Soviet bipolarity will replace the old one. The German-Soviet pact in the Caucasus on July 16, 1990 may be the most important step to avoid the emergence of the Euro-Soviet bipolarity (as described in Chapter 5). This pact also reflects new political realities of Europe.

A unified Germany is emerging as a "superpower" on the European stage. As a consequence, the geostrategic landscape of Europe will tilt toward East Central Europe and a new geopolitical reality will emerge in the geographic center of the continent. The European Community will be influenced by this development. In the 1980s, France was the political–economic engine of the EC; in the 1990s, the engine may be driven by the Germans. The European Community has difficulties in becoming a great power. Instead it seems that the EC is becoming an economic–political framework for a great power. The tendency of the EC is now primarily in "opening," not necessarily in "deepening." At least this development would facilitate for the Soviet Union an associate membership in a steadily broadening European Community.[11]

The institutionalizing of European security will primarily be a process that includes both new and old mechanisms. As described earlier (in Chapter 6), the role of the military alliances has to be changed. According to Lord Ismay, the first Secretary General of NATO, the purpose of the Atlantic Alliance was "to keep the Russians out, the Americans in, and the Germans down."[12] Now the only realistic purpose is to keep everybody in. In the final analysis, both military alliances should be gradually adapted to the European Security Organization through the CSCE. Indeed, one of the paradoxes of the end of the Cold War is the general recognition that it is imperative to keep both superpowers in Europe for the sake of stability.

The post-Cold War Europe has to adapt itself to the change in the international system. A shift toward a multipolar world has been accelerated by the revolution of 1989. In this process, the chemistry of power among nations or their coalitions has changed accordingly. At the same time, regional powers will become more influential,

certainly in anarchical parts of the globe like the Middle East, where
military power is still the paramount determinant. Indeed, in a post-
Cold War world, regional conflicts outside Europe will be the main
danger. The Iraqi invasion of Kuwait in August 1990 was a
testimony to this development. In the era of strict and global
bipolarity, both superpowers maintained leadership in world politics
through their positions within their respective "blocs." At the
Helsinki summit on September 9, 1990, Bush and Gorbachev
initiated a new international order that reached across the blocs,
rather than relying on them. In practical terms this means that the
cooperation between the superpowers in the Gulf crisis, and the
strengthening role of the United Nations in world politics in general,
could constitute a basis for a new international order of cooperation.
If this proves to be true, the most negative ramifications of the end
of the Cold War could perhaps be contained in due time.[13] In any
case, the role of the United States as the only really powerful
"superstate" became more evident in 1990. Without the strong
material and political contribution of the United States in crisis
management in the Gulf and in the building of a new architecture for
the post-Cold War Europe, no major progress could have been
achieved. This development may prove the contradictory thesis that
"the United States remains the largest and richest power with the
greatest capacity to shape the future."[14]

As another result of the change in the international system,
"Europe" and the United States have to find new premises for their
relationship. Geoeconomics matters as much as geopolitics. A
widening and opening Europe shares the same values with the
United States and even to a large extent with Japan. Yet in
economic terms these powers have to avoid the emergence of a
"new anarchical system." In the 1990s, more dialogue, even a treaty,
is needed between the United States and the European Community,
to keep the United States influential in Europe. In 1990, the United
States and the European Community have to both strengthen and
renew their mutual ties, as well as work out a new partnership for
managing global change.[15]

In the final analysis, however, the real dynamism for pursuing the
dismantling of the division must be found in Europe itself. Europe
has to regain its identity and self-confidence—a task that must be
accomplished within a system encompassing contradictory processes
of change and continuity. A European peace order can emerge if
Europe is able to avoid the repetition of its historical dilemma, that

is, if no nation should again strive for hegemony. From the 1990s on, at least all big European nations are doomed to be, then, primarily "European" and less striving for their national interests. The bipolar security order was primarily a "Soviet order," to which a counter-force was successfully established by those states supported by the U.S.

It would be unwise not to expect problems during the period of transition. Dreams and visions too often lag behind reality. Yet proceeding cautiously, although the most natural and rational advice to any of the European statesmen, may primarily strengthen the worst-case alternative. The history of Europe is full of tragic elements. Goethe was aware of this when he said to Eckermann: "Man is not born to solve the problems of the world, but to search for the starting point of the problem and then to remain within the limits of what he is able to comprehend."[16] The Europeans are, again, searching hard for the starting point of the problem.

Appendix A
Excerpts from Baker Speech on Post-Cold War Europe*

In 1945, pictures of a bombed-out Berlin brought home to us the terrible cost of war.

In 1948, the Soviet Union stalked out of the Four Power Control Commission and blockaded Berlin—the clear declaration of cold war.

In 1958, Berliners staged the first popular revolt against Soviet tyranny in Eastern Europe.

In 1961, the Berlin Wall closed the last escape hatch from the prison camp of nations which Eastern Europe had become.

In 1971, the Quadripartite Agreement on Berlin epitomized the terrible dilemma of detente—the proposition that cooperation between East and West assumed the continued division of this continent.

Then in 1989, the most important event—certainly the most dramatic—of the postwar era occurred right here in Berlin.

On November 9, the wall became a gateway. Berliners celebrated history's largest, happiest family reunion. And all of us who watched these scenes felt, once again: We are all Berliners.

Once more, images from Berlin flashed around the world, images that again heralded a new reality. This new reality has its roots in those older Berlin scenes—the scenes of West Berlin's dramatic postwar reconstruction; the scenes of Allied aircraft supplying a blockaded city; the scenes of American and Soviet tanks facing off at Checkpoint Charlie.

By standing together, in Berlin as elsewhere, Western nations created the essential preconditions for overcoming the division of this city, of this nation, and of this continent.

As these recent events have unfolded, the Soviet Union has shown a remarkable degree of realism. And President Gorbachev deserves credit for being the first Soviet leader to have the courage and foresight to permit the lifting of repression in Eastern Europe.

But the real impulse for change comes from an altogether different source: the peoples of Poland, of Hungary, of Czechoslovakia, of Bulgaria, and of East Germany. They have freed themselves.

From the Baltic to the Adriatic, an irresistible movement has gathered force—a movement of, by, and for the people. In their peaceful urgent multitude, the peoples of Eastern Europe have held up a mirror to the West

---

* Excerpts from an address by U.S. Secretary of State James A. Baker to the Berlin Press Club at the Stigenberger Hotel in Berlin, December 12, 1989.

and have reflected the enduring power of our own best values. In the words of Thomas Jefferson, the first American Secretary of State: "Nothing is more certainly written in the book of fate than that these people are to be free." The changes amount to nothing less than a peaceful revolution.

Now, as President Bush stated last week, "the task before us is to consolidate the fruits of this peaceful revolution and provide the architecture for continued peaceful change."

The first step is for free men and women to create free governments. The path may appear difficult, even confusing, but we must travel it with understanding. For true stability requires governments with legitimacy, governments that are based on the consent of the governed.

The peoples of Eastern Europe are trying to build such governments. Our view, as President Bush has told President Gorbachev, is that the political and economic reforms in the East can enhance both long-term stability in Europe and the prospects for perestroika. A legitimate and stable European order will help, not threaten, legitimate Soviet interests. An illegitimate order will provide no order at all.

Free men and free governments are the building blocks of a Europe whole and free. But hopes for a Europe whole and free are tinged with concern by some that a Europe undivided may not necessarily be a Europe peaceful and prosperous. Many of the guideposts that brought us securely through four sometimes tense and threatening decades are now coming down. Some of the diverse issues that once brought conflict to Europe are reemerging.

As Europe changes, the instruments for Western cooperation must adapt. Working together, we must design and gradually put into place a new architecture for a new era.

This new architecture must have a place for old foundations and structures that remain valuable—like NATO [North Atlantic Treaty Organization]—while recognizing that they can also serve new collective purposes. The new architecture must continue the construction of institutions—like the EC [European Community]—that can help draw together the West while also serving as an open door to the East. And the new architecture must build up frameworks—like the CSCE [Conference on Security and Cooperation in Europe]—processes that can overcome the division of Europe and bridge the Atlantic Ocean.

This new structure must also accomplish two special purposes.

First, as a part of overcoming the division of Europe, there must be an opportunity to overcome, through peace and freedom, the division of Berlin and of Germany. The United States and NATO have stood for unification for 40 years, and we will not waver from that goal.

Second, the architecture should reflect that America's security—politically, militarily, and economically—remains linked to Europe's security. The United States and Canada share Europe's neighborhood.

As President Bush stated in May: "The United States is and will remain a European power." And as he added last week: "The U.S. will maintain significant military forces in Europe as long as our Allies desire our presence as part of a common security effort." This is our commitment to a common future, a recognition of a need for an active U.S. role in Europe, a need even acknowledged by President Gorbachev.

The charge for us all, then, is to work together toward the *New Europe* *and the New Atlanticism.*

* * * * *

As we construct a new security architecture that maintains the common defense, the nonmilitary component of European security will grow. Arm control agreements, confidence-building measures, and other political con sultative arrangements will become more important. In such a world, the role of NATO will evolve. NATO will become the forum where Western nation cooperate to negotiate, implement, verify and extend agreements between East and West.

* * * * *

NATO should also begin considering further initiatives the West migh take, through the CSCE process in particular, to build economic an political ties with the East, to promote respect for human rights, to help build democratic institutions, and to fashion, consistent with Western security interests, a more open environment for East–West trade and investment.

* * * * *

Whatever security relationships the governments of Eastern Europe choose, NATO will continue to provide Western governments the optimal instrument to coordinate their efforts at defense and arms control and to build a durable European order of peace. The interests of the Soviet Union will be served by the maintenance of a vigorous North Atlantic Treaty Organization.

The future development of the European Community will play a central role in shaping the new Europe.

The example of Western cooperation through the European Community has already had a dramatic effect on Eastern attitudes toward economic liberty. The success of this great European experiment, perhaps more than any other factor, has caused Eastern Europeans to recognize that people as well as nations cooperate more productively when they are free to choose The ballot box and the free market are the fundamental instruments of choice.

* * * * *

As Europe moves toward its goal of a common internal market, and as it institutions for political and security cooperation evolve, the link between the United States and the European Community will become even more important. We want our transatlantic cooperation to keep pace with European integration and institutional reform.

To this end, we propose that the United States and the European Community work together to achieve, whether in treaty or some other form, a significantly strengthened set of institutional and consultative links Working from shared ideals and common values, we face a set of mutual challenges—in economics, foreign policy, the environment, science, and a host of other fields. So it makes sense for us to seek to fashion our responses together as a matter of common course.

We suggest that our discussions about this idea proceed in parallel with Europe's efforts to achieve by 1992 a common internal market so that plans for U.S.–EC interaction would evolve with changes in the Community.

* * * * *

The institution that brings all the nations of the East and West together in Europe, the Conference on Security and Cooperation in Europe, is in fact an ongoing process launched over 14 years ago in Helsinki. There have been different perceptions as to the functions of this CSCE process. Some saw the Helsinki Final Act of 1975 as a ratification of the status quo, the equivalent of a peace treaty concluding World War II, and thus the legitimization of Europe's permanent division. Others, however, saw this process as a device by which these divisions could be overcome.

The dynamic concept of the CSCE process has prevailed. In 1975, the governments of Eastern Europe may not have taken seriously their commitments to respect a wide range of fundamental human rights. Their populations did. The standards of conduct set by the Helsinki Final Act are increasingly being met through international pressure and domestic ferment. Last month, here in Berlin, we witnessed one of the proudest achievements of the CSCE process as the GDR [East Germany] fulfilled its commitment to allow its people to travel freely.

Now it's time for the CSCE process to advance further. We can look toward filling each of its three baskets with new substance.

First, we can give the security basket further content through the 35-nation negotiations on confidence-building measures currently underway in Vienna. The agreements under consideration there should help prevent force, or the threat of force, from being used again in an effort to intimidate any European nation. Apart from reducing further the risk of war, new confidence-building measures can create greater openness. They can institutionalize a predictable pattern of military interaction, a pattern that is difficult to reverse and that builds a new basis for trust.

Second, the relatively underdeveloped economic basket can assume new responsibilities. President Bush suggested to President Gorbachev at Malta that we could breathe new life into this CSCE forum by focusing it on the conceptual and practical questions involved in the transition from stalled, planned economies to free, competitive markets. When our nations meet in Bonn in May of next year to discuss economic cooperation, I suggest we concentrate on this issue.

Third, the CSCE process has made its most distinctive mark in the field of human rights. One fundamental right, however, has not yet been fully institutionalized. This is the right for people to choose, through regular, free, open, multiparty elections, those who will govern them.

This is the ultimate human right, the right that secures all others. Without free elections, no rights can be long guaranteed. With free elections, no rights can be long denied.

On May 31, in Mainz, President Bush announced a major new Helsinki initiative to help end the division of Europe. He called for free elections and political pluralism in all the countries of Europe. Now this is coming to pass.

In June, the United States and the United Kingdom cosponsored a free elections initiative at the CSCE human rights meeting in Paris. This proposal called on all 35 CSCE participating states to allow periodic, genuine, and contested elections based on universal and equal suffrage, by secret ballot, and with international observers. Individuals would be allowed to establish and maintain their own political parties in order to ensure fully democratic procedures.

Free elections should now become the highest priority in the CSCE process. In 1945, Joseph Stalin promised free elections and self-determination for the peoples of Eastern Europe. The fact that those elections were not free, and that those peoples were not allowed to determine their destiny, was a fundamental cause of the Cold War.

Now this Stalinist legacy is being removed by people determined to reclaim their birthright to freedom. They should not be denied. They will not be denied.

As all or nearly all the CSCE states move toward fully functioning representative governments, I suggest we consider another step: We could involve parliamentarians more directly in CSCE processes, not only as observers, as at present, but perhaps through their own meetings. To sustain the movement toward democracy, we need to reinforce the institutions of democracy.

A new Europe, whole and free, must include arrangements that satisfy the aspirations of the German people and meet the legitimate concerns of Germany's neighbors.

* * * * *

President Bush concluded that "an end to the unnatural division of Europe, and of Germany, must proceed in accordance with and be based upon the values that are becoming universal ideals, as all the countries of Europe become part of a commonwealth of free nations."

* * * * *

As Berlin has stood at the center of a divided Europe, so it may stand at the center of a Europe whole and free—no longer the embattled bastion of freedom but instead a beacon of hope for a better life.

My friends, the changes we see underway today in the East are a source of great hope. But a new era brings different concerns for all of us. Some are as old as Europe itself. Others are themselves the new products of change.

Were the West to abandon the patterns of cooperation that we have built up over four decades, these concerns could grow into problems. But the institutions we have created—NATO, the European Community, and the CSCE process—are alive. Rooted in democratic values, they fit well with the people power that is shaping history's new course.

More important, these institutions are also flexible and capable of adapting to rapidly changing circumstances. As we adapt, as we update and expand our cooperation with each other and with the nations of the East, we will create a New Europe on the basis of a new Atlanticism.

NATO will remain North America's primary link with Europe. As arms control and political arrangements increasingly supplement the still vital military component of European security, NATO will take on new roles.

The European Community is already an economic pillar of the transatlantic relationship. It will also take on, perhaps in concert with other European institutions, increasingly important political roles. Indeed, it has already done so, as evidenced by the Community's coordination of a Western effort to support reform in Eastern Europe. And as it continues to do so, the link between the United States and the European Community should become stronger, the issues we discuss more diversified, and our common endeavors more important.

At the same time, the substantive overlap between NATO and European institutions will grow. This overlap must lead to synergy, not friction. Better communication among European and transatlantic institutions will become more urgent.

The CSCE process could become the most important forum of East–West cooperation. Its mandate will grow as this cooperation takes root.

As these changes proceed, as they overcome the division of Europe, so too will the divisions of Germany and Berlin be overcome in peace and freedom.

This fall, a powerful cry went up from the huge demonstrations in Leipzig, Dresden, and Berlin: "We are the people!" the crowds chanted at the party that ruled in their name. On the other side of the globe, Lech Walesa was addressing the U.S. Congress, thanking America for supporting Polish liberty. He began with words written 200 years ago, the words that open the U.S. Constitution: "We the people."

Between 1789 and 1989, between the expressions "We the people" and "We are the people," runs one of history's deepest currents. What the American Founding Fathers knew, the people of East Germany and Eastern Europe now also know—that freedom is a blessing but not a gift; that the work of freedom is never done alone. Between the America of "We the people" and the Europe of "We are the people," there can be no division. On this basis, a new Atlanticism will flourish, and a new Europe will be born.

Appendix B
Excerpts from the Treaty between the Federal Republic of Germany and the German Democratic Republic on the Establishment of German Unity

The Federal Republic of Germany and the German Democratic Republic,

Resolved to achieve in free self-determination the unity of Germany in peace and freedom as an equal partner in the community of nations,

Mindful of the desire of the people in both parts of Germany to live together in peace and freedom in a democratic and social federal state governed by the rule of law,

In grateful respect to those who peacefully helped freedom prevail and who have unswervingly adhered to the task of establishing German unity and are achieving it,

Aware of the continuity of German history and bearing in mind the special responsibility arising from our past for a democratic development in Germany committed to respect for human rights and to peace,

Seeking through German unity to contribute to the unification of Europe and to the building of a peaceful European order in which borders no longer divide and which ensures that all European nations can live together in a spirit of mutual trust,

Aware that the inviolability of frontiers and of the territorial integrity and sovereignty of all states in Europe within their frontiers constitutes a fundamental condition for peace,

Have agreed to conclude a Treaty on the Establishment of German Unity, containing the following provisions:

Chapter 1. Effect of Accession

Article 1
Länder

(1) Upon the accession of the German Democratic Republic to the Federal Republic of Germany in accordance with Article 23 of the Basic Law taking

effect on 3 October 1990 the Länder of Brandenburg, Mecklenburg–Western Pomerania, Saxony, Saxony–Anhalt and Thuringia shall become Länder of the Federal Republic of Germany. The establishment of these Länder and their boundaries shall be governed by the provisions of the Constitutional Act of 22 July 1990 on the Establishment of Länder in the German Democratic Republic (Länder Establishment Act) (Law Gazette I, No. 51, p. 955) in accordance with Annex II.

(2) The 23 boroughs of Berlin shall form Land Berlin.

Article 2
Capital City, Day of German Unity

(1) The capital of Germany shall be Berlin. The seat of parliament and government shall be decided after the establishment of German unity.

(2) 3 October shall be a public holiday known as the Day of German Unity.

Chapter 2. Basic Law

Article 3
Entry into Force of the Basic Law

Upon the accession taking effect, the Basic Law of the Federal Republic of Germany, as published in the Federal Law Gazette Part III, No. 100-1, and last amended by the Act of 21 December 1983 (Federal Law Gazette I, p. 1481), shall enter into force in the Länder of Brandenburg, Mecklenburg–Western Pomerania, Saxony, Saxony–Anhalt and Thuringia and in that part of Land Berlin where it has not been valid to date, subject to the amendments arising from Article 4, unless otherwise provided in this Treaty.

Article 4
Amendments to the Basic Law Resulting from Accession

The Basic Law of the Federal Republic of Germany shall be amended as follows:

1. The preamble shall read as follows:

    "Conscious of their responsibility before God and men,

    Animated by the resolve to serve world peace as an equal partner in a united Europe, the German people have adopted, by virtue of their constituent power, this Basic Law.

    The Germans in the Länder of Baden–Württemberg, Bavaria, Berlin, Brandenburg, Bremen, Hamburg, Hesse, Lower Saxony, Mecklenburg–Western Pomerania, North-Rhine/Westphalia, Rhineland–Palatinate, Saarland, Saxony, Saxony–Anhalt, Schleswig–Holstein and Thuringia have achieved the unity and freedom of Germany in free self-determination. This Basic Law is thus valid for the entire German people."

2. Article 23 shall be repealed.

3. Article 51 (2) shall read as follows:

    "(2) Each Land shall have at least three votes; Länder with more than two million inhabitants shall have four, Länder with more than six million inhabitants five, and Länder with more than seven million inhabitants six votes."

4. The existing text of Article 135a shall become paragraph 1. The following paragraph shall be inserted after paragraph 1:

"(2) Paragraph 1 above shall be applied mutatis mutandis to liabilities of the German Democratic Republic or its legal entities as well as to liabilities of the Federation or other corporate bodies and institutions under public law which are connected with the transfer of properties of the German Democratic Republic to the Federation, Länder and communes (Gemeinden), and to liabilities arising from measures taken by the German Democratic Republic or its legal entities."

5. The following new Article 143 shall be inserted in the Basic Law:

"Article 143

(1) Law in the territory specified in Article 3 of the Unification Treaty may deviate from provisions of this Basic Law for a period not extending beyond 31 December 1992 in so far as and as long as no complete adjustment to the order of the Basic Law can be achieved as a consequence of the different conditions. Deviations must not violate Article 19 (2) and must be compatible with the principles set out in Article 79 (3).

(2) Deviations from sections 2, 8, 8a, 9, 10 and 11 are permissible for a period not extending beyond 3i December 1995.

(3) Notwithstanding paragraphs 1 and 2 above, Article 41 of the Unification Treaty and the rules for its implementation shall remain valid in so far as they provide for the irreversibility of interferences with property in the territory specified in Article 3 of the said Treaty."

6. Article 146 shall read as follows:

"Article 146

This Basic Law, which is valid for the entire German people following the achievement of the unity and freedom of Germany, shall cease to be in force on the day on which a constitution adopted by a free decision of the German people comes into force."

Article 5
Future Amendments to the Constitution

The Governments of the two Contracting Parties recommend to the legislative bodies of the united Germany that within two years they should deal with the questions regarding amendments or additions to the Basic Law as raised in connection with German unification, in particular

– with regard to the relationship between the Federation and the Länder in accordance with the Joint Resolution of the Minister-Presidents of 5 July 1990.

– with regard to the possibility of restructuring the Berlin/Brandenburg area in derogation of the provisions of Article 29 of the Basic Law by way of an agreement between the Länder concerned,

- with considerations on introducing state objectives into the Basic Law, and
- with the question of applying Article 146 of the Basic Law and of holding a referendum in this context.

Article 6
Exception

For the time being, Article 131 of the Basic Law shall not be applied in the territory specified in Article 3 of this Treaty.

Article 7
Financial System

(1) The financial system of the Federal Republic of Germany shall be extended to the territory specified in Article 3 unless otherwise provided in this Treaty.

(2) Article 106 of the Basic Law shall apply to the apportionment of tax revenue among the Federation as well as the Länder and communes (associations of communes) in the territory specified in Article 3 of this Treaty with the proviso that

1. paragraph 3, fourth sentence, and paragraph 4 shall not apply up to 31 December 1994;

2. up to 31 December 1996 the share of income tax revenue received by the communes in accordance with Article 106 (5) of the Basic Law shall be passed on from the Länder to the communes not on the basis of the amount of income tax paid by their inhabitants, but according to the number of inhabitants in the communes;

3. up to 31 December 1994, in derogation of Article 106 (7) of the Basic Law, an annual share of at least 20% of the Land share of total revenue from joint taxes and of the total revenue from Land taxes as well as 40% of the Land share from the German Unity Fund according to paragraph 5, item 1, shall accrue to the communes (associations of communes).

(3) Article 107 of the Basic Law shall be valid in the territory specified in Article 3 of this Treaty with the proviso that up to 31 December 1994 the provision of paragraph 1, fourth sentence, shall not be applied between the Länder which have until now constituted the Federal Republic of Germany and the Länder in the territory specified in Article 3 of this Treaty and that there shall be no all-German financial equalization between the Länder (Article 107 (2) of the Basic Law).

The Land share of turnover tax throughout Germany shall be divided up into an eastern component and a western component in such a way that the average share of turnover tax per inhabitant in the Länder of Brandenburg, Mecklenburg–Western Pomerania, Saxony, Saxony–Anhalt and Thuringia amounts

in 1991 to 55%
in 1992 to 60%
in 1993 to 65%
in 1994 to 70%

of the average share of turnover tax per inhabitant in the Länder of Baden–Württemberg, Bavaria, Bremen, Hesse, Hamburg, Lower Saxony, North-Rhine/Westphalia, Rhineland–Palatinate, Saarland and Schleswig–Holstein. The share of Land Berlin shall be calculated in advance on the basis of the number of inhabitants. The provisions contained in this paragraph shall be reviewed for 1993 in the light of the conditions obtaining at the time.

(4) The territory specified in Article 3 of this Treaty shall be incorporated into the provisions of Articles 91a, 91b and 104a (3) and (4) of the Basic Law, including the pertinent implementing provisions, in accordance with this Treaty with effect from 1 January 1991.

(5) Following the establishment of German unity the annual allocations from the German Unity Fund shall be distributed as follows:

1. 85% as special assistance to the Länder of Brandenburg, Mecklenburg–Western Pomerania, Saxony, Saxony–Anhalt and Thuringia as well as to Land Berlin to cover their general financial requirements and divided up among these Länder in proportion to their number of inhabitants, excluding the inhabitants of Berlin (West), and
2. 15% to meet public requirements at a central level in the territory of the aforementioned Länder.

(6) In the event of a fundamental change in conditions, the Federation and the Länder shall jointly examine the possibilities of granting further assistance in order to ensure adequate financial equalization for the Länder in the territory specified in Article 3 of this Treaty.

Chapter 4. International Treaties and Agreements

Article 11
Treaties of the Federal Republic of Germany

The Contracting Parties proceed on the understanding that international treaties and agreements to which the Federal Republic of Germany is a contracting party, including treaties establishing membership of international organizations or institutions, shall retain their validity and that the rights and obligations arising therefrom, with the exception of the treaties named in Annex I, shall also relate to the territory specified in Article 3 of this Treaty. Where adjustments become necessary in individual cases, the all-German Government shall consult with the respective contracting parties.

Article 12
Treaties of the German Democratic Republic

(1) The Contracting Parties are agreed that, in connection with the establishment of German unity, international treaties of the German Democratic Republic shall be discussed with the contracting parties concerned with a view to regulating or confirming their continued application, adjustment or expiry, taking into account protection of confidence, the interests of the states concerned, the treaty obligations of the Federal Republic of Germany as well as the principles of a free, democratic basic order governed by the rule of law, and respecting the competence of the European Communities.

(2) The united Germany shall determine its position with regard to the adoption of international treaties of the German Democratic Republic following consultations with the respective contracting parties and with the European Communities where the latter's competence is affected.

(3) Should the united Germany intend to accede to international organizations or other multilateral treaties of which the German Democratic Republic but not the Federal Republic of Germany is a member, agreement shall be reached with the respective contracting parties and with the European Communities where the latter's competence is affected.

Chapter 9. Transitional and Final Provisions

Article 40
Treaties and Agreements

(1) The obligations under the Treaty of 18 May 1990 between the Federal Republic of Germany and the German Democratic Republic on the Establishment of a Monetary, Economic and Social Union shall continue to be valid unless otherwise provided in this Treaty and unless they become irrelevant in the process of establishing German unity.

(2) Where rights and duties arising from other treaties and agreements between the Federal Republic of Germany or its Länder and the German Democratic Republic have not become irrelevant in the process of establishing German unity, they shall be assumed, adjusted or settled by the competent national entities.

Article 42
Delegation of Parliamentary Representatives

(1) Before the accession of the German Democratic Republic takes effect, the Volkskammer shall, on the basis of its composition, elect 144 Members of Parliament to be delegated to the 11th German Bundestag together with a sufficient number of reserve members. Relevant proposals shall be made by the parties and groups represented in the Volkskammer.

(2) The persons elected shall become members of the 11th German Bundestag by virtue of a statement of acceptance delivered to the President of the Volkskammer, but not until the accession takes effect. The President of the Volkskammer shall without delay communicate the result of the election, together with the statement of acceptance, to the President of the German Bundestag.

(3) The eligibility for election to, and loss of membership of, the 11th German Bundestag shall otherwise be subject to the provisions of the Federal Election Act as promulgated on 1 September 1975 (Federal Law Gazette I, p. 2325) and last amended by the Act of 29 August 1990 (Federal Law Gazette II, p. 813).

In the event of cessation of membership, the member concerned shall be replaced by the next person on the reserve list. He must belong to the same party as, at the time of his election, the member whose membership has ceased. The reserve member to take his seat in the German Bundestag shall, before the accession takes effect, be determined by the President of the Volkskammer, and thereafter by the President of the German Bundestag.

Article 44
Preservation of Rights

Rights arising from this Treaty in favour of the German Democratic Republic or the Länder named in Article 1 of this Treaty may be asserted by each of these Länder after the accession has taken effect.

Article 45
Entry into Force of the Treaty

(1) This Treaty, including the attached Protocol and Annexes I to III, shall enter into force on the day on which the Governments of the Federal Republic of Germany and the German Democratic Republic have informed each other that the internal requirements for such entry into force have been fulfilled.

(2) The Treaty shall remain valid as federal law after the accession has taken effect.

Done at Berlin on 31 August 1990 in duplicate in the German language.

For the
Federal Republic of Germany
Dr Wolfgang Schäuble

For the
German Democratic Republic
Dr Günther Krause

Appendix C: A Post-Divisional Europe in the Year 2000

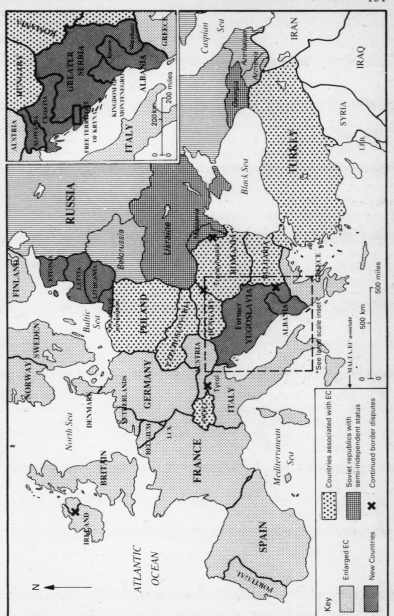

Endnotes

Introduction

1. Kenneth N. Waltz, *Theory of International Politics* (Reading, MA: Addison-Wesley, 1979), P. 190. States tend to be more motivated to protect the values they already have than to gain new ones: "The result is that protecting the status quo usually is easier than changing it; negative victories are more likely than positive ones." Quoted from Robert Jervis, "Implications of the Nuclear Revolutions," (unpublished paper, December 23, 1988).

2. The origins of the Cold War—and the division of Europe—are highly debated issues in the field of international politics in the postwar era. See Louis J. Halle, *The Cold War as History* (New York: Harper & Row, 1967); Arthur J. Schlesinger, "Origins of the Cold War," *Foreign Affairs* 46 (October 1967); Walter Lafeber, *America, Russia, and the Cold War*, 5th ed. (New York: Alfred Knopf, 1985); Wilfried Loth, *The Division of the World: 1941–1955* (London: Routledge, 1988). For a Soviet view, see Mikhail Gorbachev, *Perestroika* (New York: Harper & Row, 1987), pp. 192–193.

3. See Wolfgang Heisenberg, *Strategic Stability and Nuclear Deterrence in East–West Relations*, Institute for East–West Security Studies Occasional Paper Series, no. 10 (New York, 1989).

4. See Robert D. Blackwill, "Conceptual Problems of Conventional Arms Control," *International Security* 12, no. 4 (Spring 1988), pp. 28–47.

5. There are several well-documented descriptions of the February 1945 meeting of Joseph Stalin, Winston Churchill and Franklin Delano Roosevelt in Yalta. For a traditional scholarly interpretation, see Diane Shaver Clemens, *Yalta* (Oxford: Oxford University Press, 1970). For a recent analysis of the Yalta legacy from the East European point of view, see Ferenc Feher, "Eastern Europe's Long Revolution Against Yalta," *Eastern European Politics and Societies* 2, no. 1 (Winter 1988), pp. 1–34.

6. Lincoln Gordon et al., *Eroding Empire: Western Relations with Eastern Europe* (Washington, DC: The Brookings Institution, 1987), p. 13.

7. Zbigniew Brzezinski, *Game Plan* (Boston: The Atlantic Monthly Press, 1986) p. 197. In general terms, security means the relative absence of threat. In international relations, security can be identified as the relative absence of the threat of armed conflict, i.e., war. Security rests primarily on both political and military stability. Political stability means that there is no incentive for armed conflict on the political level, either because no major tensions exist that would require a military solution, or because the peaceful solution of conflicts has become a regular and accepted pattern of international relations. Military stability means that no state could hope to gain reasonable results by employing military

force. In the Cold War era, political stability was lacking but military stability, based upon the ability to deter aggression, prevented the outbreak of war. European security will be served if both political and military stability are high. One could say that if political stability decreases, military stability should remain high. Nevertheless the key factor in European security today is the direction of political change.

8. See K. J. Holsti, "Change in the International System: Interdependence, Integration, and Fragmentation," in *Change in the International System*, ed. Ole R. Holsti, Randolph M, Silverson and Alexander M. George (Boulder, CO: Westview Press, 1984).

9. This study approaches the process of dismantling of the Cold War structure also in "organic terms." This conceptualization draws on both the ecological perspective on international relations and on the perspective on the stable world order configured by, instance, Reinhold Niebuhr and George F. Kennan. See Reinhold Niebuhr, *Nations and Empires* (London: Faber and Faber, 1959), pp. 256–266. See also Alpo Rusi, "Assessing International Politics from an Organic Perspective," *Ulkopolitükka*, 1990, no. 1, pp. 40–46. The concept will be further elaborated in this book. In addition, see, for instance, Harold and Margaret Sprout, *Toward a Politics of the Planet Earth* (New York: Van Norstrand Reinhold, 1971), pp. 27, 30; Dennis Pirages, "The Ecological Perspective on International Relations," in *The Global Agenda*, 2nd edition, ed. Charles W. Kegley, Jr., and Eugene R. Wittkopf (New York: Random House, 1988), pp. 339–344. See also Kenneth W. Thompson, *Winston Churchill's World View* (Baton Rouge: Louisiana State University Press, 1983), p. 305. In regard to the concept of an organic state, see Zbigniew Brzezinski, *In Quest of National Security* (Boulder, CO: Westview, 1988), pp. 139, 194–196.

10. For details see Anders Stephanson, *Kennan and The Art of Foreign Policy* (Cambridge, MA: Harvard University Press, 1989), p. 117. Kennan is a strong proponent of thinking about international relations in organic terms.

I THE STATUS QUO PLUS

1 The Conflict in Retrospect

1. For a discussion of postwar superpower relations see, for example, Richard J. Barnet, "Why Trust the Soviets?" *World Policy Journal* 1, no. 3 (Spring 1984), pp. 461–482.

2. For a brief overview of postwar plans for the restoration of Europe, see, for example, Richard J. Barnet, *The Alliance* (New York: Simon & Schuster, 1983), especially pp. 95–143.

3. Andrei Zhdanov in his report to the conference of representatives of the Communist parties of Yugoslavia, Bulgaria, Hungary, Poland, the Soviet Union, France, Czechoslovakia and Italy in Schreiberhau, Poland, September 22–27, 1947 (Moscow: Inostrannaia Literatura, 1948), p. 16.

4. Quoted from Ernst Kux, "Soviet Reaction to the Revolution in Eastern Europe" (paper presented at conference on "Towards a New Eastern Europe," 1990, Bellagio, Italy).

5. Ibid.

6. See Boris Meissner, *Die "Breshnew-Doktrin"*, (Köln: Dokumentation, 1969). Regarding postwar patterns of Soviet control of Eastern Europe, see Zbigniew Brzezinski, *The Soviet Bloc: Unity and Conflict*, rev. ed. (Cambridge, MA: Harvard University Press, 1967), pp. 104–137. See also Christopher Jones, *Soviet Influence in Eastern Europe: Political Autonomy and the Warsaw Pact*, (New York: Praeger, 1981), pp. 1–4.

7. Quoted in Stanley R. Sloan, *East–West Relations in Europe* (Foreign Policy Association Headline Series, March/April 1986), pp. 5–6. For a brief analytical overview of the most recent scholarly debate that tries to combine both Eastern and Western approaches, see Allen Lynch, "Is the Cold War Over . . . Again?" (unpublished manuscript).

8. By definition, the "original" Cold War was based on a hostile relationship between two political–ideological systems, and that relationship was characterized by three developments: 1) the militarization of the relationship; 2) the globalization of commitments; and 3) ideological hysteria. This is the thesis of Allen Lynch in "Is the Cold War Over . . . Again?"

9. Quoted in Ralph B. Levering, *The Cold War, 1945 to 1972* (Arlington Heights: Harlan Davidson, 1982), p. 15.

10. Ibid.

11. See, for example, Zbigniew Brzezinski, "The Future of Yalta," *Foreign Affairs* 63, no. 2 (Winter 1984/85), pp. 279–302, and "A Proposition the Soviets Shouldn't Refuse," *The New York Times*, March 13, 1989.

12. Harto Hakovirta, *East–West Conflict and European Neutrality* (New York: Oxford University Press, 1988), pp. 37–44.

13. Regarding postwar bipolarity as a basis for a stable peace order, see John Lewis Gaddis, "The Long Peace: Elements of Stability in the Postwar International System," *International Security* 10, no. 4 (Spring 1986), pp. 99–142.

14. Michael Mandelbaum, "Is the Cold War Over?" *Foreign Affairs* 68, no. 2 (Spring 1989), pp. 16–36.

15. Lynch, "Is the Cold War Over . . . Again?"

16. See for example André Fontaine, *History of the Cold War* (New York: Vintage, 1970), pp. 11–24. The concept of the Cold War was introduced to the public debate by the noted American Bernard Baruch in 1947, but it had already been making the rounds in Western capitals in 1945–1946.

17. The Americans realized in the spring of 1947 that Europe was on the verge of economic collapse. Secretary of State George Marshall was convinced that the Soviet leaders had a political interest in seeing the economies of Western Europe fail under anything other than communist leadership. For a brilliant background to the Marshall Plan preparations, see George F. Kennan, *Memoirs: 1925–1950* (Boston: Little, Brown, 1967), p. 388. Scholarly interest in the Marshall Plan has been strong. For a brief overview of the most recent literature, see William Diebold, Jr., "The Marshall Plan in Retrospect: A Review of

Recent Scholarship," *Journal of International Affairs* 41, no. 2 (1988), pp. 421–435.

18. George F. Kennan ("Mr X"), "The Sources of Soviet Conduct," *Foreign Affairs* 25 (July 1947), pp. 566–582.

19. Kennan, *Memoirs, 1925–1950*, p. 417. War and conquest have played a large part in shaping modern Europe. The European state system from the outset was characterized by war. The 1648 Treaty of Westphalia, which laid down the basis for that system, was certainly not the work of Germans. The treaty enshrined and made permanent German disunity by creating "the mosaic of petty States which conventionally forms the immemorial background of Germany," as A. J. P. Taylor characterizes the issue. The paradox of history demonstrated its triumph during the coming centuries in the numerous small German states that remained outsiders for decades in the European war games. The inhabitants of these states escaped the burdens of military service and taxation. In addition, German culture and art remained free from absolutism and militarism—but, as Taylor puts it, "free from reality" too. Indeed, the German states owed their existence not to German sentiment but to the determination of the great powers, Russia, France and Britain. It can be said that throughout modern European history, the basic geopolitical problem has remained by and large the same: Russia, France and Britain have constituted nationally unified great powers, and Germany, although "great" in terms of size, economic power and cultural innovation, has been subject to disunity, and as a consequence, has held equal footing with other great powers only temporarily. For a comprehensive analysis of the history of Germany in Europe, see A. J. P. Taylor, *Europe: Grandeur and Decline* (London: Penguin, 1971), in particular pp. 121–123.

20. For the most judicious treatment of the origins of the division of Europe, see John Lewis Gaddis, *Strategies of Containment* (New York: Oxford University Press, 1982). In fact, at the end of the war neither superpower had a clear conception of Germany's future.

21. Quoted from Gaddis, *Strategies of Containment*, p. 75.

22. Kennan, *Memoirs, 1925–1950*, p. 448.

23. Ibid.

24. Gaddis, *Strategies of Containment*, p. 88.

25. For a responsible discussion, see Adam Ulam, *Expansion and Coexistence*, 2nd ed. (New York: Praeger, 1974), pp. 504–514, 535–537. As late as March 19, 1952, Stalin expected that Germany could be unified at some point. In Stalin's view, a "Rapallo" policy—the Russo-German agreement in the 1920s—would have offered a number of advantages. First of all, a neutral Germany could form part of a group of neutral states that could act as a "Cordon Stalinaire" between the Soviet sphere of influence and the West. See F. Stephen Larrabee, "The View from Moscow," in *The Two German States and European Security*, ed. F. Stephen Larrabee (New York: St. Martin's Press, for the Institute for East–West Security Studies, 1989), pp. 184–185.

26. See Larrabee, "The View from Moscow," p. 186. Wilfried Loth argues that the Soviet Union accepted the division of Germany after the

disturbances in East Berlin in June 1953. See Wilfried Loth, *The Division of the World: 1941–1955*. Loth emphasizes that both superpower conflict and the subsequent formation of European blocs were a result of the hopes and fears aroused by consideration of the German problem.

27. Eric G. Frey provides a brief overview of the postwar West German foreign policy in *Division and Detente*, pp. 3–7, as does George F. Kennan in *Memoirs, 1950–1963* (New York: Pantheon, 1972), pp. 229–266. See also George F. Kennan, *The German Problem: A Personal View* (Washington, DC: American Institute of Contemporary German Studies, Johns Hopkins University, 1989), pp. 2–3.

28. Helga Haftendorn, *Security and Detente: Conflicting Priorities in German Foreign Policy* (New York: Praeger, 1985), p. 60.

29. In the final analysis Adenauer's Deutschlandpolitik was characterized by a dual nature and followed contradictory designs. In rhetoric and ideology, reunification was a sine qua non. Meanwhile, Adenauer adopted a policy that made reunification essentially impossible: Western integration. In the future this dualism was, however, subject to permanent testing, which the policy of Ostpolitik—and the de facto end of the process of isolation—triggered in the late 1960s. See, for example, Frey, *Division and Detente*, pp. 4–5.

30. For an overview of European history, and Germany's role in Europe, see Gordon A. Craig, *Europe Since 1815* (New York: Holt & Winston, 1974); Anton DePorte, *Europe Between the Superpowers: The Enduring Balance*, 2nd ed. (New Haven: Yale University Press, 1986).

31. Haftendorn, *Security and Detente*, p. 2.

32. In a historical perspective, the so-called German question was, and to a certain extent still is, how to constrain Germany so that it could not seek European hegemony from its Central European base. Regarding the role of geopolitics in German history, see, for example, Hans J. Morgenthau, *Politics Among Nations*, 5th ed. (New York: Alfred Knopf, 1978), pp. 164–165.

33. Haftendorn, *Security and Detente*, p. 3.

34. Ibid, p. 4.

35. Ibid., p. 6. By the mid-1950s the institutional organization of the two military alliances had been completed, with the two German states included in them. On the evolution of the European postwar system, see F. Roy Willis, *France, Germany and the New Europe, 1945–1963* (Palo Alto, CA: Stanford University Press, 1965); Alfred Grosser, *The Western Alliance: European–American Relations since 1945* (New York: Continuum Publishing, 1980); and David P. Calleo, *Beyond American Hegemony* (New York: Basic Books, 1987).

36. See Catherine McArdle Kelleher, "Germany and NATO: The Enduring Bargain," in *West Germany's Foreign Policy: 1949–1979*, ed. Wolfram F. Hanrieder (Boulder, CO: Westview, 1980), pp. 43–60.

37. See Haftendorn, *Security and Detente*, p. 9.

38. Ibid., p. 68.

39. The Soviet leaders used nuclear blackmail repeatedly during the Berlin crisis of 1958–1959. Soviet Foreign Minister Gromyko stated on Christmas Day, 1958 that "any provocation in West Berlin" could start "a big

war, in the crucible of which millions upon millions of people would perish and which would bring devastation incomparably more serious than the last world war. The flames of war would inevitably reach the American continent." Quoted from Halle, *The Cold War as History*, p. 353.

40. See, for example, Haftendorn, *Security and Detente*, p. 68.

41. See Halle, *The Cold War as History*, p. 359.

42. For the FRG, the building of the Berlin Wall in August 1961 meant, at least temporarily, the breakdown of a long-term reunification concept that had been based on maintaining an "open status quo." For a more detailed analysis of the construction of the Berlin Wall, see Haftendorn, *Security and Detente*, pp. 76–78. The building of the wall was ordered by the GDR in a declaration of August 12, 1961, which was based on a Warsaw Pact resolution of the same day.

43. In regard to the impact of the Cuban and Berlin crises on international politics and East–West relations in particular, see, for example, Robert J. Jordan and Werner J. Feld, *Europe in the Balance* (London and Boston: Faber and Faber, 1986), pp. 211–264.

44. Lynch, "Is the Cold War Over . . . Again?" For a comprehensive analysis of the impact of the Berlin crisis on FRG–U.S. relations and as a source of permanent mistrust, see Walter Lafeber, *The American Age: United States Foreign Policy at Home and Abroad Since 1750* (New York and London: W. W. Norton, 1989), pp. 565–566.

2 The Rise of Detente

1. Urho Kekkonen, *President's View* (London: Heinemann, 1982), pp. 114–115.

2. Regarding the Finnish–Soviet "note crisis" of the fall of 1961, see Max Jakobson, *Veteen Piirretty Viiva* (Helsinki: Otava, 1980), pp. 247–292. Jakobson does not insist that the Soviets would have threatened to deploy—in compliance with the 1948 Finnish–Soviet Treaty on Friendship, Cooperation and Mutual Assistance—nuclear weapons on Finnish territory. President Kekkonen, in fact, bluntly disputed speculations about the possibility that the Soviets would have sent a note to Helsinki in order to get permission to deploy Soviet nuclear weapons on Finnish soil after his arrival from Novosibirsk. Yet these speculations have never really ceased. In fact, Kekkonen's initiative to establish a nuclear-free zone in Scandinavia could be seen as a logical step toward a multilateral arrangement to eliminate the deployment option definitively. Of course, Finland would not permit the deployment, although no agreement could be reached on the zone. For a Finnish scholarly work dealing with the "note crisis," see Risto E. J. Penttila, *Finland's Search for Security Through Defence, 1944–89* (London: Macmillan, 1990), pp. 93–110. See also Alpo Rusi, "The Note Crisis as an Incident of Nuclear Politics" (in Finnish), *Turun Sanomat*, April 8, 1990. With respect to Soviet military policy in the early 1960s, see, for example, Raymond L. Garthoff, *Soviet Military Policy* (London: Faber and Faber, 1966), pp. 113–123.

3. Kenneth Dyson, ed., *European Detente* (New York: St. Martin's Press, 1986), p. 4.

4. Ibid., pp. 5–6.

5. See Hakovirta, *East–West Conflict and European Neutrality*, pp. 40–41. It can be stated that detente sought to broaden the terms of East–West debate beyond ideological and military categories to the political balance of interest. But this kind of "enlightened" philosophy of detente was developed much later.

6. See, for example, Paul Kennedy, *The Rise and Fall of the Great Powers* (New York: Random House, 1987), p. 339, or more generally, Willy Brandt, *People and Politics: The Years 1960–1975*, (Boston: Little, Brown, 1978).

7. See Dyson, *European Detente*, p. 11.

8. John Erickson, "The Soviet Union and European Detente," in *European Detente*, ed. Dyson, pp. 172–197. In the 1960s and 1970s, in the Soviet perspective, detente embodied elements of both cooperation and conflict; hence it can be regarded as only a modus vivendi between the two antagonistic systems. Detente even involves an intensification of ideological competition while the increasingly pointless arms race is phased out and subjected to monitoring. See Klaus von Beyme, *The Soviet Union in World Politics* (New York: St. Martin's Press, 1987), p. 65.

9. For brief accounts of the development of the CSCE process, see Kenneth Dyson, "The CSCE: Europe Before and After the Helsinki Final Act," in *European Detente*, ed. Dyson, pp. 83–112; and John Borawski, *From the Atlantic to the Urals* (New York: Pergamon Brassey's, 1986), pp. 6–11.

10. Lafeber, *The American Age*, pp. 588–589. It has been emphasized in U.S. scholarly works about postwar U.S. diplomacy that the seeds of detente were sown in 1967–1968, when U.S. forces suffered setbacks in Vietnam. According to this interpretation, "detente did not signal an American retreat from world affairs but was a new—and necessary—tactic for carrying traditional containment policy." See Lafeber, *America, Russia and the Cold War*, p. 253. Detente began a bit earlier, however; see the next chapter for details.

11. See Erickson, "The Soviet Union and European Detente," in *European Detente*, ed. Dyson, pp. 176–177.

12. Borawski, *From the Atlantic to the Urals*, pp. 8–9.

13. See J. Sizoo and R. T. Jurrjens, *CSCE Decision-Making: The Madrid Experience* (The Hague, Boston and Lancaster: Martinus Nijhoff Publishers, 1983), pp. 24–27; see also Borawski, *From the Atlantic to the Urals*, pp. 8–9.

14. Quoted from J. Sizoo and R. T. Jurrjens, *CSCE Decision-Making*, p. 27. The CSCE process will be dealt with in greater detail later in this study. In May 1969, the Finnish government sent a memorandum to 32 governments, including those of the United States and Canada, offering to act as host for an East–West European security conference. The Finnish government argued that its initiative was completely independent because Finland was a small neutral state and because its action was taken out of a sense of responsibility for "the peaceful development

of Europe." On the bases of the responses to the memorandum, the Finnish government appointed Ambassador Ralph Enckell, a highly esteemed career diplomat, to visit the capitals of all the countries involved to further elaborate the agenda and other details related to the conference. Ambassador Enckell's "shuttle diplomacy" was successful and on the basis of his report the Finnish government sent invitations to 35 countries to meet in Espoo, a town near Helsinki, to discuss the details of convening the CSCE in the fall of 1972. For the documents related to the preliminary talks on the CSCE, see Leo Tujunen, "A Conference on European Security? Background to the Finnish Government's Proposal," *European Review* 19, no. 4 (Autumn 1969), pp. 15–16.

15. For a classical analysis of this type, see Arnold Horelick and Myron Rush, *Strategic Power and Soviet Foreign Policy* (Chicago: University of Chicago Press, 1966), chapters 11 and 12.

16. See Graham Allison, *Essence of Decision: Explaining the Cuban Missile Crisis* (Boston: Little, Brown, 1971), in particular, pp. 45–46. Allison tried to place the Cuban missile crisis in a wider and much more complicated context, which rules out simplistic and clear-cut explanations of the crisis.

17. This observation was made by Charles R. Planck in *The Changing Status of German Unification in Western Diplomacy, 1946–1966* (Baltimore: Johns Hopkins University Press, 1967), pp. 43–44. See also Timothy W. Stanley and Darnell M. Whitt, *Detente Diplomacy: The United States and European Security in the 1970s* (New York: The Dunellen Publishing Company, 1970), p. 29.

18. On the Kennedy administration's hopes for detente, see Arthur Schlesinger, *A Thousand Days: John F. Kennedy in the White House* (Boston: Houghton Mifflin, 1965), pp. 891–892. In the late 1950s and early 1960s, an academic theory of convergence encouraged such hopes. Briefly, the convergence theory hypothesized that both the socialist and capitalist socioeconomic systems could, in the longer term, approach each other and constitute a "unified" system. John Kenneth Galbraith, one of the proponents of the theory, was close to President Kennedy. For a classical examination of convergence, see Zbigniew Brzezinski and Samuel Huntington, *Political Power: USA/USSR* (New York: Viking Press, 1965), pp. 419–436.

19. Calleo, *Beyond American Hegemony*, p. 50.

20. Ibid., p. 51. Regarding the motivations for de Gaulle's "Europeanism," see also Kennedy, *The Rise and Fall of the Great Powers*, pp. 400–401. For a historical analysis of France's European policy between 1945 and the mid-1960s, see, for example, Hans A. Schmitt, *European Union: From Hitler to de Gaulle* (New York: Van Nostrand Reinhold, 1969), pp. 78–83.

21. Stanley and Whitt, *Detente Diplomacy*, p. 30.

22. For a general study of West German Ostpolitik under Kurt Georg Kiesinger and Willy Brandt, see William Griffith, *The Ostpolitik of the Federal Republic of Germany* (Cambridge, MA: MIT Press, 1978). See also Boris Meissner, *Die Deutsche Ostpolitik 1961–1970* (Köln: Verlag Wissenschaft und Politik, 1970).

23. Kennedy, *The Rise and Fall of the Great Powers*, pp. 400–401.

24. Frank A. Ninkovich, *Germany and the United States* (Boston: Twayne, 1988), p. 151.

25. The so-called Harmel Exercise was initiated in 1966 by the Belgian Foreign Minister Pierre Harmel. There was a great deal of West German input in the exercise, and Willy Brandt was particularly influential in its formulation. For an in-depth analysis of the formulation of the report, see Haftendorn, *Security and Detente*, pp. 117–123. The Harmel Report will be dealt with again later in this book.

26. For the text of the Harmel Report, see *Texts of Final Communiques Issued by Ministerial Sessions of the North Atlantic Council, the Defense Planning Committee, and the Nuclear Planning* (Brussels: NATO Information Service, 1975), pp. 198–202. For a discussion, see Roger Morgan, *The United States and West Germany: A Study in Alliance Politics* (Oxford: Oxford University Press, 1974), pp. 179–180.

27. This book does not deal in greater detail with the process of rapprochement between the two German states in 1969–1973, but does try to define its status within the general process of detente in Europe. For discussion, see Helmut Kistler, *Die Ostpolitik der Bundesrepublik Deutschland, 1966–1973* (Bonn: Bundeszentrals für Politische Bildung, 1982), pp. 27–28.

28. Richard Lowenthal, "The German Question Transformed," *Foreign Affairs* 63, no. 2 (Winter 1984-85) pp. 307–308.

29. See W. Richard Smyser, "American Interests and the German–German Dialogue," in *The Two-German States*, ed. Larrabee, pp. 212–213.

30. Quoted in Renata Fritsch-Bournazel, "The Changing Nature of the German Question," in *The Two German States*, ed. Larrabee, p. 52.

31. Willy Brandt, *People and Politics*, p. 99. On U.S. suspicions regarding Ostpolitik, see Henry Kissinger, *The White House Years* (Boston: Little Brown, 1979), pp. 408–409. See also Kissinger's discussions of Bahr, Brandt and Ostpolitik in the second volume of his memoirs, *Years of Upheaval* (Boston: Little, Brown, 1982), pp. 144–147.

32. Ninkovitch, *Germany and the United States*, p. 150.

33. For further discussion, see Alpo Rusi, "Finlandization without Finland?" in *Yearbook of Finnish Foreign Policy, 1987* (Helsinki: Finnish Institute of International Affairs, 1988), pp. 13–16.

34. Quoted from Rusi, "Finlandization Without Finland?" p. 14. From the outset of the Finlandization debate, it was clear that Finland itself had little to do with the essence of the term. Finland was never Finlandized; rather, it functioned as a Western image of the situation that might occur if the Soviet peace campaign successfully "softened" the Western policy toward the Soviet Union and Western strategy overemphasized detente instead of military preparedness.

35. See the interview with Honecker in *The New York Times*, November 25, 1972; and his closing address to the eighth meeting of the Central Committee of the SED (Socialist Unity Party of Germany), *Neues Deutschland*, December 8, 1972. See Haftendorn, *Security and Detente*, p. 229.

36. Statement by Foreign Minister Walter Scheel on the day of the signing of the Basic Treaty, November 7, 1972, in Haftendorn, *Security and Detente*, p. 230.
37. On the increasing support for Ostpolitik, see Gebhard L. Schweigler, *National Consciousness in Divided Germany* (Beverly Hills: Sage, 1975), p. 144 ff; for various pertinent opinion polls see Elizabeth Noelle-Neumann, *The Germans: Public Opinion Polls, 1967–1980*, rev. ed. (Westport, CT: Greenwood Press, 1981), pp. 119 ff.
38. For a detailed analysis of the domestic process of the approval of Ostpolitik in the FRG, see Haftendorn, *Security and Detente*, p. 230.
39. Address by Chancellor Willy Brandt to the fifth Franco-German conference of Chambers of Commerce in Hamburg, September 3, 1971, in *Bundeskanzler Brandt: Reden und Interviews* (Bonn: Press und Informationsamt des Bundesregierung, 1971), pp. 326–332.
40. This is particularly evident in retrospect. See, for example, William E. Griffith, "The Security Policies of the Social Democrats and the Greens in the FRG," in *Security Perspectives of the West German Left*, ed. William Griffith et al. (Washington, DC: Pergamon-Brassey's, 1989), pp. 1–20, particularly p. 1.
41. Kissinger, *Years of Upheaval*, pp. 144–147.
42. Ibid., pp. 146–148.
43. Indeed, Henry Kissinger delivered his first major foreign policy speech on the "Year of Europe" on April 23, 1973, in which he announced an unequivocal U.S. commitment to the promotion of East–West interaction. Kissinger also expressed his support for "European unity," which in essence meant supporting the maintenance of the status quo and the division of Europe. For details, see Kissinger, *Years of Upheaval*, pp. 151–154.
44. The CSCE took place in several phases between July 3, 1973 and August 1, 1975, in Helsinki, Geneva and Helsinki again. The Final Act, signed in Helsinki in 1975, included the renunciation of the use of force and the possibility of peaceful alteration of borders—in fact, the cornerstones of Ostpolitik. On the U.S. motivations and doubts regarding the CSCE, see, for example, Kissinger, *Years of Upheaval* pp. 710, 1124–1125.
45. Haftendorn, *Security and Detente*, p. 246.

II CHANGE IN EUOPE

1. The "security community" concept was introduced by Richard W. Van Wagenen in his *Research in the International Organization Field: Some Notes on a Possible Focus* (Princeton, NJ: Princeton University Center for Research on World Political Institutions, 1952).
2. Robert Gilpin, *War and Change in World Politics* (New York: Cambridge University Press, 1981), p. 9.
3. Kennedy, *The Rise and Fall of the Great Powers*, pp. 536–537. There is strong evidence to show that the West has been unwilling to support any

major change in Europe since 1956. "Western desire for stability has prevailed over Western interest in changing the European order," according to Gregory Flynn in "Problems in Paradigm," *Foreign Policy* 74 (Spring 1989), pp. 63–84.

4. See Dieter Senghaas, *Die Zukunft Europas: Probleme der Friedens-gestaltung* (Frankfurt-am-Main: Suhrkamp, 1987), p. 7. See also *Beyond 1992: U.S. Strategy Toward the European Community*, Final Report of the CSIS Steering Committee on the Strategic Implications of EC 1992, (Washington D.C.: CSIS, 1990). The report states as follows: "The U.S. lag in grasping these changes [in particular the emergence of the EC as a political power center, etc.] did not signify a lack of interest in Europe during the 1980s but rather a primary focus on a European security agenda. Not only did NATO provide the dominant framework for U.S. involvement in Europe, but also the most important challenges seemed to be in the realm of security."

3 The Europeanization of the East–West System

1. On the structural components of the East–West system, see Ray Maghroori and Bennett Ramberg, *Globalism Versus Realism: International Relations' Third Debate* (Boulder, CO: Westview, 1982), p. 223.
2. See Holsti, *Change in the International System*, pp. 23–54. Regarding the origins of the theory of interdependence, see Robert O. Keohane and Joseph Nye, "Complex Interdependence, Transnational Relations, and Realism: Alternative Perspectives on World Politics," in *The Global Agenda: Issues and Perspectives*, ed. Kegley and Wittkopf, pp. 257–271.
3. François Heisbourg, "The General State of European Security" in *Conventional Arms Control and East–West Security*, ed. Robert D. Blackwill and F. Stephen Larrabee, IEWSS Research Volume (Durham and London: Duke University Press, 1989) p. 1.
4. Lafeber, *The American Age*, p. 618.
5. Interview with Henry Kissinger in *U.S. News & World Report*, March 15, 1976, p. 28; see also Lafeber, *The American Age*, p. 620. In fact, the superpower rivalry became more global in the heyday of the detente years, 1972–1974. President Nixon used his "China card" shrewdly against Leonid Brezhnev, hindering the Soviet Union from further gains in the developing world. Further analysis of international development goes beyond the scope of this book; however, regarding European security, superpower relations no longer played as important a role as at the end of the 1960s.
6. In regard to Western doubts vis-à-vis the CSCE, see, for instance, Philip Williams, "Britain, Detente and the CSCE," in *European Detente*, ed. Dyson, pp. 221–236. On the *Foreign Affairs* editorial and similar views, see Rusi, "Finlandization Without Finland?" in *Yearbook of Finnish Foreign Policy, 1987*, pp. 13–16.
7. See Flora Lewis, "Peace and its Implications," *The New York Times*, June 1, 1989. Henry Kissinger, for example, does not consider the Kennedy era to constitute any kind of beginning of superpower

rapprochement: "The Kennedy era will be seen as the last flowering of the previous era rather than as the beginning of a new era," *Department of State Bulletin*, May 12, 1975, p. 606.

8. See Lafeber, *The American Age*, pp. 637–638.

9. By the term system, as a key concept related to systemic changes, etc., this study refers to the network of interactions (political, economic, cultural and otherwise) that knits a group of states together into an integrated unit with regard to the external world.

10. *International Herald Tribune*, January 29, 1990.

11. See Sizoo and Jurrjens, *CSCE Decision-Making*, pp. 23–48.

12. See Margarita Mathiapoulos, "Neither Barbarian nor Angel of Peace. The Common European Home: Resurrection of Change through Rapprochement" (paper prepared for the Aspen Institute Berlin Study Group on "A Common European Home" within the CSCE process, September 21–25, 1988, Paris).

13. See, for example, Robert Jervis, "From Balance to Concert: A Study of International Security Cooperation," *World Politics* 38 (October 1985), pp. 58–79. For a general discussion of the problems of cooperation in the absence of supranational sovereignty, see Robert Jervis, "Cooperation under the Security Dilemma," *World Politics* 30 (January 1978), pp. 167–214.

14. Eric G. Frey, *Division and Detente*, p. 77.

15. See S. J. Flanagan, "The CSCE and the Development of Detente," in *European Security: Prospects for the 1980s*, ed. Derek Leebaert (Lexington, MA: Heath, 1979), p. 190. Ernst Kux concludes that "the turning point for the Eastern European countries and for their relations with the Soviet overlord was reached at the CSCE. For the first time they were allowed to act at least in outside appearance as equal and independent partners in the circle of the 35 participants of the CSCE." In 1976, Brezhnev agreed at a conference of 29 European Communist and Workers Parties in East Berlin to new principles for the relations between "the fraternal parties." In fact, these new principles to a certain extent abrogated indirectly the Brezhnev Doctrine. Such abrogation was requested, for example, by the so-called Eurocommunists. See Kux, "Soviet Reaction to the Revolution in Eastern Europe," pp. 7–8.

16. See, for instance, "Soviets Propose Three-Stage Cuts in European Arms," *The New York Times*, March 7, 1989. See also Markku Reina, "The Significance of the CSCE Yesterday and Now," in *Yearbook of Finnish Foreign Policy, 1989* (Helsinki: Finnish Institute of International Affairs, 1990), pp. 20–25.

17. See also Otmar Hoell, "Cooperation within the CSCE Context," in *CSCE: N + N Perspectives*, ed. Hanspeter Neuhold (Vienna: W. Bramueller, 1987), p. 127.

18. In the longer term, the CSCE will at least remain a "safety net." If the superpowers were once again to break off their dialogue, the CSCE would constitute a forum for East–West interaction to promote detente, as was the case in the early 1980s. See Heinz Gaertner, "Entspannung, Europa und die KSZE-in thematischer Überblick," *Oesterreichische Zeitschrift für Politikwissenschaft* 3 (1986), pp. 245–256.

19. See, for example, Sizoo and Jurrjens, *CSCE Decision-Making*, p. 21. Regarding the development of the confidence-building measures (CBM) regime within the CSCE structure, see Rolf Berg and Daniel Rotfeld, *Building Security in Europe*, Institute for East–West Security Studies Monograph Series, no. 2 (New York, 1985), pp. 24–27 and 76–93.

20. Laszlo Lang, *International Regimes and the Political Economy of East–West Relations*, IEWSS Occasional Paper Series, no. 13 (New York, 1989). Lang does not see the CSCE as playing any significant role in solving East–West trade problems in the future.

21. K.J. Holsti, "Bargaining Theory and Diplomatic Reality: The CSCE Negotiations," *Review of International Studies*, 1982, no. 8, p. 167.

22. Quoted in Michael D. Intriligator and Hans-Adolf Jacobsen, ed. *East–West Conflict* (Boulder, CO: Westview, 1988) p. 14. Interpretations of how the provisions of the Final Act should affect the relations between the signatory powers can be roughly divided into two main types: the Western states see the Final Act as a "code of conduct," while the East sees it as a "political commitment." This division must not be interpreted as waterproof, however, but as a hypothetical assessment of the approaches of various signatory powers to the provisions of the Final Act. See for a brief analysis, Esko Antola, "Order and Change in the CSCE," *Oesterreichische Zeitschrift für Politikwissenschaft*, 1986, no. 3, pp. 271–283.

23. Ibid., pp. 275–276.

24. See for discussion Kennedy, *The Rise and Fall of the Great Powers*, p. 439.

25. Holsti, *Change in the International System*, pp. 23–54.

26. Bruce Russett and Harvey Starr, *World Politics: The Menu for Choice* (New York: W.H. Freeman and Co., 1985), p. 499.

27. Jack Snyder, "The Gorbachev Revolution: A Waning of Soviet Expansionism," *International Security* 12, no. 3 (Winter 1987–88), pp. 93–131. For a timely and critical assessment of the confusion regarding the use of the concept of interdependence and related connotations, in particular if applied in Europe, see Gerhard Wettig, "New Thinking on Security and East–West Relations," *Problems of Communism* 38, no. 1 (January–February 1989), pp. 1–14.

28. A West German opinion poll released in January 1989 said that 88% of those polled do not feel militarily threatened by the Soviet bloc. This kind of change in traditional threat perceptions led to a bitter political debate in the FRG between the opposition party SPD and the government about the repercussions for West German security policy. See Rolf Soderlin, "What if the Cold War Is Over?" *Armed Forces Journal International* (March 1989). Literature on the theory of interdependence is abundant. The theory of interdependence underscores the need to develop international institutions and rules for economic interdependence. See for background, Robert O. Keohane, *After Hegemony: Cooperation and Discord in the World Political Economy* (Princeton: Princeton University Press, 1984), pp. 5–17; this book also contains strong criticism in regard to certain conclusions of the functionalist school of thought. See Oran R. Young, "Interdepen-

dences in World Politics," in *Globalism Versus Realism: International Relations' Third Debate*, ed. Maghroori and Ramberg, pp. 57–79. In regard to the concept of "ecological interdependence" and some other new trends toward interdependence, see Marvin S. Soroos, "Global Interdependence and the Responsibilities of States: Learning from the Japanese Experience," *Journal of Peace Research* 25, no. 1 (1988), pp. 17–29.

29. Charles Yost, *The Insecurity of Nations: International Relations in the Twentieth Century* (New York: Praeger, 1968), pp. 50–51.

30. Quoted from Philip Hanson, *Western Economic Statecraft in East–West Relations*, Royal Institute of International Affairs Chatham House Papers 40 (London, 1988). In regard to the concept of "economic security," see, for instance, Laszlo Lang, "International Financial Security: Concepts and Outlines," *Kuelpolitika* (1988), pp. 83–101.

31. Hanson, *Western Economic Statecraft in East–West Relations*.

32. Ibid., pp. 19–25.

33. Jozsef Bognar, "Economic Forces in the History of East–West Relations," in *Technology and Change in East–West Relations*, ed. F. Stephen Larrabee, IEWSS Monograph Series, no. 6 (New York, 1988), pp. 165–180.

34. Angela E. Stent, "East–West Economic Relations: An East–West or a West–West Problem?" in *Europe and the Superpowers*, ed. Stephen Bethlen and Ivan Volgyes (Boulder, CO: Westview, 1985), pp. 141–145.

35. Ellen L. Frost and Angela E. Stent, "NATO's Troubles with East–West Trade," *International Security* 8, no. 1 (Summer 1988), pp. 179–200. See H. J. Seeler, "Die Beziehungen zwischen der Europaeischen Gemeinschaft und dem Rat für gegenseitige Wirtschaftshilfe," *Europa Archiv* 7 (1987), p. 198.

36. Lang, *International Regimes and the Political Economy of East–West Relations*. The current study does not make an in-depth analysis of the state of East–West economic relations, but tries to draw some general conclusions on the questions that may have an impact on the general security situation in Europe. Regarding the general trends of East–West trade, see Hanson, *Western Economic Statecraft in East–West Relations*, pp. 20–25. Of course, in the wake of the 1989 revolutions, the East–West trade setting is rapidly changing. This is due in particular to the reunification of Germany. This development will be assessed later in this volume.

37. Regarding the history of COCOM coordination, see, for instance, Hanson, *Western Economic Statecraft in East–West Relations*, pp. 26–37. See also, *How Should America Respond to Gorbachev's Challenge?*, IEWSS Special Report (New York, 1987), p. 19.

38. Frost and Stent, "NATO's Troubles with East–West Trade," pp. 179–200.

39. In 1987 the already low level of economic interaction between the CMEA and the OECD countries declined further. The proportion of East–West trade in overall international trade declined also from 4% to 3.4% within one year (1987). The German Economic Research Institute (DIW) stated, when publishing East–West trade figures in November

1988, that the CMEA's lack of export potential proved to be its Achilles heel. *Foreign Broadcast Information Service Daily Report—West Europe Update* (FBIS-WEU-88-213), Nov. 12, 1988, p. 3.

40. In the early 1970s, Henry Kissinger espoused the concept of positive linkage as part of his overall approach to detente. He believed that it was possible to use trade effectively as both carrot and stick. His primary goal was to maintain Soviet interest in moderating its foreign policy behavior—in short, to get the Soviet Union permanently committed to detente. Kissinger, *Years of Upheaval*, pp. 985–986. See also Frost and Stent, "NATO's Troubles with East–West Trade," p. 191.

41. Michael Dobroczynski, "Rapprochement of the Peoples of Europe: Difficulties and Prospects," *International Affairs* 63, no. 3 (February 1989), p. 37. See also Jànos Màtyàs Kovàcs, "Reform Economics: The Classification Gap," *Daedalus* 119, no. 1 (Winter 1990), pp. 215–248.

42. See document CSCE/KWZEB. 15/Rev. 1 (Bonn: April 11, 1990).

43. The question of economic integration and its impact on European security will be dealt with in greater detail later in this volume.

4 The Imperatives of Political Change

1. Thompson, *Winston Churchill's World View*, pp. 235–249. There are plenty of definitions of "Europe." In this context, when dealing with an "all-European" perspective, the following clarification is provided: "Eastern" and "Western" Europe are only political terms that refer to the political realities of Europe during the postwar era. They reflect neither geographical nor prewar historical realities but simply a kind of temporary settlement of affairs reflecting to a certain extent socioeconomic realities (which are, however, changing due to other processes). By definition "political Europe" consists of "Eastern" and "Western" Europe, but not as such the two superpowers. In order to cope with the security issues of Europe, the Conference on Security and Cooperation in Europe (CSCE) was created. The CSCE process represents an interplay of these four entities plus the NNA countries (this study emphasizes five entities instead of four as main actors in the CSCE process), while the *core* of the systemic transformation in Europe involves the bridging of the split between Eastern and Western Europe.

2. See Stephanson, *Kennan and the Art of Foreign Policy*, pp. 145–146.

3. See Thompson, *Winston Churchill's World View*, pp. 5, 7, 25, 207 and 310. It is widely agreed among Western scholars that the division of Europe was laid down in the meeting between Churchill and Stalin in Moscow in October 1944. See Feher, "Eastern Europe's Long Revolution against Yalta," pp. 1–34.

4. For details see von Beyme, *The Soviet Union in World Politics*, p. 109. Sonnenfeldt spoke to a group of U.S. ambassadors in an off-the-record State Department briefing in December 1975 and said that "it must be our policy to strive for an evolution that makes the relationship between Eastern Europe and the Soviet Union an organic one . . . . Our policy must be a policy responding to the clearly visible aspirations in Eastern

Europe for a more autonomous existence within the context of a strong Soviet geopolitical influence." Summary of remarks, *The New York Times*, April 6, 1976. See also Gaddis, *Strategies of Containment*, p. 342.

5. Seweryn Bialer, "Harsh Decade: Soviet Policies in the 1980s," *Foreign Affairs* 59, no. 5 (Summer 1981), pp. 999–1020.

6. See Ernst Kux's brilliant analysis, "Soviet Reaction to the Revolution in Eastern Europe," p. 9.

7. Eric Hobsbawm, "1989: To the Victor the Spoils," *The Independent*, October 2, 1990, p. 19.

8. Bulgaria, Czechoslovakia, the GDR, Hungary, Poland and Romania. This paper does not consider Yugoslavia and Albania, each unique in its own way, as part of Eastern Europe.

9. F. Stephen Larrabee, "Eastern Europe: A Generational Change," *Foreign Policy* 70 (Spring 1988), pp. 42–64.

10. See Brzezinski, *The Soviet Bloc: Unity and Conflict*.

11. See Kux, "Soviet Reaction to the Revolution in Eastern Europe," pp. 9–10.

12. See Pierre Hassner, "Soviet Policy in Western Europe: The East European Factor," in *Soviet Policy In Eastern Europe*, ed. Sarah Meiklejohn Terry (New Haven: Yale University Press, 1984).

13. A. Ross Johnson, *The Impact of Eastern Europe on Soviet Policy Toward Western Europe*, A Project Air Force Report. (Santa Monica, CA: The RAND Corporation, March 1986), pp. 4–5.

14. See Paul Marantz, "Changing Soviet Conceptions of International Security" (paper presented at the American Association for the Advancement of Slavic Studies annual meeting, November 19, 1988, Honolulu.

15. Marantz, "Changing Soviet Conceptions of International Security."

16. For discussion, see Lafeber, *The American Age*, pp. 638–639. Lafeber states that Brezhnev's policies "stressed detente with the United States, military support for 'wars of liberation', and at home, the exiling of dissenters to Siberian prisons." Indeed, Brezhnev's policies constituted a combination of a Stalininst world view and Machiavellian power politics applied in a modern world.

17. Quoted from Marantz, "Changing Soviet Conceptions of International Security." For discussion of the changes in Soviet foreign-policy thinking since the end of World War II, see Allen Lynch, *The Soviet Study of International Relations* (Cambridge: Cambridge University Press, 1987).

18. Marantz, "Changing Soviet Conceptions of International Security."

19. H. Fiedler, "Bundnissystem und Vertragsbeziehungen," in *Sowjetunion Aussenpolitik III*, ed. D. Geyer and B. Meissner (Köln: Bohlau, 1976), pp. 130–162, here p. 139).

20. A heated debate was triggered in 1989, particularly in the United States, regarding the internal situation of the Soviet Union. Martin Malia published an article (under the pseudonym Z), which predicted that "further crises will most likely be necessary to produce further, and more real, reforms" in the Soviet Union. See Z, "'To the Stalin Mausoleum," *Daedalus* 199, no. 1 (Winter 1990), pp. 195–344. Z's article was seen in Moscow as an attempt to attack Gorbachev and, in fact, to deepen

national tensions in the Soviet Union. In the winter of 1990 the situation in Lithuania in particular proved at least some of Z's predictions.

21. See, for example, Aurel Braun, "Whither the Warsaw Pact in the Gorbachev Era?" *International Journal* 43 (Winter 1987/1988), pp. 63–105.

22. *The New York Times*, December 12, 1988.

23. Zbigniew Brzezinski, "The Soviet Union: Three Scenarios," *U.S. News & World Report*, April 23, 1990. The problems of the Soviet Union will be further analyzed in the concluding chapter of this book.

24. In most Western analyses it has been underscored that the unity of the Warsaw Pact will certainly remain an inalienable principle of policy throughout the bloc. While this view might be true, it does not necessarily contradict the more far-reaching goal of establishing a new relationship between the Soviet Union and Eastern Europe.

25. For a background analysis of the future of Eastern Europe in light of Gorbachev's efforts, see Timothy Garton Ash, "The Empire in Decay," *The New York Review of Books*, September 29, 1988. On the reorientation of the WTO toward defensive and national postures, see Daniel N. Nelson, "Military Effort in the WTO: Extractive and Performance Dimensions, 1975–85" (unpublished paper prepared at the University of Kentucky, March 1989); Kent D. Lee, "Changes in Soviet Military Doctrine and Changes in Soviet Military History: A Connection?" (unpublished paper, 1989). The situation within the WTO in light of the revolutions of 1989 will be dealt with later in this book.

26. See Stephanson, *Kennan and the Art of Foreign Policy*, pp. 137–141.

27. Ibid., p. 143. Kennan's proposals regarding the reunification of Germany were in the final analysis based on the withdrawal of the occupation forces from German soil. In short, Kennan took the step of proposing a settlement based on "indigenous German rule," which would "avoid congealment of Europe along the present lines." Power had to be given back to the Germans if the division was to be dismantled.

28. Mary N. Hampton, "West German Foreign Policy and the Bifurcation of the Western Security Regime," in *East–West Conflict* ed. Intriligator and Jacobsen, p. 171.

29. Christoph Bertram, "Europe's Security Dilemmas," *Foreign Affairs* 65, no. 5 (Summer 1987), pp. 942–957.

30. A. W. DePorte, "The Atlantic Alliance Won't Die of Its Feud," *The New York Times*, July 30, 1982.

31. A. W. DePorte, *Europe Between the Super Powers*, pp. 190, 198.

32. See CSIS, *Beyond 1992: U.S. Strategy toward the European Community*, p. 40. The concept of political integration (and political union) is often used in a different sense, referring to the creation of a federal European state with common democratic institutions. The EPC will be discussed in detail later. For a historical analysis see C. Hill, *National Foreign Policies and European Political Cooperation* (London: Routledge & Kegan Paul, 1983); Helen Wallace, *Widening and Deepening, the EC and the New European Agenda*, Royal Institute of International Affairs Discussion Paper, no. 23 (London, 1989); Thomas Pedersen, "Problems of Enlarge-

ment: Political Integration in a Pan-European EC," *Cooperation and Conflict* 25 (1990), pp. 83–99.

33. See Baard Bredrup Knudsen, "Europe Between Superpowers: An All-European Model for the End of the 20th Century," *Cooperation and Conflict* 20 (1985), pp. 91–112.

34. The reunification of Germany and its impact on NATO must be omitted from this volume to a large extent because the details of that process are still being negotiated both between the FRG and GDR as well as between the two German states and the Four Powers in the so-called two-plus-four process. This process, however, will be dealt with later in this volume.

35. Lothar Ruehl, "Franco-German Military Cooperation: An Insurance Policy for the Alliance," *Strategic Review* (Summer 1988), pp. 48–54.

36. The debate on the future role of NATO beyond containment and the Cold War was triggered in the aftermath of U.S. President George Bush's visit to NATO headquarters and the FRG in May–June 1989. See "Bush Asks an End to Divided Europe," and "Excerpts from President's Address," *The New York Times*, June 1, 1989. See also "Bush in Europe: Looking to Germans," *The New York Times*, June 2, 1989. For a brief account of the problems of NATO reflecting the challenges stemming from Gorbachev's disarmament and political proposals in regard to Europe, as well as German reunification, see, for example, R. W. Apple, Jr., "Arms and Germany," *The New York Times*, April 29, 1990.

37. As changes in Eastern Europe and the Soviet Union became more concrete, two distinct approaches have emerged in the U.S. debate as to how the West should respond to the risks and opportunities posed by these historic developments. Henry Kissinger proposed a "superpower track" for negotiations on the future of Central Europe. See *The Washington Post*, "A Kissinger Plan for Central Europe," February 12, 1989. Zbigniew Brzezinski, for his part, proposed "some form of East–West dialogue—which could then include American–Soviet dialogue." See, "Has 'Post-Communist Era' Arrived?" *The Christian Science Monitor*, March 20, 1989. Since the end of 1989, however, the U.S. view has become more unified by accepting the developments on "European terms."

38. Robert Jervis, *The Symbolic Nature of Nuclear Politics* (Urbana, IL: University of Illinois at Champaign-Urbana, 1985), p. 6.

39. Marie-France Garaud, "The Lure of the East," *Géopolitique* 21 (Summer 1988).

40. The process of "de-Stalinization" of the Soviet system is one of the major features of Gorbachev's reform policy in general.

41. Quoted from Ronald Steel "Europe's Superpower Problem," *SAIS Review* (Summer 1988), pp. 137–147.

42. The concept of a "common European home" is not new. What is new, however, is Gorbachev's commitment to de Gaulle's concept of Europe "from the Atlantic to the Urals." Yet Gorbachev has further elaborated his design for the concept. He stated before the House of Commons in London in December 1984 that "Europe is our common home [*nash obshchii dom*], a home and not a theater of military operations." In

Gorbachev's understanding, the common European home has remained an open-ended concept. He once proposed a "pan-European roundtable of the best minds to prepare a draft of the 'Common European Home'." Quoted from Stephan Kux, "Soviet–West European Relations: The Promises of a Common European Home" (unpublished paper, The Institute for East–West Security Studies, 1989). In regard to Gorbachev's performance at the Council of Europe, see "Gorbachev Spurns Armed Aggression as Tool in Europe," *The New York Times*, July 7, 1989.

43. De Gaulle's conception of "European Europe" was aimed at undoing the partition of Europe with political means and excluding the superpowers. See, for example Zbigniew Brzezinski, "The Framework for East–West Reconciliation," *Foreign Affairs* 46, no. 2 (1968), pp. 256–275. To a certain extent, the present process of "Europeanization" of European security matters fulfills the criteria of de Gaulle's vision.

44. Ernst Haas has noted that military alliances, even with permanent organs and broad competence, have historically triggered little or no permanent interaction between members. Ernst Haas, "The Study of Regional Integration—Reflections on the Joy and Anguish of Pretheorizing," *International Organization* 24 (Spring 1970), pp. 618–639.

45. See, for instance, Zbigniew Brzezinski, "Beyond Chaos: A Policy for the West," *The National Interest*, no. 19 (Spring 1990), pp. 3–12.

46. See, for example, J. Noetzold, A. Inotai and K. Schroeder, "East–West Trade at the Crossroads," *Aussenpolitik* 37, no. 4 (1986), pp. 400–412.

47. See, for example, Edward N. Luttwak, "The Shape of Things to Come," *Commentary* 89, no. 6 (June 1990), pp. 17–25.

48. Timothy Garton Ash, "Reform or Revolution?" *The New York Review of Books*, October 27, 1988.

49. See David Gress, *Peace and Survival: West Germany, the Peace Movement and European Security* (Stanford: Hoover Institution, 1985), pp. 151–152.

50. Jacques Rupnik, "Central Europe or Mitteleuropa?" *Daedalus* 119, no. 1 (Winter 1990), pp. 249–278.

III BIPOLARITY IN TRANSITION

1. See, for instance, Istvan Deak, "Eastern Europe's Dark History," *Orbis* 33, no. 1 (Winter 1989), pp. 51–68.

2. For a timely analysis of this problem, see, for instance, Ken Booth, "Steps Toward Stable Peace in Europe: A Theory and Practice of Coexistence," *International Affairs* 66, no. 1 (1990), pp. 6–46.

3. Charles W. Kegley, Jr. and Gregory A. Raymond, "The End of Alliances?" *USA Today*, May 1990, pp. 32–34.

5 The Changing Geostrategic Landscape of Europe

1. This book does not address arms control issues in detail but tries to draw certain conclusions from the ongoing negotiations. For background

discussions see, for example, Joachim Krause, *Prospects for Conventional Arms Control in Europe*, IEWSS Occasional Paper Series, no. 8 (New York, 1988); Ian M. Cuthbertson & David Robertson, *Enhancing European Security* (New York: St. Martin's Press, 1990).

2. Brzezinski, "Beyond Chaos—A Policy for the West," pp. 3–12.

3. Conference on "Democratization and Institution-building in Eastern Europe" in Warsaw, March 1–3, 1990 by the Institute for East–West Security Studies. See Meeting Report by Mary Albon. The building of market economies was started in Central Europe with only marginal results. Poland, for instance, introduced the convertibility of its currency on January 1, 1990. See Jeffrey Sachs and David Lipton, "Poland's Economic Reform," *Foreign Affairs* 69, no. 2 (Spring 1990), pp. 47–66. The economic reform of Central Europe and the Soviet Union goes beyond the scope of this study. As part of the phenomena of the system change it has been dealt with in Chapter 3.

4. Stephen S. Rosenfeld, "Finlandization: A Prudent Step for Small Nations?", *International Herald Tribune*, January 12, 1990.

5. See Kennan, *The German Problem: A Personal View*, pp. 3–4.

6. In military terms the WTO has been a "one-pillar" structure skewed toward Moscow. The power of the WTO "was directed towards readdressing Moscow's incomplete power—the USSR required an adjunct to its own armed might to deny nations within the Soviet cordon sanitaire the capacity to defend themselves against intervention." Daniel M. Nelson, "Power at What Price: The High Cost of Security in the WTO" (unpublished paper, the University of Kentucky, 1989).

7. See Braun, "Whither the Warsaw Pact in the Gorbachev Era?"

8. Kristi Bahrenburg, "Peter Hardi on the Current Political Situation in Hungary," IEWSS Meeting Report, November 15, 1989.

9 See Mary Albon, "Valentin Larionov and Alexander Konovalov on Changes in Soviet Military-Security Thinking," IEWSS Meeting Report, January 9, 1990. In the West it was generally taken as a starting point for the conventional arms control negotiations that the West will reduce its troops and forces in compliance with the process of democratization in the Soviet Union. See Michael Howard, "The Remaking of Europe," *Survival* 32, no. 2 (March/April 1990). In a nutshell, political change will be "tested" with military changes. See also Fred Charles Iklé, "The Ghost in the Pentagon," *The National Interest*, no. 19 (Spring 1990), pp. 13–20. Iklé is strongly critical about whether this kind of linkage is necessary at all.

10. Sergei Karaganov, "Our Common European House Within the East–West Structure" (unpublished paper, 1988).

11. Karaganov underscores perestroika's difference from Stalinism by implicitly hinting at the possibility of also reconsidering intra-alliance relations within the Soviet bloc: "Perestroika in my country, its democratization, doing away with the vestiges of Stalinism, are creating an especially favourable climate for change *in all spheres of relations* between East and West." Sergei Karaganov, "Our Common European Home Within the East–West Structure." See also the Joint Declaration signed by Mikhail S. Gorbachev and Helmut Kohl of the FRG on June

13, 1989, which clearly is aimed at finding ways and means to overcome the division on the basis of the common European home.

12. See Robert Legvold, "The Soviet Union in Transition: Update on Perestroika and Glasnost" (Colombia University, School of International and Public Affairs, A Memo, February 6, 1989), where Legvold stated that Moscow was relenting on imposing a single system in Eastern Europe and was evolving a "political laissez-faire," a fundamental alteration of the Brezhnev Doctrine. These changes stemmed from four basic causes, two commonly recognized, two less often considered. First, the Soviet Union's enormous domestic problems were forcing it to modify its external posture and approaches. Second, the force of Gorbachev's own personality and beliefs in this area contributed significantly to the Soviet Union's position in the world. Third, the effects of foreign policy failures of the past, and fourth, the "imperative of the international setting itself" also have had an impact.

13. Brzezinski, "The Framework for East–West Conciliation."

14. Ibid.

15. Knudsen, "Europe Between Superpowers," pp. 91–112.

16. Henry Kissinger, "A Memo to the Next President," *Newsweek*, September 19, 1988. For a timely argument in this direction, see also, for example, Richard A. Bitzinger, "Neutrality for Eastern Europe? An Examination of Possible Western Role Models" (paper prepared for the RAND Corporation Symposium on European Security, Santa Monica, February 2, 1990). See also Heinz Timmermann, "The Soviet Union and Eastern Europe: Dynamics of 'Finlandization'," *Radio Liberty, Report on the USSR* 2, no. 33 (August 17, 1990), pp. 15–18.

17. In 1948 Finland signed the Treaty of Friendship, Co-operation and Mutual Assistance (FCMA) with the Soviet Union. It reflected a historical appraisal of the situation prevailing at the time of its signing. The president of Finland, Dr. Mauno Koivisto, stated in the protocol of the Council of State on September 21, 1990 that such a situation no longer existed. The reference to Germany in the FCMA treaty had become especially obsolete. Koivisto confirmed, however, that the essential purpose of the treaty remains unchanged, i.e., Finland will not allow her territory to be used for an attack against the Soviet Union. The treaty continues to serve Finnish security interests. See Press Releases by the Ministry for Foreign Affairs of Finland, no, 277 and 278, September 21, 1990. For a theoretical analysis of Finnish foreign policy, especially in a European setting, see Raimo Väyrynen, "Stability and Change in Finnish Foreign Policy," Research Reports, Series A, no. 60 (1982), Department of Political Science, University of Helsinki. See also Alpo Rusi, "Finnish Foreign Policy on the Threshold of the 1990s," Ministry for Foreign Affairs, October 1989. Since the early 1990s Finland has stressed her neutrality in the military field as an important aspect of her foreign policy in general. For the role of the military component of Finnish security policy, see a timely and challenging analysis by Thomas Ries, *The Cold Will* (London: Brassey's Defence Publishers, 1988).

18. See, for example, Knudsen, "Europe Between Superpowers," pp. 91–112.

President Vaclav Havel of Czechoslovakia proposed such a cooperative approach to all "new democracies" in Central Europe in January 1990. See "Havel Asks Coordinated Bid by East to 'Return to Europe'," *International Herald Tribune*, January 26, 1990.

19. Timothy Garton Ash, "The Empire in Decay."

20. Geoffrey Parker, in *The Geopolitics of Domination* (London: Routledge, 1988), pp. 71–74, stated that the USSR was in geopolitical decline, which was why the years of Soviet domination were likely to be coming to an end. Parker elaborated a geopolitical interpretation of Gorbachev's new thinking which, if applied in Eastern Europe, would result in a new relationship among the member-states of the WTO.

21. Charles Gati, "Gorbachev and Eastern Europe," *Foreign Affairs* 65, no. 5 (Summer 1987), pp. 958–975.

22. William Safire, "Raise and Call," *The New York Times*, June 1, 1989.

23. It is thought that there exists a "neutralist" view (in particular in the West German left) toward the countries of Eastern Europe. The emergence of a neutral Central Europe would realize the old Rapallo diplomacy. See Rupnik, "Central Europe or Mitteleurope," p. 269.

24. Curt Gasteyger, "Neutrality in Europe: The End or a New Beginning?" *European Affairs* no. 4 (Winter 1989), pp. 87–92. Finland, for its part, may become a country with a neutral history and a "proactive and non-aligned" role within the European structures of cooperation and integration.

25. See Craig R. Whitney, "Gen-scher-ism: n. 1. Innuendo. 2. Mass Movement," *International Herald Tribune*, July 21–22, 1990.

26. The concept of the resurgence of Europe is defined here as a political resurrection of Europe, the division of which is gradually losing its significance in both East and West. The resurgence of Europe is underway both at the all-European level (systemic changes) and at the national level. The level of perceptions (i.e., an increased European identity) should also be mentioned; this is dealt with in this book in the relevant context. The concept of the resurgence of Europe was originally elaborated by Hans-Dieter Heumann in "Political Resurgence of Europe," (paper prepared at IEWSS, 1988).

27. See Haftendorn, *Security and Detente*, pp. 253–254.

28. See Frey , *Division and Detente*, p. 154.

29. Gordon Craig, "After the Reich," *The New York Review of Book*, October 9, 1987, from Richard von Weizsäcker, *A Voice from Germany*, trans. Karin von Abrams (London: Weidenfeld and Nicolson, 1987). Regarding the progress of inner-German trade and general ties, see Kennedy, *The Rise and Fall of the Great Powers*, pp. 478–479. During the 1980s the GDR experienced economic setbacks in spite of its wide interaction with the FRG economy. As a consequence, this trend pushed the GDR closer to its Western neighbor. Trade between the German states was called "inner-German" trade, which allowed East German products duty-free entry into the FRG.

30. See Peter Bender, *Das Ende des Ideologischen Zeitalters: Die Europae-isierung Europas* (Berlin: Severin und Siedler, 1981), p. 229.

31. For a detailed and informative description of the events of 1989 in

Eastern Europe, see, for example, Jackson Diehl and Jim Hoagland, "A Year of Revolt in Eastern Europe," *International Herald Tribune*, January 15, 1990. GDR head of state Erich Honecker was forced to resign on October 18, 1989, in favor of Egon Krenz. Despite his radical moves to change the East German political system, Krenz was also forced to resign six weeks later.

32. See "Kohl Demands Eradication of the Economic and Social Gap between East and West in Europe," *Helsingin Sanomat*, February 4, 1990. Kohl also said in his Davos speech that a unified Germany cannot be neutral but must be an integral part of the European Community and also remain an ally of the Soviet Union. See also Graham Allison, "German Reunification On Acceptable Terms," *International Herald Tribune*, February 5, 1990; Allison advocated the acceptance of Kohl's terms on reunification, but only as the result of negotiations with Moscow.

33. See Appendix B.

34. Joachim Krause, "Force Structures, Force Levels and Force Deployments in a Changing European Strategic Landscape" (paper presented at the IEWSS 9th Annual Conference, June 7–9, 1990, Stockholm).

35. See Krause, "Force Structures, Force Levels."

36. See details about the Caucasus agreement, *International Herald Tribune*, "Gorbachev Agrees to United Germany in NATO," July 17, 1990.

37. See, for example, Jim Hoagland, "Talks in the Caucasus: Just How Good Was the News?", *International Herald Tribune*, July 19, 1990.

38. Scott Sullivan, "Can Germany be Contained?" *Newsweek*, July 30, 1990. About an emerging "power vacuum" in Central Europe as the result of the Soviet withdrawal and German "denuclearization," see Jim Hoagland, "Why France's Defense Minister Still Feeds the Lions," *International Herald Tribune*, July 12, 1990.

39. Keith Wind, "Rita Süssmuth on German Unification and the Future Political Architecture of Europe" IEWSS Meeting Report, March 20, 1990.

40. In France in particular the German question is equated with the European question. Furthermore, as Alain Minc reasons, the German drift toward the East is transforming "Atlantic Europe" into "continental Europe." Minc combines the emergence of the single market with the German drift eastward and states: "We are going to have a big free-trade zone in a strategically soft Europe. In terms of their deeper evolution, the single market does not interest the Germans at all." James M. Markham, "When Europe's Walls Tumble, Who'll Rush In?" *The New York Times*, March 21, 1989.

41. Kennedy, *The Rise and Fall of the Great Powers*, pp. 471–472.

42. For a brief background history of the emergence of the EC, see, for example, Hans A. Schmitt, *European Union: From Hitler to de Gaulle*. For a timely and comprehensive analysis concerning the history and the future of European political cooperation, see Panagiotis Isestos, *European Political Cooperation* (Avebury: Gower Publishing, 1987).

43. See Appendix A.

44. Regarding the details of the "Single European Act" used here, see Lutz

G. Stavenhagen, "Political Priorities of the German EC Presidency," *Aussenpolitik* 39, no. 1 (1988), pp. 13–23. The role of West German Foreign Minister Hans-Dietrich Genscher was decisive in starting the drafting of the "Single European Act" in the early 1980s, which, of course, reflects the special interest of the FRG in European integration.

45. Joseph C. Rallo, *Defending Europe in the 1990s* (New York: St. Martin's Press, 1986), pp. 109–127.

46. See "London Declaration on A Transformed North Atlantic Alliance", issued by the heads of state and government participating in the meeting on the North Atlantic Council in London on July 5–6, 1990.

47. With respect to the West European contribution in the Gulf, see, for example, "A Strange and Motley Army," *The Economist*, September 22, 1990. For a timely review of the debate on strengthening the role of WEU as the military wing of the EC, see John Palmer, "With a Security Role, Metamorphosis from Club to Community is Complete", *The European*, September 21–23, 1990. In fact, the Gulf crisis was also a setback to European unity. See Giles Merritt, "A Wind From the Gulf is Emptying Europe's Sails," *International Herald Tribune*, September 21, 1990. See also Dominique Moisi and Lawrence Freedman, "It's Time for French–British Security Partnership," *International Herald Tribune*, September 24, 1990.

48. See, for example, Robert Rudney, "France: Preparing for European Leadership," *The National Interest* (Fall 1987), pp. 33–48.

49. Quoted from *The National Interest* (Fall 1987), p. 44 and originally published in *The Economist*, July 18, 1987.

50. George Will, "The Opiate of Arms Control," *Newsweek*, April 27, 1987. For a timely analysis of European nuclear security, see *Europe in Transition. Politics and Nuclear Security*, ed. Vilho Harle and Pekka Sivonen (London and New York: Pinter Publishers, 1989). With respect to the need to reappraise the role of nuclear weapons in the post-Cold War era, especially in light of the Gulf crisis of 1990, see, for example, Pierre Lellouche, "So What are the Nuclear Armories for Now?", *International Herald Tribune*, September 27, 1990. Lellouche asks what kind of strategy and weapons will be needed to effectively deter nuclear threats from the South. He prefers to stick to a "realistic view" of the role of accurate, nuclear or non-nuclear, weapons to meet this challenge. One could say that the Gulf crisis may bring the "nukes" back to the core of the debate about European security identity. To further elaborate this question would go beyond the scope of this book.

51. See Calleo, *Beyond American Hegemony: The Future of the Western Alliance*, pp. 183, 214. Quoted from Stanley Hoffman's review in *Political Science Quarterly* 103, no. 3 (1988), pp. 547–548.

52. Regarding the economic decline of the EC, see Joel Kotkin and Yoriko Kishimoto, *The Third Century* (New York: Crown Publishers, 1988), pp. 75–83. For an ambiguous vision regarding the EC and the year 1992, see Albert Bressand, "Beyond Interdependence: 1992 as a Global Challenge," *International Affairs* 66, no. 1 (1990), pp. 47–65.

53. See CSIS, *Beyond 1992: U.S. Strategy toward the European Community*, pp. 14–15. The socioeconomic and political situation in the Soviet Union

became more catastrophic in the course of 1990 and even the prospect of civil war became more real. See, for example, *Soviet Prospects*, CSIS Report on the USSR & Eastern Europe, no. 1 (September 1990); John Kohan, "Beyond Perestroika," *Time*, September 24, 1990; for Soviet developments, see above.

54. Pierre Hassner, "Europe Beyond Partition and Unity: Disintegration or Reconstitution?" *International Affairs* 66, no. 3 (1990), pp. 461–475.

55. Pedersen, "Problems of Enlargement: Political Integration in a Pan-European EC." See also Werner Ungerer, "Die Entwicklung der EG und ihr Verhältnis zu Mittel- und Osteuropa," *Aussenpolitik* 3 (1990), pp. 225–235.

56. This view draws on the theory that in the 19th century Europe consisted mainly of "three European communities": tsarist Russia, imperial Germany and Austria–Hungary. Regarding the debate related to the "organic basis" of Europe, see *Foreign Broadcast Information Service Daily Report—West Europe Update* (FBIS-WEU-89-036), Feb. 24, 1990, pp. 30–32. The CSIS Steering Committee states that it does not believe the EC will emerge as a multidimensional superpower during the 1990s. "Nevertheless, the Community has established itself as a powerful framework for defining West European economic and political interests. Under any circumstances, the EC poses a new reality to which the United States must respond." *Beyond 1992: U.S. Strategy toward the European Community*, p. 8.

57. To further elaborate this issue would go beyond the goal of this book.

58. It would be wrong to claim that each of the Euroneutrals would pursue exactly the same kind of security policy. The similarity addresses itself, however, most visibly within the framework of the postwar East–West conflict. Also, the differences between the concepts of neutrality, neutralism and nonalignment should be stressed. One of the main differences between nonalignment and neutrality lies in the attitude toward the Western values of democracy and fundamental freedoms. Since its foundation in the mid-1950s, the nonaligned movement has been characteristically "anti-Western." For timely and comprehensive analyses see, for example, Nils Orvik, *The Decline of Neutrality, 1914–1941*, 2nd ed. (London: Frank Cass and Company, 1971), pp. 279–304 (Appendix) as well as S. Victor Papacosma and Mark R. Rubin, eds., *Europe's Neutral and Nonaligned States* (Wilmington, DE: Scholarly Resources, Inc., 1989). Altogether ten European countries (Austria, Cyprus, Finland, Ireland, Liechtenstein, Malta, San Marino, Sweden, Switzerland and Yugoslavia) have either legally instituted permanent neutrality or conduct a de facto policy of neutrality. However, the most prominent representatives of the so-called *armed neutrality* are the four Euroneutrals. For this analysis, see Wolfgang Danspeckgruber, "Armed Neutrality: Its Application and Future," in *Securing Europe's Future*, ed. Stephen J. Flanagan and Fen Osler Hampson (Dover, MA: Auburn House Publishing Company, 1986), pp. 242–279. Neutrality has also been dealt with within the tradition of small-state research, which often equates small states with weak states. Hans Vogel has elaborated a policy model for small states, in which he describes a path of a self-

increasing deficit of autonomy: 1) structural scarcity, 2) external economic dependence, 3) external sensitivity, and 4) probability of foreign penetration. See Hans Vogel, "Small States' Efforts in International Relations: Enlarging the Scope," in *Small States in Europe and Dependence*, ed. Otmar Hoell (Boulder, CO: Westview, 1983), pp. 54–58. This study is built on a more historical view of the premises of a policy of neutrality in Europe, which emphasizes differences of neutrality vis-à-vis small-nation policies in general.

59. The Marstrand Study Group, "Neutrality in Need of Conceptual Revision" (unpublished paper, 1988.)

60. Mauno Koivisto, "Changing Europe" (speech delivered to the Hungarian parliament, June 8, 1988).

61. The Marstrand Study Group, "Neutrality in Need of Conceptual Revision." See Harto Hakovirta, "Neutral States in East–West Economic Cooperation," *Co-Existence* 8 (1981), pp. 95–119.

62. The logic of this attitude derives from neutrality itself. Neutralist thinking addresses itself most often against one of the superpowers. The neutrals—at least in the cases of Finland and Switzerland, and often Austria and Sweden too—do not want to be mixed up with Schaukelpolitik, which would mean siding with one of the superpowers. As Urho Kekkonen, a long-time president of Finland, bluntly put it: "In implementing a policy of neutrality, one should always bear in mind that we are neither a Western bridgehead in the East nor an Eastern bridgehead in the West." Kekkonen, *President's View*, p. 194.

63. Knudsen, "Europe between Superpowers."

64. Gaddis, "The Long Peace."

65. The European neutrals—except Ireland—have used two basic methods to manage and solve the problems of neutrality arising from regional integration: 1) they have abstained from or have chosen limited forms of participation; and 2) they have denied that the forms of participation they have chosen (or have been allowed to choose) compromise or change neutrality. See Hakovirta, *East–West Conflict and European Neutrality*, pp. 128–132.

66. Austria is the only one of the Euroneutrals that had already applied for membership in the EC in 1989. This question became, however, a major topic in 1990 in all neutral states.

67. For a timely and comprehensive compilation of the most recent studies on questions of the economic and political integration in Europe from the neutral point of view, see Kari Mottola and Heikki Patomaki, eds., *Facing the Change in Europe* (Helsinki: Finnish Institute of International Affairs, 1989). See, in this connection in particular, the chapters by Esko Antola, "The Finnish Integration Strategy: Adaptation with Restrictions," pp. 55–70; and Geoffrey Edwards, "European Political Cooperation, EFTA Countries and Integration," pp. 79–89.

68. See Hans Thalberg, "The European Neutrals and Regional Stability," in *The European Neutrals in International Affairs*, ed. Hanspeter Neuhold and Hans Thalberg (Boulder, CO: Westview, 1989), pp. 125–131.

69. The EC and EFTA formed a huge free-trade area in 1973. EFTA and the EC have been negotiating the establishment of the EES extending to the

EFTA nations "four freedoms" (the unrestricted movement of goods, capital, services and people) of the single market. A link-up between the EC and EFTA would unite the 320 million people of the EC with the 30 million of EFTA. In effect, the EFTA nations would have a special relationship with the EC without being full members—an arrangement that could open the way for the East European states, with a combined population of 110 million, to make similar links in the future.

70. Pedersen, "Problems of Enlargement: Political Integration in a Pan-European EC."

71. See, for example, Palmer, "With a Security Role, Metamorphosis from Club to Community is Complete." The debate about the relevance of the concept of neutrality has become a hot topic in the Euroneutrals in 1990. See, for example, Dietrich Schindler, "Neutralität am Wendepunkt?" *Neue Züricher Zeitung*, September 23/24, 1990. In Sweden Per Gyllehammer, Chairman of the Volvo Corporation, proposed in August 1990 that Sweden should reject neutrality altogether in order to join the EC as soon as possible. See John Edin, "Vi har aldrig varit neutrala," *Dagens Nyheter*, September 26, 1990. In Finland many prominent scholars of international relations have proposed that Finland should apply for membership in the EC, even "for security reasons." See Paavo Pipponen, "EY-jäsenyys lisäisi suomen turvallisuutta" (EC membership would strengthen Finland's security), *Turun Sanomat*, October 2, 1990. There is no unanimity, however, in any of the Euroneutrals with respect to the application for membership.

6   The Outlook for European Security in the 1990s

1. See Philip Marchand, *Marshall McLuhan: The Medium and the Messenger* (New York: Ticknor & Fields, 1989), p. 276.

2. Robert Jervis, "Conclusions: Winning and Losing—Clausewitz in the Nuclear Era" (forthcoming), p. 43. I am grateful to Professor Jervis for taking the time to read my manuscript before its publication.

3. For a timely analysis of the problems related to the changes of military doctrines, see Pal Dunay, *Military Doctrine: Change in the East?*, IEWSS Occasional Paper Series, no. 15 (New York, 1990).

4. This study does not deal with the problem of the redefinition of security in greater detail. However, that debate has exploded in recent years, particularly in Europe, and the literature is expanding. On the need to redefine security on the basis of ecological arguments, see, for example, James G. Speth, *Environment, Economy, Security: The Emerging Agenda* (Washington, DC: Center for National Policy, 1985). Decision-makers throughout the world have rapidly recognized the importance of "ecological thinking." For a systemic analysis of the impact of the threat of environmental catastrophes on interdependence, see Norman Meyers, "Emergent Aspects of Environment: A Creative Challenge," *The Environmentalist* 7, no. 3 (1987), pp. 163–174. See Michael MccGwire, *Military Objectives in Soviet Foreign Policy* (Washington, DC: The Brookings Institution, 1987).

5. A case in point was the need of West German leaders to promote FRG

national interests over those of NATO in the 1989 debate on modernization of short-range nuclear weapons. On the conflict over short-range missiles and the West German position vis-à-vis the interests of the alliance, see "Bonn's Dovish Nuclear Stand Winning Support in NATO," *The New York Times*, April 26, 1989; Irving Kristol, " A Smug NATO Is Letting Germany Secede," *Wall Street Journal*, May 2, 1989; also Doug Bandow, "The Germans Need A Nuclear Arsenal," *The New York Times*, May 2, 1989. Henry Kissinger, in "Reversing Yalta," *The Washington Post*, April 16, 1989, reflects the fears that the withdrawal of U.S. troops from Europe and the reluctance of the FRG to modernize its short-range nuclear arsenals would move NATO toward denuclearizing Central Europe, which, as a consequence, would increase ferment in Eastern Europe, and also a realization of the concept of the common European home, which in Kissinger's view, "relegates to the U.S. a secondary status, establishes the Soviet claim to economic assistance based on geography, and provides a basis for Soviet domination of a denuclearized Central Europe." In fact, Kissinger links the emergence of German national sentiment with the consequent increase of the Soviet domination of a denuclearized Central Europe.

6. Raimo Väyrynen, "Common Security and the State System" (forthcoming).

7. The concept of common security was elaborated by the Palme Commission in 1982, and its report was published in The Independent Commission on Disarmament and Security Issues Staff, *Common Security: A Blueprint for Survival* (New York: Simon & Schuster, 1982).

8. The conceptual starting point is that "common security" must be sought within the system of "all-encompassing security," that is, a system that includes all countries and extends to all spheres of mutual interest. The creation of such a system is presented as being particularly imperative in Europe.

9. See Lee Wilkins and Philip Patterson, "Reporting Chernobyl: Cutting the Government Fog to Cover the Nuclear Cloud" (unpublished paper, 1987); also Ilkka Timonen, *Suomi ulkomaisessa lehdistossa Tshernobylin yoimalaonnet-tomuuden jalkeen*, Tampereen yliopisto, Sarja B 52/1988.

10. Gaddis, "The Long Peace," p. 140.

11. See Dobroczynski, "Rapprochement of the Peoples of Europe: Difficulties and Prospects," p. 41.

12. Gress, *Peace and Survival*, p. 197.

13. For a historical analysis, see Raymond Garthoff, *Detente and Confrontation: American–Soviet Relations from Nixon to Reagan* (Washington, DC: The Brookings Institution, 1985).

14. Kenneth Boulding, *The Image* (Ann Arbor, MI: University of Michigan Press, 1956).

15. Ole R. Holsti, "The Beliefs of American Leaders About the Soviet Union and Soviet–American Relations, 1976–1984," in *East–West Conflict: Elite Perceptions and Political Options*, ed. Intriligator and Jacobsen, pp. 45–105.

16. See Laszlo Molnar, "On the Adequacy of Negotiation Processes in European Conventional Arms Control," (paper prepared at the IEWSS,

1989). This book does not deal with the problem of conventional balance in Europe in detail.

17. John D. Steinbruner, "The Prospect of Cooperative Security," *The Brookings Review* (Winter 1988/89), pp. 53–62.

18. Quoted from Flora Lewis, "Moscow Steady Ahead," *The New York Times*, June 7, 1989.

19. There is no common NNA policy on conventional arms control in Europe. Each country has its own policy based on its own national postulates. Within the CSCE process the NNA group has introduced a common proposal on this matter. During the next few years conventional arms control, covering the area from the Atlantic to the Urals, will be negotiated within the CSCE. The issue will be dealt with in two separate negotiations, one with the members of NATO and the members of the WTO on Conventional Arms Forces in Europe (CFE) and the other with the participation of all the CSCE states (35 altogether) on Confidence- and Security-Building Measures. On the security policies of the neutral states of Europe referred to in particular in this context, see, for example, *Parlamentarisen Puolustuskkomitean (III) Mietinto* (Helsinki: 1980), pp. 27, 35–36; Ermei Kanninen, "Suomen sotilaallinen doktriini," *Strategian kasikirja* (Helsinki: 1983), pp. 188–192; "Finland's Military Doctrine," in *A Handbook of Strategy* (Helsinki: Department of Military Studies, Ministry of Defense, 1983), pp. 188–192. See also, "Sweden's Security Policy Entering the 90s," *Report by the 1984 Defense Committee*, SOU (Swedish Official Reports Series 6), 1985 (Stockholm: Ministry of Defense, 1985).

20. Jessica T. Mathews, "Preparing for a Global 'Green' Era," *The New York Times*, June 11, 1989. See also Rupnik, "Central Europe or Mitteleuropa."

21. For an indication of the present development, see, for example, Sheila Rule, "Politics as Usual Over the Dutch Environment," *The New York Times*, June 11, 1989.

22. Henry Kissinger, *A World Restored* (London: Victor Gollancz Ltd., 1974, orig. 1957), pp. 144–145. I am grateful to Professor Robert Jervis for drawing my attention to Kissinger's book.

23. Ibid, p. 145.

24. On the merits of the bipolar system, see in particular Gaddis, "The Long Peace." Among those who have emphasized the instability of bipolarity, see Morgenthau, *Politics Among Nations*, pp. 350–354. On the transition from bipolarity to multipolarity, see also Gilpin, *War and Change*, pp. 10–15 and Waltz, *Theory of International Relations*, p. 162.

25. John Mueller, "The Essential Irrelevance of Nuclear Weapons," *International Security* 13, no. 2 (Fall 1988), pp. 57–90.

26. See in particular Kenneth Boulding, *Stable Peace* (Austin: University of Texas Press, 1979). See Karl Kaiser, "A View from Europe: The U.S. Role in the Next Decade," *International Affairs* 65, no. 2 (Spring 1989), pp. 209–223. Kaiser puts great emphasis on the maintenance of nuclear deterrence as a precondition for stable peace in Europe by speaking about "a sufficient capacity for deterrence."

27. See Henry Kissinger, "Observations on U.S.–Soviet Relations," speech

delivered at the Heritage Foundation in Washington, DC, January 14, 1988. *The Heritage Lectures*, no. 174 (1988). This argument is emphasized by, for example, Fred Charles Iklé in his "The Ghost in the Pentagon," 1990.

28. Gaddis, "The Long Peace," pp. 99–142, here p. 142.

29. On the foundation of the European nation-state system, see, for example, William H. McNeill, *The Pursuit of Power: Technology, Armed Forces, and Society Since A.D. 1000* (Chicago: University of Chicago Press, 1982), p. 125. McNeill argues that as a result of the Treaty of Westphalia, national armies were established that finally became guarantors of order and peace in Europe between the states. Yet political disputes between states were not eliminated by the Treaty of Westphalia and no permanent peace ensued, although a certain degree of order was established.

30. See Lawrence J. Goodrich, "Restructuring European Security," *The Christian Science Monitor*, May 30, 1989.

31. See in particular Henry Kissinger, "Reversing Yalta," *The Washington Post*, April 16, 1989; Zbigniew Brzezinski, "A Proposition the Soviets Shouldn't Refuse," *The New York Times*, March 13, 1989; and excerpts from an address by President Bush at Texas A&M University, May 12, 1989, *The New York Times*, May 13, 1989.

32. The author has developed this model of three or four European political entities in his article "Europe's Security Structure in Disintegration: Power Politics, Stability and Political Change," *Rauhantutkimu* 1989, no. 1 (in Finnish). See also Valéry Giscard d'Estaing, Yasuhiro Nakasone and Henry A. Kissinger, "East–West Relations," *Foreign Affairs* 68, no. 3 (Summer 1989), pp. 1–21, in which a model of three "political entities" is proposed.

33. About the two paths to peace in conceptual terms, see Charles W. Kegley, Jr. and Eugene R. Wittkopf, *World Politics—Trend and Transformation*, 3rd ed. (New York: St. Martin's Press, 1989), pp. 423–492.

34. See Appendix A.

35. See Richard H. Ullman, "Institutionalizing European Security," (paper presented at the IEWSS 9th Annual Conference, June 7–9, 1990, Stockholm).

36. The philosophy of Jacques Attali is illustrative with respect to the foundation of EBRD. Attali is of the opinion that Western Europe would become one of the two or three power centers of a new world not dominated any more by the two postwar superpowers. He predicts a major decline in particular of the Soviet Union, but also of the United States. In Attali's vision, a united Germany does not exist as a power center comparable with Western Europe (which would be a France-like Western Europe). See Jacques Attali, *Lignes d'Horizon* (Paris: Librairie Arthème Fayard, 1990).

37. See Charlotte Savidge, "Theodore Malloch on Eastern Europe and International Economic Organizations" (IEWSS Meeting Report, January 30, 1990).

38. See Charles W. Kegley, "The New Containment Myth: Realism and Anomaly of European Integration" (paper presented at the Carnegie

Council on Ethics and International Affairs Conference on "Ethics and Foreign Policy," July 2–6, 1990, Wilton Park International Conference Centre, Wiston House, Great Britain).

39. Quoted from Kegley, "The New Containment Myth."

40. See Lawrence Malkin, "G-7 Leaders Leave Loose Ends on World Trade and Soviet Aid," *International Herald Tribune*, July 12, 1990.

41. Quoted from Kegley and Raymond, "The End of Alliances?"

42. This view is expressed by Richard H. Ullman in his "Institutionalizing European Security."

43. Henry Kissinger, "The End of NATO?" *The Washington Post*, July 24, 1990.

44. Ewa Nowotny, "The Role of the CSCE and the Council of Europe in Facilitating a Stable Transition Towards New Political Structures in Europe" (paper presented at the IEWSS 9th Annual Conference, June 7–9, 1990, Stockholm).

45. See Victor-Yves Ghebali, "The Institutionalization of the CSCE Process: Towards an Instrument for the 'Greater Europe'" (paper presented at meeting of the Finnish Institute of International Affairs (FIIA) and Washington Center for Strategic and International Studies (CSIS) on "New Security Arrangements in Europe: Developing the CSCE Framework," September 27–28, 1990, Helsinki. For a timely analysis that tries to combine the collective security arrangements with the existing security institutions, see Gregory Flynn and David J. Scheffer, "Limited Collective Security," *Foreign Policy* 80 (Fall 1990), pp. 77–101.

46. About the allocation of tasks between the CSCE and the present security and related institutions, see Edward Mortimer, "Springtime for Euro-institutions," *Financial Times*, June 12, 1990; also Ullman, "Institutionalizing European Security."

47. See in particular F. Stephen Larrabee, "The United States and the New European Security Order" (paper presented at the IEWSS 9th Annual Conference, June 7–9, 1990, Stockholm).

48. See Nowotny, "The Role of the CSCE."

49. A number of visions related to the establishment of a European Confederation have been introduced. See, for example, French President François Mitterrand's idea of a confederation in his December 31, 1989 speech, *Bulletin d'Information* (Washington, DC: Embassy of France), pp. 1–2; or Italian Foreign Minister Gianni de Michelis' concept of regionalism in "Reaching Out to the East," *Foreign Policy* 79 (Summer 1990). EC president Jacques Delors has blended these two concepts of confederation and regionalism. See, for example, his speeches to the European Parliament on January 17, 1989 (Washington, DC: Delegation of the Commission of the European Communities), pp. 29–36; and on January 17, 1990 (Washington, DC: Delegation of the Commission of the European Communities), pp. 18–37.

50. An array of ideas was proposed about the secretariat of the CSCE in 1990. It seems obvious that the Central European states are especially eager to host the secretariat. President Vaclav Havel has proposed the establishment of the CSCE Security Commission, which could gradually replace the military alliances.

7 Europe in Transition

1. Excerpt from the speech by Vaclav Havel, President of the Czech and Slovak Federal Republic, to a joint session of the U.S. Congress, February 21, 1990.
2. Excerpt from a speech by Hans-Dietrich Genscher at the United Nations, September 26, 1990.
3. Ralf Dahrendorf, "Roads to Freedom: Democratization and Its problems in East Central Europe," in *Uncertain Futures: Eastern Europe and Democracy*, ed. Peter Volten, Institute for East–West Security Studies Occasional Paper Series, no. 16 (New York, 1990), p. 12.
4. Luttwak, "The Shape of Things to Come."
5. Samuel P. Huntington, "No Exit—The Errors of Endism," *The National Interest*, no. 17 (Fall 1989), pp. 3–11.
6. Alexei Iziumov and Andrei Kortunov, "The Monolith is Cracking," *Newsweek*, August 13, 1990.
7. Martin Malia, "The Soviet Union is Dead: Thus Spake 'Z'," *International Herald Tribune*, September 1–2, 1990.
8. Seweryn Bialer, "The Passing of the Soviet Order?" *Survival* 32, no. 2 (March/April 1990), pp. 107–120.
9. The future of the Soviet Union as a Great Russia has been illustrated by Aleksandr Solzhenitsyn in his 16,000-word essay of September 1990. He is impatient with parliaments and elections, and urges instead a paternal autocracy rooted in Orthodox religion and Russian nationalism. See "Choice for Russians," *International Herald Tribune*, October 1, 1990. See also William H. Luers, "The Cost of Soviet Disintegration," *The New York Times*, June 29, 1990. Ambassador Luers proposed that, in the event of major Soviet disintegration, "the key to managing these dilemmas [all possible problems related to that situation] is to work toward a democratic and economically healthy Russia, one that does not feel threatened by the new Europe in which it must ultimately find a home. And we should pursue this goal with or without Mr. Gorbachev."
10. Martin Roberts, *Machines and Liberty: A Portrait of Europe 1789–1914* (Hong Kong: Oxford University Press, 1980), p. 205.
11. See, for example, Joseph Fitchett, "Europe: A U.S. Map of Moscow's Hopes," *International Herald Tribune*, March 26, 1990. Also Philip A. Petersen, "The Emerging Soviet Vision of European Security," (unpublished paper, 1990).
12. Quoted from Kegley and Raymond, "The End of Alliances?"
13. See, for example, Amos Perlmutter and Benjamin Frankel, "The Helsinki Effect: A Soviet Foot in the Mideast Door," *International Herald Tribune*, September 17, 1990.
14. See Joseph S. Nye, *The Changing Nature of American Power* (New York: Basic Books, 1990).
15. See CSIS, *Beyond 1992: U.S. Strategy Toward the European Community*, pp. 20–21.
16. Quoted from Hans J. Morgenthau, *Scientific Man vs. Power Politics* (Chicago: The Chicago University Press, 1946), p. 207.

Bibliography

BOOKS

Allison, Graham. *Essence of Decision: Explaining the Cuban Missile Crisis.* Boston: Little, Brown, 1971.

Attali, Jacques. *Lignes d'Horizon.* Paris: Librairie Arthème Fayard, 1990.

Barnet, Richard J. *The Alliance.* New York: Simon & Schuster, 1983.

Bender, Peter. *Das Ende des Ideologischen Zeitalters: Die Europaeisierung Europas.* Berlin: Severin und Siedler, 1981.

Berg, Rolf, and Daniel Rotfeld. *Building Security in Europe.* Institute for East–West Security Studies Monograph Series, no. 2. New York, 1985.

Bethlen, Stephen, and Ivan Volgyes, eds. *Europe and the Superpowers.* Boulder, Colorado: Westview, 1985.

Blackwill, Robert D., and F. Stephen Larrabee, eds. *Conventional Arms Control and East–West Security.* Durham, North Carolina: Duke University Press, 1989.

Borawski, John. *From the Atlantic to the Urals.* New York: Pergamon Brassey's, 1986.

Boulding, Kenneth. *The Image.* Ann Arbor, Michigan: University of Michigan Press, 1956.

———. *Stable Peace.* Austin, Texas: University of Texas Press, 1979.

Brandt, Willy. *Bundeskanzler Brandt: Reden und Interviews.* Bonn: Press und Informationsamt des Bundesregierung, 1971.

———. *People and Politics: The Years 1960–1975.* Boston: Little, Brown, 1978.

Brzezinski, Zbigniew. *Game Plan.* Boston: Atlantic Monthly Press, 1986.

———. *In Quest of National Security.* Boulder, Colorado: Westview, 1988.

———. *The Soviet Bloc: Unity and Conflict.* Rev. ed. Cambridge, Massachusetts: Harvard University Press, 1967.

Brzezinski, Zbigniew, and Samuel Huntington. *Political Power: USA/USSR.* New York: Viking Press, 1965.

Calleo, David P. *Beyond American Hegemony.* New York: Basic Books, 1987.

Center for Strategic and International Studies. *Beyond 1992: U.S. Strategy Toward the European Community.* Washington, DC, 1990.

Clemens, Diane Shaver. *Yalta.* Oxford: Oxford University Press, 1970.

Craig, Gordon A. *Europe Since 1815.* New York: Holt & Winston, 1974.

Cuthbertson, Ian M., and David Robertson. *Enhancing European Security.* New York: St. Martin's Press, 1990.

DePorte, Anton. *Europe Between the Super Powers: The Enduring Balance.* 2nd ed. New Haven, Connecticut: Yale University Press, 1986.

Dunay, Pal. *Military Doctrine: Change in the East?* Institute for East–West Security Studies Occasional Paper Series, no. 15. New York, 1990.

Dyson, Kenneth, ed. *European Detente.* New York: St. Martin's Press, 1986.

Flanagan, Stephen J., and Fen Osler Hampson, eds. *Securing Europe's Future.* Dover, Massachusetts: Auburn House Publishing Co., 1986.

Fontaine, André. *History of the Cold War*. New York: Vintage Books, 1970.

Frey, Eric G. *Division and Detente: The Germanies and Their Alliances*. New York: Praeger, 1987.

Gaddis, John Lewis. *Strategies of Containment*. New York: Oxford University Press, 1982.

Garthoff, Raymond L. *Detente and Confrontation: American-Soviet Relations from Nixon to Reagan*. Washington, DC: The Brookings Institution, 1985.

———. *Soviet Military Policy*. London: Faber & Faber, 1966.

Geyer, D., and B. Meissner, eds. *Sowjetunion Aussenpolitik III*. Köln: Bohlau, 1976.

Gilpin, Robert. *War and Change in World Politics*. New York: Cambridge University Press, 1981.

Gorbachev, Mikhail. *Perestroika*. New York: Harper & Row, 1987.

Gordon, Lincoln et al. *Eroding Empire: Western Relations With Eastern Europe*. Washington, DC: The Brookings Institution, 1987.

Gress, David. *Peace and Survival: West Germany, the Peace Movement and European Security*. Stanford, California: Hoover Institution, 1985.

Griffith, William. *The Ostpolitik of the Federal Republic of Germany*. Cambridge, Massachusetts: MIT Press, 1978.

Griffith, William, et al., eds. *Security Perspectives of the West German Left*. Washington, DC: Pergamon Brassey's, 1989.

Grosser, Alfred. *The Western Alliance: European-American Relations Since 1945*. New York: Continuum Publishing, 1980.

Haftendorn, Helga. *Security and Detente: Conflicting Priorities in German Foreign Policy*. New York: Praeger, 1985.

Hakovirta, Harto. *East–West Conflict and European Neutrality*. New York: Oxford University Press, 1988.

Halle, Louis J. *The Cold War as History*. New York: Harper & Row, 1967.

A Handbook of Strategy. Helsinki: Department of Military Studies, Ministry of Defense, 1983.

Hanrieder, Wolfram F., ed. *West Germany's Foreign Policy: 1949 to 1979*. Boulder, Colorado: Westview, 1980.

Hanson, Philip. *Western Economic Statecraft in East–West Relations*. Royal Institute of International Affairs Chatham House Papers 40. London, 1988.

Harle, Vilho, and Pekka Sivonen, eds. *Europe in Transition: Politics and Nuclear Security*. London and New York: Pinter Publishers, 1989.

Heisenberg, Wolfgang. *Strategic Stability and Nuclear Deterrence in East–West Relations*. Institute for East–West Security Studies Occasional Paper Series, no. 10. New York, 1989.

Hill, C. *National Foreign Policies and European Political Cooperation*. London: Routledge & Kegan Paul, 1983.

Hoell, Otmar, ed. *Small States in Europe and Dependence*. Boulder, Colorado: Westview, 1983.

Holsti, Ole R., Randolph M. Silverson and Alexander M. George, eds. *Change in the International System*. Boulder, Colorado: Westview, 1984.

Horelick, Arnold, and Myron Rush. *Strategic Power and Soviet Foreign Policy*. Chicago: University of Chicago Press, 1966.

Independent Commission on Disarmament and Security Issues Staff. *Common Security: A Blueprint for Survival*. New York: Simon & Schuster, 1982.

Institute for East–West Security Studies. *How Should America Respond to Gorbachev's Challenge?* Special Report. New York, 1987.

Intriligator, Michael D., and Hans-Adolf Jacobsen, eds. *East–West Conflict.* Boulder, Colorado: Westview, 1988.

Isestos, Panagiotis. *European Political Cooperation.* Avebury: Gower Publishing, 1987.

Jakobson, Max. *Veteen Piirretty Viiva.* Helsinki: Otava, 1980.

Jervis, Robert. *The Symbolic Nature of Nuclear Politics.* Urbana, Illinois: University of Illinois at Champaign-Urbana, 1985.

Johnson, A. Ross. *The Impact of Eastern Europe on Soviet Policy Toward Western Europe.* Santa Monica, California: RAND Corporation, 1986.

Jones, Christopher. *Soviet Influence in Eastern Europe: Political Autonomy and the Warsaw Pact.* New York: Praeger, 1981.

Jordan, Robert J. and Werner F. Feld. *Europe in the Balance.* London and Boston: Faber & Faber, 1986.

Kegley, Charles W., Jr., and Eugene R. Wittkopf. *World Politics–Trend and Transformation.* 3rd ed. New York: St. Martin's Press, 1989.

————, eds. *The Global Agenda.* 2nd ed. New York: Random House, 1988.

Kekkonen, Urho. *President's View.* London: Heinemann, 1982.

Kennan, George F. *The German Problem: A Personal View.* Washington, DC: American Institute of Contemporary German Studies, Johns Hopkins University, 1989.

————. *Memoirs: 1925–1950.* Boston: Little, Brown, 1967.

————. *Memoirs: 1950–1963.* New York: Pantheon, 1972.

Kennedy, Paul. *The Rise and Fall of the Great Powers.* New York: Random House, 1987.

Keohane, Robert O. *After Hegemony: Cooperation and Discord in the World Political Economy.* Princeton, New Jersey: Princeton University Press, 1984.

Kissinger, Henry. *The White House Years.* Boston: Little, Brown, 1979.

————. *A World Restored.* London: Victor Gollancz Ltd, 1974.

————. *Years of Upheaval.* Boston: Little, Brown, 1982.

Kistler, Helmut. *Die Ostpolitik der Bundesrepublik Deutschland, 1966–1973.* Bonn: Bundeszentrals für Politische Bildung, 1982.

Kotkin, Joel, and Yoriko Kishimoto. *The Third Century.* New York: Crown Publishers, 1988.

Krause, Joachim. *Prospects for Conventional Arms Control in Europe.* Institute for East–West Security Studies Occasional Paper Series, no. 8. New York, 1988.

Lafeber, Walter. *America, Russian, and the Cold War.* 5th ed. New York: Alfred Knopf, 1985.

————. *The American Age: United States Foreign Policy at Home and Abroad Since 1750.* New York and London: W.W. Norton, 1989.

Lang, Laszlo. *International Regimes and the Political Economy of East–West Relations.* Institute for East–West Security Studies Occasional Paper Series, no. 13. New York, 1989.

Larrabee, F. Stephen, ed. *Technology and Change in East–West Relations.* Institute for East–West Security Studies Monograph Series, no. 6. New York, 1988.

———, ed. *The Two German States and European Security*. New York: St. Martin's Press, 1989.

Leebaert, Derek, ed. *European Security: Prospects for the 1980s*. Lexington, Massachusetts: D. C. Heath, 1979.

Levering, Ralph B. *The Cold War, 1945 to 1972*. Arlington Heights, Virginia: Harlan Davidson, 1982.

Loth, Wilfried. *The Division of the World: 1941–1955*. London: Routledge, 1988.

Lynch, Allen. *The Soviet Study of International Relations*. Cambridge: Cambridge University Press, 1987.

Maghroori, Ray, and Bennett Ramberg. *Globalism Versus Realism: International Relations' Third Debate*. Boulder, Colorado: Westview, 1982.

Marchand, Philip. *Marshall McLuhan: The Medium and the Messenger*. New York: Ticknor & Fields, 1989.

MccGwire, Michael. *Military Objectives in Soviet Foreign Policy*. Washington, DC: The Brookings Institution, 1987.

McNeill, William H. *The Pursuit of Power: Technology, Armed Forces, and Society Since A.D. 1000*. Chicago: University of Chicago Press, 1982.

Meissner, Boris. *Die "Breshnew-Doktrin."* Köln: Dokumentation, 1969.

———. *Die Deutsche Ostpolitik, 1961–1970*. Köln: Verlag Wissenschaft und Politik, 1970.

Morgan, Roger. *The United States and West Germany: A Study in Alliance Politics*. Oxford: Oxford University Press, 1974.

Morgenthau, Hans J. *Politics Among Nations*. 5th ed. New York: Alfred Knopf, 1978.

———. *Scientific Man Versus Power Politics*. Chicago: University of Chicago Press, 1946.

Mottola, Kari, and Heikki Patomaki, eds. *Facing the Change in Europe*. Helsinki: Finnish Institute of International Affairs, 1989.

Neuhold, Hanspeter, ed. *CSCE: N + N Perspectives*. Vienna: W. Braumueller, 1987.

Neuhold, Hanspeter, and Hans Thalberg, eds. *The European Neutrals in International Affairs*. Boulder, Colorado: Westview, 1989.

Niebuhr, Reinhold. *Nations and Empires*. London: Faber & Faber, 1959.

Ninkovich, Frank A. *Germany and the United States*. Boston, Massachusetts: Twayne Publishers, 1988.

Noelle-Neumann, Elizabeth. *The Germans: Public Opinion Polls, 1967–1980*. Rev. ed. Westport, Connecticut: Greenwood Press, 1981.

Nye, Joseph S. *The Changing Nature of American Power*. New York: Basic Books, 1990.

Orvik, Nils. *The Decline of Neutrality, 1914–1941*. 2nd ed. London: Frank Cass and Company, 1971.

Papacosma, S. Victor, and Mark R. Rubin, eds. *Europe's Neutral and Nonaligned States*. Wilmington, Delaware: Scholarly Resources, Inc., 1989.

Parker, Geoffrey. *The Geopolitics of Domination*. London: Routledge, 1988.

Penttila, Risto E.J. *Finland's Search for Security Through Defence, 1944–89*. London: Macmillan, 1990.

Planck, Charles R. *The Changing Status of German Unification in Western Diplomacy, 1946–1966.* Baltimore, Maryland: Johns Hopkins University Press, 1967.

Rallo, Joseph C. *Defending Europe in the 1990s.* New York: St. Martin's Press, 1986.

Report by the 1984 Defense Committee. Swedish Official Reports Series 6. Stockholm: Ministry of Defense, 1985.

Ries, Thomas. *The Cold Will.* London: Brassey's Defense Publishers, 1988.

Roberts, Martin. *Machines and Liberty: A Portrait of Europe, 1789–1914.* Hong Kong: Oxford University Press, 1980.

Rusi, Alpo. *Finnish Foreign Policy on the Threshold of the 1990s.* Helsinki: Ministry of Foreign Affairs, 1989.

Russett, Bruce, and Harvey Starr. *World Politics: The Menu for Choice.* New York: W.H. Freeman and Co., 1985.

Schlesinger, Arthur. *A Thousand Days: John F. Kennedy in the White House.* Boston: Houghton Mifflin, 1965.

Schmitt, Hans A. *European Union: From Hitler to de Gaulle.* New York: Van Nostrand Reinhold, 1969.

Schweigler, Gebhard L. *National Consciousness in Divided Germany.* Beverly Hills, California: Sage, 1975.

Senghaas, Dieter. *Die Zukunft Europas: Probleme der Friedensgestaltung.* Frankfurt-am-Main: Suhrkamp, 1987.

Sizoo, J., and R.T. Jurrjens. *CSCE Decision-Making: The Madrid Experience.* The Hague: Martinus Nijhoff Publishers, 1983.

Sloan, Stanley R. *East–West Relations in Europe.* Foreign Policy Association Headline Series. March/April 1986.

Speth, James G. *Environment, Economy, Security: The Emerging Agenda.* Washington, DC: Center for National Policy, 1985.

Sprout, Harold and Margaret. *Towards a Politics of the Planet Earth.* New York: Van Nostrand Reinhold, 1971.

Stanley, Timothy W. and Darnell M. Whitt. *Detente Diplomacy: The United States and European Security in the 1970s.* New York: Dunellen Publishing Co., 1970.

Stephanson, Anders. *Kennan and the Art of Foreign Policy.* Cambridge, Massachusetts: Harvard University Press, 1989.

Taylor, A.J.P. *Europe: Grandeur and Decline.* London: Penguin, 1971.

Terry, Sarah Meiklejohn, ed. *Soviet Policy in Eastern Europe.* New Haven, Connecticut: Yale University Press, 1984.

Thompson, Kenneth W. *Winston Churchill's World View.* Baton Rouge, Louisiana: Louisiana State University Press, 1983.

Timonen, Ilkka. *Suomi ulkomaisessa lehdistossa Tshernobylin yoimalaonnettomuuden jalkeen.* Tampereen yliopisto, Sarja B52, 1988.

Ulam, Adam. *Expansion and Coexistence.* 2nd ed. New York: Praeger, 1974.

van Wagenen, Richard. *Research in the International Organization Field: Some Notes on a Possible Focus.* Princeton, New Jersey: Princeton University Center for Research on World Political Institutions, 1952.

Volten, Peter, ed. *Uncertain Futures: Eastern Europe and Democracy.* Institute for East–West Security Studies Occasional Paper Series, no. 16. New York, 1990.

von Beyme, Klaus. *The Soviet Union in World Politics.* New York: St. Martin's Press, 1987.

von Weizsäcker, Richard. *A Voice from Germany.* London: Weidenfeld & Nicholson, 1987.

Wallace, Helen. *Widening and Deepening: The EC and the New European Agenda.* Royal Institute of International Affairs Discussion Paper, no. 23. London, 1989.

Waltz, Kenneth N. *Theory of International Politics.* Reading, Massachusetts: Addison-Wesley, 1979.

Willis, F. Roy. *France, Germany and the New Europe, 1945–1963.* Palo Alto, California: Stanford University Press, 1965.

Yearbook of Finnish Foreign Policy, 1987. Helsinki: Finnish Institute of International Affairs, 1988.

Yearbook of Finnish Foreign Policy, 1989. Helsinki: Finnish Institute of International Affairs, 1990.

Yost, Charles. *The Insecurity of Nations: International Relations in the Twentieth Century.* New York: Praeger, 1968.

ARTICLES, ESSAYS, UNPUBLISHED WORK, ETC.

Albon, Mary. "Democratization and Institution-Building in Eastern Europe." Institute for East–West Security Studies Meeting Report, March 1–3, 1990.
———. "Valentin Larionov and Alexander Konovalov on Changes in Soviet Military-Security Thinking." Institute for East–West Security Studies Meeting Report, January 9, 1990.

Antola, Esko. "Order and Change in the CSCE." *Oesterreichische Zeitschrift für Politikwissenschaft*, 1986, no. 3.

Bahrenburg, Kristi. "Peter Hardi on the Current Political Situation in Hungary." Institute for East–West Security Studies Meeting Report, November 15, 1989.

Barnet, Richard J. "Why Trust the Soviets?" *World Policy Journal* 1, no. 3 (Spring 1984).

Bertram, Christoph. "Europe's Security Dilemmas." *Foreign Affairs* 65, no. 5 (Summer 1987).

Bialer, Seweryn. "Harsh Decade: Soviet Policies in the 1980s." *Foreign Affairs* 59, no. 5 (Summer 1981).
———. "The Passing of the Soviet Order?" *Survival* 32, no. 2 (March/April 1990).

Bitzinger, Richard A. "Neutrality for Eastern Europe? An Examination of Possible Western Role Models." Paper prepared for the RAND Corporation Symposium on European Security, Santa Monica, February 2, 1990.

Blackwill, Robert D. "Conceptual Problems of Conventional Arms Control." *International Security* 12, no. 4 (Spring 1988).

Booth, Ken. "Steps Toward Stable Peace in Europe: A Theory and Practice of Coexistence." *International Affairs* 66, no. 1 (1990).

Braun, Aurel. "Whither the Warsaw Pact in the Gorbachev Era?" *International Journal* 43 (Winter 1987/88).

Bressand, Albert. "Beyond Interdependence: 1992 as a Global Challenge." *International Affairs* 66, no. 1 (1990).

Brzezinski, Zbigniew. "Beyond Chaos: A Policy for the West." *The National Interest*, no. 19 (Spring 1990).

————. "The Framework for East–West Reconciliation." *Foreign Affairs* 46, no. 2 (1968).

————. "The Future of Yalta." *Foreign Affairs* 63, no. 2 (Winter 1984/85).

Deak, Istvan. "Eastern Europe's Dark History." *Orbis* 33, no. 1 (Winter 1989).

de Michelis, Gianni. "Reaching Out to the East." *Foreign Policy* 79 (Summer 1990).

Diebold, William, Jr. "The Marshall Plan in Retrospect: A Review of Recent Scholarship." *Journal of International Affairs* 41, no. 2 (Summer 1988).

Dobroczynski, Michael. "Rapprochement of the Peoples of Europe: Difficulties and Prospects." *International Affairs* 63, no. 3 (February 1989).

Feher, Ferenc. "Eastern Europe's Long Revolution Against Yalta." *Eastern European Politics and Societies* 2, no. 1 (Winter 1988).

Flynn, Gregory. "Problems in Paradigm." *Foreign Policy* 74 (Spring 1989).

Flynn, Gregory, and David J. Scheffer. "Limited Collective Security." *Foreign Policy* 80 (Fall 1990).

Frost, Ellen L., and Angela E. Stent. "NATO's Troubles with East–West Trade." *International Security* 8, no. 1 (Summer 1988).

Gaddis, John Lewis. "The Long Peace: Elements of Stability in the Postwar International System." *International Security* 10, no. 4 (Spring 1986).

Gaertner, Heinz. "Entspannung, Europa und die KSZE–in thematischer Überblick." *Oesterreichische Zeitschrift für Politikwissenschaft* 3 (1986).

Garaud, Marie-France. "The Lure of the East." *Géopolitique* 21 (Summer 1988).

Garton Ash, Timothy. "The Empire in Decay." *The New York Review of Books*, September 29, 1988.

————. "Reform or Revolution?" *The New York Review of Books*, October 27, 1988.

Gasteyger, Curt. "Neutrality in Europe: The End or a New Beginning?" *European Affairs*, no. 4 (Winter 1989).

Gati, Charles. "Gorbachev and Eastern Europe." *Foreign Affairs* 65, no. 5 (Summer 1987).

Ghebali, Victor-Yves. "The Institutionalization of the CSCE Process: Towards an Instrument for the 'Greater Europe'." Paper presented at the meeting of the Finnish Institute of International Affairs (FIIA) and the Center for Strategic and International Studies on "New Security Arrangements in Europe: Developing the CSCE Framework," Helsinki, September 27–28, 1990.

Giscard d'Estaing, Valèry, Yasuhiro Nakasone, and Henry Kissinger. "East–West Relations." *Foreign Affairs* 68, no. 3 (1989).

Haas, Ernst. "The Study of Regional Integration–Reflections on the Joy and Anguish of Pre-theorizing." *International Organization* 24 (Spring 1970).

Hakovirta, Harto. "Neutral States in East–West Economic Cooperation." *Co-Existence* 8 (1981).

Hassner, Pierre. "Europe Beyond Partition and Unity: Disintegration or Reconstitution?" *International Affairs* 66, no. 3 (1990).

Heumann, Hans-Dieter. "Political Resurgence of Europe." Unpublished paper, Institute for East–West Security Studies, 1988.

Holsti, K.J. "Bargaining Theory and Diplomatic Reality: The CSCE Negotiations." *Review of International Studies*, 1982, no. 8.

Howard, Michael. "The Remaking of Europe." *Survival* 32, no. 2 (March/April 1990).

Huntington, Samuel P. "No Exit–The Errors of Endism." *The National Interest*, no. 17 (Fall 1989).

Iklé, Fred Charles. "The Ghost in the Pentagon." *The National Interest*, no. 19 (Spring 1990).

Iziumov, Alexei, and Andrei Kortunov. "The Monolith is Cracking." *Newsweek*, August 13, 1990.

Jervis, Robert. "Conclusions: Winning and Losing–Clausewitz in the Nuclear Era." Forthcoming.

———. "Cooperation under the Security Dilemma." *World Politics* 30 (January 1978).

———. "From Balance to Concert: A Study of International Security Cooperation." *World Politics* 38 (October 1985).

———. "Implications of the Nuclear Revolutions." Unpublished paper, December 23, 1988.

Kaiser, Karl. "A View from Europe: the U.S. Role in the Next Decade." *International Affairs* 65, no. 2 (1989).

Karaganov, Sergei. "Our Common European House Within the East–West Structure." Unpublished paper, 1988.

Kegley, Charles W., Jr. "The New Containment Myth: Realism and Anomaly of European Integration." Paper presented at the Carnegie Council on Ethics and International Affairs Conference on "Ethics and Foreign Policy." Wiston House, England, July 2–6, 1990.

Kegley, Charles W., Jr., and Gregory A. Raymond. "The End of Alliances?" *USA Today*, May 1990.

Kennan, George F. ("Mr. X"). "The Sources of Soviet Conduct." *Foreign Affairs* 25 (July 1947).

Kissinger, Henry. "A Memo to the Next President." *Newsweek*, September 19, 1988.

———. "Observations on U.S.–Soviet Relations." *The Heritage Lectures*, no. 174 (1988).

Knudsen, Baard Bredrup. "Europe Between Superpowers: An All-European Model for the End of the 20th Century." *Cooperation and Conflict* 20 (1985).

Kohan, John. "Beyond Perestroika." *Time*, September 24, 1990.

Kovàcs, Jànos Màtyàs. "Reform Economics: The Classification Gap." *Daedalus* 119, no. 1 (Winter 1990).

Krause, Joachim. "Force Structures, Force Levels and Force Deployments in a Changing European Strategic Landscape." Paper presented at the Institute for East–West Security Studies Ninth Annual Conference, Stockholm, June 7–9, 1990.

Kux, Ernst. "Soviet Reaction to the Revolution in Eastern Europe." Paper presented at the conference on "Towards a New Eastern Europe," Bellagio, Italy, 1990.

Kux, Stephan. "Soviet–West European Relations: The Promises of a Common European Home." Unpublished paper, 1989.

Lang, Laszlo. "International Financial Security: Concepts and Outlines." *Kuelpolitika* (1988).

Larrabee, F. Stephen. "Eastern Europe: A Generational Change." *Foreign Policy* 70 (Spring 1988).

———. "The United States and the New European Security Order." Paper presented at the Institute for East–West Security Studies Ninth Annual Conference, Stockholm, June 7–9, 1990.

Lee, Kent D. "Changes in Soviet Military Doctrine and Changes in Soviet Military History: A Connection?" Unpublished paper, 1989.

Legvold, Robert. "The Soviet Union in Transition: Update on Perestroika and Glasnost." Columbia University School of International and Public Affairs, memo, February 6, 1989.

Lowenthal, Richard. "The German Question Transformed." *Foreign Affairs* 63, no. 2 (Winter 1984/85).

Luttwak, Edward N. "The Shape of Things to Come." *Commentary* 89, no. 6 (June 1990).

Lynch, Allen. "Is the Cold War Over . . . Again?" Unpublished paper.

Mandelbaum, Michael. "Is the Cold War Over?" *Foreign Affairs* 68, no. 2 (Spring 1989).

Marantz, Paul. "Changing Soviet Conceptions of International Security." Paper presented at the American Association for the Advancement of Slavic Studies annual meeting, November 19, 1988, Honolulu.

Marstrand Study Group. "Neutrality in Need of Conceptual Revision." Unpublished paper, 1988.

Mathiapoulos, Margarita. "Neither Barbarian nor Angel of Peace. The Common European Home: Resurrection of Change through Rapprochement." Paper prepared for the Aspen Institute Berlin Study Group meeting on "A Common European Home," September 21–25, 1988, Paris.

Meyers, Norman. "Emergent Aspects of Environment: A Creative Challenge." *The Environmentalist* 7, no. 3 (1987).

Molnar, Laszlo. "On the Adequacy of Negotiation Processes in European Conventional Arms Control." Paper prepared at the Institute for East–West Security Studies, 1989.

Mueller, John. "The Essential Irrelevance of Nuclear Weapons." *International Security* 13, no. 2 (Fall 1988).

Nelson, Daniel N. "Military Effort in the WTO: Extractive and Performance Dimensions, 1975–85." Unpublished paper, 1989.

———. "Power at What Price: The High Cost of Security in the WTO." Unpublished paper, 1989.

Noetzold, J., A. Inotai, and K. Schroeder. "East–West Trade at the Crossroads." *Aussenpolitik* 37, no. 4 (1986).

Nowotny, Eva. "The Role of the CSCE and the Council of Europe in Facilitating a Stable Transition Towards New Political Structures in Europe." Paper presented at the Institute for East–West Security Studies Ninth Annual Conference, Stockholm, June 7–9, 1990.

Palmer, John. "With a Security Role: Metamorphosis from Club to Community is Complete." *The European*, September 21–23, 1990.

Pedersen, Thomas. "Problems of Enlargement: Political Integration in a Pan-European EC." *Cooperation and Conflict* 25 (1990).

Petersen, Philip A. "The Emerging Soviet Vision of European Security." Unpublished paper, 1990.

Rudney, Robert. "France: Preparing for European Leadership." *The National Interest* (Fall 1987).

Ruehl, Lothar. "Franco-German Military Cooperation: An Insurance Policy for the Alliance." *Strategic Review* (Summer 1988).

Rupnik, Jacques. "Central Europe or Mitteleuropa?" *Daedalus* 119, no. 1 (Winter 1990).

Rusi, Alpo. "Assessing International Politics from an Organic Perspective." *Ulkopolitükka*, 1990, no. 1.

———. "Europe's Security Structure in Disintegration: Power Politics, Stability and Political Change." *Rauhantutkimu*,1989, no. 1.

———. "The Note Crisis as an Incident of Nuclear Politics." *Turun Sanomat*, April 8, 1990.

Sachs, Jeffrey, and David Lipton. "Poland's Economic Reform." *Foreign Affairs* 69, no. 2 (Spring 1990).

Savidge, Charlotte. "Theodore Malloch on Eastern Europe and International Economic Organizations." Institute for East–West Security Studies Meeting Report, January 30, 1990.

Schlesinger, Arthur J. "Origins of the Cold War." *Foreign Affairs* 46 (October 1967).

Seeler, H.J. "Die Beziehungen zwischen der Europaeischen Gemeinschaft und dem Rat für gegenseitige Wirtschaftshilfe." *Europa Archiv* 7 (1987).

Snyder, Jack. "The Gorbachev Revolution: A Waning of Soviet Expansionism." *International Security* 12, no. 3 (Winter 1987-8).

Soderlin, Rolf. "What If the Cold War Is Over?" *Armed Forces Journal International* (March 1989).

Soroos, Marvin S. "Global Interdependence and the Responsibilities of States: Learning from the Japanese Experience." *Journal of Peace Research* 25, no. 1 (1988).

Stavenhagen, Lutz G. "Political Priorities of the German EC Presidency." *Aussenpolitik* 39, no. 1 (1988).

Steel, Ronald. "Europe's Superpower Problem." *SAIS Review* (Summer 1988).

Steinbruner, John D. "The Prospect of Cooperative Security." *The Brookings Review* (Winter 1988/89).

Sullivan, Scott. "Can Germany Be Contained?" *Newsweek*, July 30, 1990.

Timmermann, Heinz. "The Soviet Union and Eastern Europe: Dynamics of 'Finlandization'." *Radio Liberty Report on the USSR* 2, no. 33 (August 17, 1990).

Tujunen, Leo. "A Conference on European Security? Background to the Finnish Government's Proposal." *European Review* 19, no. 4 (Autumn 1969).

Ullman, Richard H. "Institutionalizing European Security." Paper presented at the Institute for East–West Security Studies Ninth Annual Conference, Stockholm, June 7–9, 1990.

Ungerer, Werner. "Die Entwicklung der EG und ihr Verhältnis zu Mittel- und Osteuropa." *Aussenpolitik* 3 (1990).

Väyrynen, Raimo. "Common Security and the State System." Forthcoming.

―――. "Stability and Change in Finnish Foreign Policy." Department of Political Science, University of Helsinki Research Reports Series A, no. 60 (1982).

Wettig, Gerhard. "New Thinking on Security and East–West Relations." *Problems of Communism* 38, no. 1 (January-February 1989).

Wilkins, Lee, and Philip Patterson. "Reporting Chernobyl: Cutting the Government Fog to Cover the Nuclear Cloud." Unpublished paper, 1987.

Will, George. "The Opiate of Arms Control." *Newsweek*, April 27,1987.

Wind, Keith. "Rita Süssmuth on German Unification and the Future Political Architecture of Europe." Institute for East–West Security Studies Meeting Report, March 20, 1990.

"Z" [Martin Malia]. "To the Stalin Mausoleum." *Daedalus* 119, no. 1 (Winter 1990).

Index